THE
COLLISION

*A pursuit
of sacred light*

OF
GRIEF AND
GRATITUDE

A 366-DAY JOURNEY

ROSANNE LIESVELD

FOREWORD BY JOHN LIESVELD

THE
COLLISION

A pursuit
of sacred light

OF
GRIEF AND
GRATITUDE

A 366-DAY JOURNEY

ROSANNE LIESVELD
FOREWORD BY JOHN LIESVELD

Illum||natio
Press
Lincoln, NE

THE COLLISION OF GRIEF AND GRATITUDE: A PURSUIT OF SACRED LIGHT

For publishing inquiries, contact:
Illuminatio Press
c/o Concierge Marketing
13518 L. Street
Omaha, NE 68137
(402) 884-5995

Hardcover ISBN: 978-0-9988610-1-2
Paperback ISBN: 978-0-9988610-2-9
Mobi ISBN: 978-0-9988610-3-6
EPUB ISBN: 978-0-9988610-4-3
Audio ISBN: 978-0-9988610-5-0

Publishing and production services by Concierge Marketing Inc.

Library of Congress Cataloging Number: 2017938045

Cataloging-in-Publication data on file with the publisher.

Printed in the USA

10 9 8 7 6 5 4 3 2 1

To my grandchildren Johnny and Norah.

May you live with the hope and confidence that when you look for gratitude in each day, there will always be a brilliant Light to guide your path.

Contents

Foreword

I work in talk radio, which probably means a lot of things to a lot of people, but at its core, I spend my days discussing problems and how to fix them. In the process of doing that for over a decade, I've learned a lot about how we collectively address our societal issues, and the inefficiencies and misplaced blame latent in those methods. Among those is our tendency to simplistically trace the origin of specific societal ills exclusively to certain things, usually relatively new things, that are simply conduits that produce reflections of our human brokenness, but are nonetheless often regarded as inherently counterproductive, if not evil.

Those things have been different from generation to generation, but today, the one scapegoat that takes it on the chin more than any other is social media. And those punches are leveled from all sides—from those longing for the return to the simpler, less wired good old days, to those who lament its deleterious effects on high-level discourse. And while we've all found ourselves reading or even participating in discussions in the most cesspool-like corners of Facebook or its counterparts, I've gained an unexpected alternate perspective on the unbelievable, life-changing value of this technology that connects us socially in an entirely different way.

My dad was my ultimate role model for reasons you'll read about in the coming pages. He was also my biggest cheerleader. The grief I felt when he died unexpectedly was, as you might expect, devastating and sometimes bitter. But almost worse than those feelings were the times I spent imagining what my mom was going through in those darkest moments alone in the days and weeks after Dad died. And while I know those moments were terrible for her—and saying goodbye to her at the end of a night when I knew that loneliness and grief were coming her way felt hopeless, there was a small light that developed as the days went on. A light that didn't erase but mitigated the darkness of those moments, at least for me. That light, as corny as it sounds, was Facebook. Or more specifically, the real-time human interactions, listening ears, and comfort that it provided for my mom at nearly any hour of the day or night.

After Dad died, I remember saying several times that I couldn't bear to imagine how much darker and lonelier those days would have been had it happened even five or ten years earlier when we didn't have this technology that connects us. I think you'll understand that sentiment as you read the pages ahead, filled with Mom's daily posts from an entire year of finding gratitude while grieving. While there's no shortage of days where she described feeling unbearably sad—maybe even hopeless—for each of those there was a cadre of friends, family, co-workers, and even acquaintances who shared a bit of the brunt of those moments by reading, responding, sympathizing, remembering, or just knowing they happened. Our hope is that sharing those moments here will, in some small way, do the same thing for those who read them.

My dad was always heartily skeptical of those who spent life casting blanket, all-encompassing critiques on every new thing that came along. His ability to see the unique and very real good in people made him a legend in his field, but that ability extended beyond people. He wouldn't be surprised that an oft-maligned, relatively new thing like Facebook could take on and multiply the best attributes of human love and be a vital source of something he sought until the day he died—a light in the darkness.

—*John Liesveld*

Prelude

Do you ever look back on something and marvel at how unplanned it was, yet how its impact on your life was profound?

This journey of grief and gratitude started with unexpected loss. I never imagined myself a widow at sixty-three. My husband's death was a shock. It left me reeling and trying to figure out how to move from the future I had planned and hoped for with my soul mate to the messy ugliness of grief.

A few days after Curt's funeral, I thought my heart couldn't hold any more grief or heaviness. Then I felt a new wave of grief over the fear that I'd never be able to adequately express my gratitude to the people who made such a difference for me in the darkest hours. So, I wrote a Facebook post thanking my son. And the next day, I thanked someone else. And I felt better after I wrote those short messages and shared them.

Through that process, I soon realized that what I needed was to look hard for some gratitude each day, no matter how miserable, angry, weak, or confused I felt.

I certainly had no plan to post my deepest grief on Facebook for 366 days—it was a leap year. Some may have questioned my willingness to emotionally undress in front of so many people, but what I knew was that when I communicated my deepest and most authentic feelings, I ended up feeling better.

Even more, when I searched for the grain of gratitude, I could face the day. Day by day by day, that revelation of grief and the hunt for gratitude changed me.

I discovered it changed others too. Many suggested I put these posts in a book. I thought they were crazy until I realized that, at least in part, a book could be my greatest tribute to Curt's life. Perhaps telling part of the story could encourage a life well-lived for others.

In the end, writing these posts connected me with people who held me up, who encouraged me, who prayed for me, and who simply "liked" my posts.

Curt was on a quest during the last few months of his life for light. He chose *light* as his word for the year. Little did he know that he would see the Creator of Light just six months into his journey. And little did I know that the light would eventually come for me through grief and gratitude colliding, almost violently, to produce new meaning and hope for me—and I hope for you.

—Rosanne

Anne, Norah, Rosanne, John, Meagan, John, and Curt Liesveld

A Book Emerges

Life takes us on unexpected journeys. This book has been one of them.

I have known Curt and Rosanne Liesveld since they walked into the church where I worked one Sunday morning in 2000. I was intrigued by this power couple who were never anything other than authentically interested in other people.

We shared a love of good wine and great sports. Rosanne showed me how a backyard can be transformed into a slice of Eden. Curt introduced me to my strengths and spoke life-changing words to me: "You belong at the table."

We talked about writing. Both Curt and Rosanne are published authors, and we dreamed of a marriage book they would write together.

With Curt's sudden death (my Competition theme is still a bit irked that Curt got to heaven first), that dream died—at least as we had originally imagined it. Then Rosanne began to write—raw, soulful words that she shared on Facebook. I watched my friend fight for light, fall, and get up to fight again. I read her words as my own husband, Kirk, mourned one of his closest friends. *What if...* began to nudge my Ideation.

What if a new book was emerging? A book that pulled back the curtain on a strong marriage? A book that allowed us to follow the process of grief? A journal of a courageous woman's search for gratitude in the messiness of grief? Yes, this was the book that would tell at least part of Curt and Rosanne's love story.

Rosanne didn't intend to write a book. She didn't even intend to share her grief and gratitude on Facebook every day for a year. We've done some editing, but tried to retain the raw emotion of her original posts.

So, this book is for you, wherever you are on your journey. If you are new to grief, you may want to read it straight through. It may offer you a roadmap of how to navigate loss by looking for bits of gratitude. If you have loved and lost, you may want to read a post daily, following the dates on the calendar as you walk through the seasons. Some of you may use it as a guide that offers insight into how to care for those who are tender with grief. For many of you, it will be a guidebook for how to love more deeply and live with more purpose.

At the end of each post, Rosanne has included a nudge. My dear friend is a teacher at heart and wants to leave you with challenges and inspiration each day. Mostly, she wants to leave you with hope—hope that strong marriages can and do exist. Hope that transformation is not only possible, but probable. Hope that you will find faith in God, who will sustain you through life's greatest joys and deepest sorrows. Hope that when the future you imagined is ripped away, something new and sweet can emerge.

—Cindy Conger
  Editor

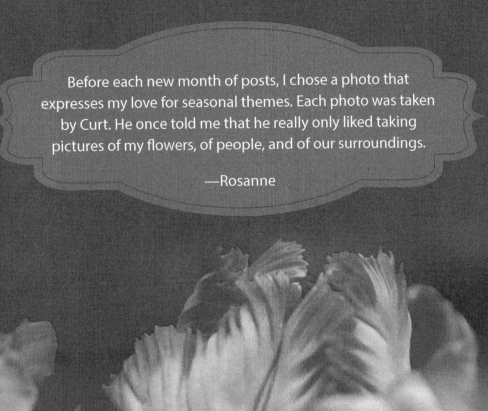

Before each new month of posts, I chose a photo that expresses my love for seasonal themes. Each photo was taken by Curt. He once told me that he really only liked taking pictures of my flowers, of people, and of our surroundings.

—Rosanne

Each fall Curt would help me plant hundreds of tulips. It was his ultimate act of love; the soil was hard, the bulbs were too many, and my planting designs were specific. This photo of his favorite flower, the tulip, gives a nod to our Dutch heritage and to the arrival of spring.

May 24

Day 1: Rock

How will I ever thank everyone for what they've done for me and my family in the past week?

It was a week ago today that Curt went to meet the Creator of his amazing life. Curt loved Facebook. He loved to post his pictures. But he also loved reading about others, learning things, and the beautiful way Facebook connects people with one another.

I know not everyone needs or wants public recognition, but I would like to use this venue as a way to occasionally express some gratitude and post my profound appreciation for others. My first thought is of the person who has been a rock for me—my rock star son, John.

Within minutes of knowing Curt had died, John said, "Mom, I will be there for you for anything you will ever need." And he has been. His greatest gift, of course, is the gift of being himself—except an even better version of his already bright, funny, serious, initiating, passionate, honest, and people-needing, loving self. Curt always said, "You can't be someone else, but you can be more of who you already are," and John has been that over the last few days.

Curt was always so proud of him, and this last week, he would have been bursting at the seams with that pride. I know I am.

Who is your rock?

Rosanne and John

Day 2: Comforter

Today is our daughter Anne's birthday. She is so special in many ways. She grieved, but found great comfort in her sweet friends, family, her work family, and her church. People are important to her just like they were to Curt. She always has been my steadfast company, and although I am thrilled she has her own apartment now, I'm so glad she is near so I can lean on her as well.

She wrote these memories of her dad that were read at his memorial service:

"When I think about my dad I think about all the things we did together as a bigger family… I also remember a large part of my life being about Hope Church, listening to him talk, and seeing the connection to people that he loved. I loved that he always seemed interested in others.

"…I remember sitting outside at my mom and dad's house watching him and Johnny play games and ping-pong in the summer. In the winter, we'd skate on the pond behind my parents' house. Any excuse to be outside and connect.

"My dad had such a way with words. No matter where he was, he impacted lives. He impacted mine with connecting, time away, play, and laughter."

Happy birthday, Anne. And thanks for being you.

Who's your comfort?

Curt and Anne

May 26

Day 3: The Place

Only three days after Curt died, his dad Owen passed away. Yesterday was Owen's funeral. He was ninety-two and had been married for almost seventy years—a very long and full life. Curt would have loved to have preached his dad's funeral sermon. Instead, John got to talk about his grandfather's relentless positivity and where that came from. It was such a sweet moment for me.

So, today's gratitude is focused on Curt's family: his mom and dad; his sister Sandy and her family, Rich and Emily; his brother Claude and his family, Cherise, Katie, Megan, Troy, and little Owen; his sister Cori and her family, Chris, Lizzie, and Alec. I don't know how you've handled all this death, having two loved ones to grieve. What I do know is there are no regrets. This family always got along, always considered each other's opinions, always honored their parents, and always loved me as one of their own.

Our home was often "the place" where the Liesvelds gathered for holidays or family events, and I want more than ever to still make it "the place" where you all will come and bring a part of Curt.

Thank you, Liesvelds. I love you.

> **Where is the place you gather with your family?**
> **Should you work at finding or creating that place?**

Day 4: Work and Worth

Gallup. Not just a place to work, but a place to match your soul to your role. (Didn't someone great say that?)

I faced a first again today when I went to my office in Omaha to deal with the legalities of Curt's death. I found much more than forms and paperwork. I found my colleagues there waiting for me with open arms. My grandson, Johnny, rode with me. I thought he'd be company for what felt like too long a ride, and everyone there embraced him like their own. Curt would have loved watching everyone love on him.

I will take another time to single individuals out from Gallup; today is more about the organization, and what it has been to me for over twenty-nine years, and what it was for Curt in the last fifteen years. It gave him a pulpit. It gave me an audience. It helped feed his Learner. It helped me to impact schools. It gave him smart and enlightened colleagues. It gave me friends. But mostly, it gave us both purpose—a place to live out our mission.

This is no ordinary company that Don Clifton started about forty-five years ago—it is the best church outside of the church I know. Thanks, friends.

> *Is your work a place of purpose? What meaning is there in your workplace? Have you told your coworkers what they mean to you?*

May 28

Day 5: Be Strong

One day about ten years ago, I walked into a nail salon that had just opened. The woman in charge there—who also did my nails—was Leslie. Her husband, D'ai, helped manage the salon. She always greeted me by name as soon as I walked in the door. I grew to love this couple and their stories of the courage, and strength, and hard work it took to be in this new country. We enjoyed having them in our home, treating their kids like our grandkids, and were so honored to be a part of their daughter's first communion and dinner—the only people there who weren't Vietnamese.

They sold their business, and I went on to have my nails done with Mya, at a new salon. She also became a friend, and I admired her and her husband's hard work and love of our country. Curt often thought it was a little weird how I fell in love with my nail ladies and their families.

Anyway, here is my gratitude part. While almost everyone was telling me to take time and take care of myself (which I do think is wise advice), D'ai whispered in my ear when they came to visit, and Mya wrote to me on Facebook, one thing: "Be strong." Most Americans wouldn't say that, but it was so comforting for someone to say that to me. Some may need to be told to take it easy, but I appreciated that challenge to be strong.

My love of country is most deep in my heart when I see people like these Vietnamese Americans who came to our country because we as a nation opened our arms to them. And we treat them well (at least Nebraskans do). And they love what America stands for while still loving their homeland.

So, today, at least for a time, I think about what they said—"be strong"—and it helps me be grateful for these Vietnamese friends and my God-given strength.

When is it necessary to be strong? What does strong look like to you?

May 29

Day 6: Plain Jane

Plain as an adjective: not decorated or elaborate; simple or ordinary in character. Plain as in "plain Jane." Plain as an adverb: clearly and absolutely, as in "Jane is plainly the most amazing person in the world."

My sister Jane has been a rock for me in the almost two weeks since I lost the love of my life. I don't know what I would have done without her. I also know my life will be better in the future—even though it's hard to see it now—with her in it. We are not the same personality type. She is steady, thoughtful, empathetic, hard-working, faith-driven, and loyal. But, much like Curt and me, the two of us make a great pair.

I can't even begin to thank her for her love and support. Yesterday, she knew I'd need my yard tended to, but also knew I probably didn't have the strength or motivation to do it. But she came, and together we dead-headed the flowers, pulled weeds, cleaned off the patio, and with that, she breathed a breath of life in me that I needed badly.

Thank you. You are no "Plain Jane." You are plainly the best in the world.

> *Who is the Jane in your life? Who is different from you,*
> *but almost like a sister?*

Jane and Rosanne

Day 7: Eat and Drink

As you can probably tell, my posts are not in any order of significance. I decided to let God speak to me about what I felt grateful for each day, so today's may seem odd to you.

I am thankful for coffee shops and restaurants.

I'm not a good cook and do not like to cook, but Curt never, ever made me feel guilty about that. Rather, he was the first one to say, "Let's go out for coffee," or "Let's go out to eat tonight." He liked eating, and I was glad I didn't have to cook. And I like good wine. One of the things I will miss most is sitting with him at our favorite spots discussing either grandkids, our work with strengths, or just not talking at all.

This morning my sisters and John's family ended up at local restaurant Bread and Cup, and it reminded me of how Curt loved that place and the awesome owners, Kevin and Karen. So, here's to the Lincoln restaurants that Curt and I loved: Lazlo's, La Paz, Venue Restaurant & Lounge, Culvers, Taco Inn, Scooters, Blue Orchid, Nu Vibe, Misty's, Val's, and probably many more I can't think of now. Those places are like holy ground in some ways. These are places where you can be nourished physically, spiritually, and relationally as you talk, eat, laugh, drink, and share deeply.

> *Go out for coffee or a meal sometime soon and think of how it nourishes your soul and deepens relationships.*

May 31

Day 8: A Lush Lawn

Curt was mowing our lawn when he died. Our association mows lawns, and in our eleven years in our home, Curt had never mowed. It had been so rainy that our backyard hadn't been mowed for two and a half weeks. The grass was so long. Curt wanted to mow so we could be outside the next day—as was our Sunday custom. He went to borrow a mower from our son and proceeded to mow the grass. As I watched him mowing, I thought he looked happy.

Here's the gratitude part; he had just a little left to mow, and after we left for the hospital, our friend Craig and his son Cole, came over, finished the undone strip, and took John's mower back. They were the last people to touch what Curt touched, so I think their hands may never be the same. Then they proceeded to mow my son's yard, which was very wet and very large. Such help is the kind that only comes from generous and loving hearts and hands. Thanks, Cole and Craig.

Admire a beautiful, green lawn today and think of Curt. He liked them too.

Backyard of the Liesveld Lottage

June 1

Day 9: The Bed

The bed. I have a feeling it's one of the toughest things to face after losing a spouse. I have very consciously slept only on my side and haven't even looked at Curt's pillow. The smell, the look, the memories of our bed may be one of the hardest things I face each night.

Last night, I asked if my grandkids, Johnny and Norah, wanted to sleep over. I offered them any bed in the house. They've recently liked getting to sleep upstairs in Anne's old room, but they both wanted to sleep in our bed. Norah fell asleep fast and Johnny struggled at first to find sleep. We cuddled tightly in a queen-sized bed. And then they laid their heads on Curt's pillow. And I finally could look at it again.

Here's my gratitude for the day: Grandkids that can sleep over and transform a bed and pillow into something healing and precious.

Rest easy on your pillows tonight and thank God for what you have.

Johnny and Norah

June 2

Day 10: Broken

There is a broken toilet seat in my bathroom. As if someone wanted to torment me, just days after Curt died, not only did this toilet seat break, but so did the one upstairs.

When my heart is breaking, anything else that breaks makes me feel like giving up. But I have a brother-in-law, Doug, who swooped in to take the broken seats off and get new ones ordered. This is the same guy who pulled together the choir for the final song at Curt's service. Yes, he has many talents and offers them when needed.

I have amazing brothers-in-law. You will hear more about them later, but today I am grateful for a new toilet seat. It helps with my broken heart.

Thank an in-law today for something. They are the best.

The broken toilet

June 3

Day 11: Grace for Your Personality

Today I want to revisit the words John spoke about his dad at the funeral. It was a powerful tribute that captured the essence of Curt's life message. Consider these words from a son who was powerfully shaped by his father.

> "We believe in grace. And it's a pretty wonderful and central concept that probably too often takes a backseat these days. A lot of times people will get up behind the pulpit and say we need to get back to basics. I agree. Grace. We have the unmerited favor of God despite the fact that we constantly screw up. It's a wonderful idea, but so often, grace is only positioned as being about what we've done, not who we are. There's value in having past wrongs forgiven absolutely, your slate wiped clean. It's wonderful, but it's an incomplete view of grace.

> "We all have flaws about who we are. We all have weaknesses, but my dad showed us that we're designed in a way such that we don't have to be defined by those. We don't have to frustratingly confront them every new day. In the same way, we believe that all the stupid things we regret doing are wiped away by grace; my dad believed all our systemic shortcomings that we don't like about ourselves can also be wiped away by our God-given strengths. This might be a clunky term—I couldn't think of the perfect term, but he taught 'grace for personalities.'

> "Once you experience grace for your personality, just like grace for your actions, it's unbelievably freeing. That's how I felt when he did all these things that we were talking about—free. You can be you. You're supposed to be you…Soak in that freedom today. My hope is that you're going to leave here—and yes, there's still grieving to be done—inspired to carry on my dad's ministry in your family, in your community, or just inside yourself.

"My dad looked at people the way God looks at people. That's his legacy. And he's gone, but the great news is that the freedom of looking at yourself and others with personality grace—the way God looks at you—lives on. Some of you are probably in some level of darkness now. Some of you may not think much of yourself right now. I've been there. Stop doing that. And if you don't know how to stop doing that, find your Curt Liesveld."

> *Amen. Be yourself. Embrace your personality and revel in the strengths God gave you. Find someone who will give you help, understanding, and inspiration along the way. Find your Curt Liesveld.*

June 4

Day 12: Beauty

If you were at Curt's funeral, you saw how peaceful the front of the church looked. As odd as it seemed, one of my most difficult decisions was about flowers as memorials. I love flowers, but I was concerned that a stage loaded with them would be overwhelming. I also wondered about the money being spent wisely. On the other hand, I did want some flowers.

Long story short, my friend Cindy was a part of the A Team to plan Curt's funeral. She had the idea to have lanterns in the front since Curt's one word for the year was light. But here's another amazing piece. Kim, who lost her son ten years ago, had asked me at that time to help make the stage of the church "not look like a funeral." This time the roles were reversed, and I asked Kim to be the creative design person. Patty did tons of running for lanterns, etc., and the three women made the front of the church look like what so many told me—our backyard on a beautiful summer night.

As we walked into the church, John asked, "Mom, does it look like you imagined it would?" I said, "No, it's more beautiful than I could imagine." I'm so grateful for the beauty.

> *Today, light a candle or buy a lantern. Then buy some flowers just for the heck of it. Do it in honor of Curt.*

June 5

Day 13: Dreams

Someone asked me if I've had bad dreams since Curt died. Only the night before last do I remember any dream.

In that dream, I was in a large room with a lot of people I knew. We all had suitcases, and I was trying to get mine closed and just couldn't do it. I remember something about a large wooden fish I'd bought that I was trying to force into the suitcase. (That makes sense since I was always buying stuff on trips and trying to shove it into a too-small suitcase.) I remember that I kept wondering how I would ever get that suitcase shut, and if anyone in that room would notice that I could use help. Then someone knocked at the door to the room. It was Curt. He said to me, "We've got to go home." I remember thinking he was upset with me because I didn't have my suitcase packed. And then he said, "It's okay. We have to go home. There's something really good there."

I have no idea what that meant. Curt was good at interpreting my dreams. I wish I could ask him what he thought was in my subconscious to produce that dream. But I can't, and I hate that. I can feel good that in the dream, he seemed happy about "going home."

> *Today, love your home. Embrace your home, and think about how your home can be like heaven to someone. Maybe even entertain angels unaware.*

Day 14: The Closet

Today we cleaned out Curt's closet. Everyone warned me how hard it would be. And it was. He was not the most organized person in the world, but piece by piece, John and my daughter-in-law, Meagan, helped sort. Anne volunteers at Barnabas, a non-profit here in Lincoln, and they are always in need of clothes, so we will donate many of the items there.

The man loved his hats. I often bought him a hat when we went on vacations or to ballgames. I always thought he looked so handsome in a ball cap. John and Johnny will keep some of their favorites, and a few found their way into my closet.

Curt's closet is bare now except for dozens and dozens of cards and notes that Curt received from the kids and me. Those will stay there. The love notes are powerful, and sensuous, and full of life. So, in the grief of Curt's too-early death, I'm grateful that the words on those notes and cards will stay in the closet and fill it forever with life, and love, and beautiful memories.

> **What does your closet say about you? Where do you keep your precious possessions?**

Curt's collection of hats

Day 15: Leave the Lights On

What's the hardest part about losing Curt? How much time do you have? As Shakespeare said, "Let me count the ways."

One of the hardest things is coming home alone to a dark house. I have figured out that leaving some lights on helps a little. I don't even know why it is so difficult since I came home alone many nights when Curt was traveling. Now I fight off fear of many things—sometimes intense fear and slight paranoia. But John does something for me. He texts me on those nights when he thinks I'm afraid, and those texts tell me I'm never alone. Even more, he assures me he isn't afraid. It feels like Jesus wrapping his arms around me late at night.

Hey, wait a minute. Maybe John is my light on those nights!

> **Be a light to somebody today. And leave a light on if that makes it easier for you.**

John

Just my nightly reminder that you're not alone. It's still sad but it's not dark.

Love you so so

Me too. Whenever you feel helplessly alone I will make sure to end that. I'm not scared.

John's texts

Day 16: Sundays

Yesterday may have been my hardest day yet. Most grief experts say one goes through a time of anger. I had not done that because I truly want to avoid that emotion. But yesterday when I saw Johnny, he was in a deep place of sadness. Sundays will never be the same for him. No more fun with Poppo, doing all those rest and recreation things like fishing, ping-pong, paddle boat, basketball, Scrabble, watching the Royals, watching any sport for that matter.

He simply said, "I miss Poppo so much."

For the first time, I felt cheated and angry, but I tried to do what might make Johnny smile. I invited Great Grandma Liesveld over for both their benefit. Then I told him to invite some friends. Cole and Jack and their dad Bret came to fish and paddle boat. Johnny had a good day. And although Sundays will never be the same, I am determined to make them good again.

> *Please come over on Sunday if you are lonely or like to fish or shoot hoops.*
> *We need you. Maybe you will feel better for coming too.*

Day 17: Cars

Neither Curt or I are "car people." As long as we had a reasonable vehicle that could haul flowers, grandchildren, Christmas trees, and baseball equipment, we were fine. Today when I was in Omaha starting to get back a little to work, Anne texted me to say her car was not working right. She had taken it to the nearest mechanic, whom she knew was honest. I was so proud of her for being so responsible.

Then I remembered that my sister Marlene and her husband, Ron, had asked how they could help right after Curt's death. I had answered quickly, "Help me with the cars." You see, Ron was a car mechanic expert for much of his career. I didn't expect I would need this help while everything else was being piled on, but I called them from Omaha, and they went to check on Anne's car, take her to work, and arrange for her to pick up one of our cars.

They did what everyone should do when helping those in grief—do what you do best. In fact, Ron had the car towed to their house so he could check it out himself and work on it (if it's fixable).

My tears today are flowing a lot again—most of them because I miss my precious husband, but a few are tears of gratitude for people like Ron and Marlene, who helped me when I felt such a load of despair and frustration. And tears of gratitude for Anne. I love them all.

Today, take your car in for a tune-up, or oil change, or whatever you do with cars. And thank your mechanic. They are important people in my life.

Day 18: Switzerland

Nine days from now, Curt and I would have been leaving for Switzerland on a trip we both were so excited about taking. We were going there to teach for a couple days, but I had planned about ten days of vacation in the one country Curt said he most wanted to see.

Today, I went to Cheryl, my travel agent at AAA, to turn in final paperwork and bring a death certificate. Cheryl always insisted we buy insurance for bigger trips. She lost her husband suddenly and much-too-young as they were just ready to go to France. I so hated walking into that office, but Cheryl greeted me with a hug. Hugs from other widows feel different. They know what this feels like. Cheryl then spent an hour helping me to hear a bit of her story so I could do my new normal a bit more easily. In the end, she worked her magic and all the costs of our trip were refunded.

I walked out of that travel agency a bit stronger and with admiration for another woman who does her work beautifully and shares her own story in such a helpful way. And I had to remember what my granddaughter, Norah, told me last night: "I bet Poppo can see Switzerland from heaven. I'm pretty sure you can see all the countries once you get to heaven."

Hope you love the Alps, Curt. My heart is with you.

> *And for the rest of you, buy travel insurance if your agent suggests it. And go take that trip you've always wanted to take, maybe even to Switzerland.*

Day 19: Neighbors

I've learned to hate getting the mail. You cannot even imagine all the bills that come with death, and today was no exception. No cards, just a massive bill from the hospital. When I walked into the house with that bill in my hand, I felt crushed again. I cried. I vomited. I cried some more. Then I tried to figure out where there was any tiny bit of light in this grief today.

I thought about my next-door neighbors. I had run to Debbie for help once I realized Curt was down. She is a nurse. A healthcare professional. She gave him CPR because my shaking arms could not do it. And then my other neighbor Becky ran over and held me and prayed. I will never forget how important those two women were to me that Saturday. Today, Becky took me for coffee. She said things that felt like Curt was saying them to me. She gave me a little glimmer of hope.

After dealing with the hospital bill, I will take time to let in a tiny bit of light remembering that healthcare professionals do such important jobs. But even more, that friends who happen to be neighbors are friends for life. They knelt on holy ground (better known as our yard) with me when Curt died.

Today, go meet your neighbor, or forgive a neighbor for something stupid they did. Or, help them when their lives have just fallen apart. Wasn't it Jesus who said, "Love your neighbor as yourself"?

June 12

Day 20: Sports

Photography and sports were Curt's hobbies, and sports were big for him. He was a Husker fan through and through. And Royals. And KC Chiefs—especially in the days of Will Shields. He loved to watch, read about, and attend all types of sporting events. He liked to watch one game on TV and another game on his iPad. It was about the only time I saw him multi-task.

I didn't ever think I'd say I miss having sports on the TV all the time, but oddly, the droning sound of ESPN is now something I miss. I don't regret now that I was usually willing to have Curt watch whatever sports were on TV while I sat in the chair next to him reading or working. The NBA finals are going on now and all I can think is, "What team would Curt be for?" Or "What time is the game so I know what time we'll need to be home tonight?" So, last night when our friends Cindy, Kirk, and Rita came over with a bottle of wine and box of Ritz crackers, ready to watch the NBA game, I felt a little normal for a bit.

I wish Curt would have been there with us so I'd know which team he'd be cheering for, but I have my hunches.

Maybe you can learn to like some sports if you don't currently and your spouse does. Or maybe you can simply cheer for the Huskers and the Royals when they play since we need a lot of great fans to take Curt's place.

Day 21: People vs. Mountains

Four weeks ago today Curt died. As I re-read my posts, they sound a lot stronger than I really am. It's not because I'm not being honest in what I write, I think it's because the posts are typed, and the font looks more stable, more balanced, more perfect than handwriting. It looks more clear and more focused than I feel.

Last week was so hard. Yesterday between 4:00 and 6:00 p.m., my cries turned into wails. Let me be clear; I'm not as strong and I'm not doing as well as the typed words indicate. I feel much more like the handwriting I had to do when signing my name to documents like the mortuary agreement, or the organ donor form, or the bill from the EMT. It was weak, messy, and lacked strength.

Yes, the grief is as real as it can be, but I do know I have people who have been there for me in huge ways. I have a family who never stops taking care of me. I have friends at Gallup who are supportive and understanding. I have a church that ministers to me daily. I have a small group that hugs and feeds me. My friends make sure I stay busy. I have people. I've always said, "Mountains and oceans don't show up at your funeral, but people do." As wonderful as even these natural beauties are, they are never as important as the people in our lives.

Think about your relationships today. Ask yourself if they are the most important thing in your life. If not, someday you will regret it.

June 14

Day 22: Re-gifted Life

Yesterday I worked in my yard like we always did on Saturdays. It was the first time I tried to do the job of two people. I usually tended to the flowers and yard while Curt sprayed, dug out weeds, cleaned off the patio etc. I managed to get some things done, but it was lonely.

My motivation came from knowing I was having guests over. Mark and Jami, good friends from many years ago, have come back to Lincoln. Many weeks ago, I asked if I could host a gathering in our yard so they could see their friends. Jami, of course insisted they not use our house after Curt died, but I insisted they come. You see, Mark is sporting a new heart from a transplant he had in January. He is a walking miracle, and they have returned to Lincoln because he is the new Executive Director of the Strengths Institute at the University of Nebraska. Wow!

Minutes after the physician confirmed Curt was dead, I asked if any of his organs could be harvested. God and Mark prompted that idea. And even though the immediate thirty-minute organ transplant interview was hellish, I was glad they could use parts of Curt's precious body for someone like Mark.

> *Today, think about becoming an organ donor. Get on a registry. Talk to your loved ones. Save someone's life like I know Curt has.*

Day 23: Sensuous Rain

I woke up this morning to clouds and rain once again. I have always loved days like this because my dad, who was a farmer, was always the happiest when it was raining in the summer. It meant the crops would grow. His livelihood depended on the rain. That was before irrigation, and he didn't have much control over the amount of water his crops got.

But in the past four weeks, I have learned to dread waking up to clouds and rain. I hate waking up to the darkness inside and outside. The rain means I can't go outside when I need to distract myself with gardening. The pond gets filled with debris. I look outside and my flowers look smashed. I need to take a walk, but I'll get wet. My love of rainy days has lessened significantly.

The rain does bring back one great memory. Just a few days before Curt died, the rain was coming down gently but consistently. Curt and I always loved to watch it rain on the pond, the drops on the water so rhythmic and calming. That evening, we stood arm in arm under the eaves with our patio door open, watching it rain. It was one of the sweetest memories I now have.

He teased me about how I thought the rain was sensuous. We felt such affection and love for each other standing there watching and listening to the rain. The evening ended in a sweet way for us. Little did I know it would be one of my last and best memories of our time together. So even though I am tired of rain right now and need the sun, I have a memory of rain, and passion, and emotion that will never be erased.

Today, let your kids jump in a rain puddle. Buy a rain gauge—a really big one. Or just thank God for the rain that sustains us in every way.

Rain on Liesveld Pond

June 16

Day 24: Co-Grandparenting

Last night, Johnny's baseball game was rained out (again), so the kids took pity on me (again), and invited me over for dinner (again). I had gotten through the day feeling okay until I overheard Johnny talking on the phone to his grandpa in Grinnell.

As I listened, it sounded just like he could have been talking to Curt and telling him about his games, his day at Vacation Bible School, and all the rain. In an instant, I felt ugly emotions. I felt jealous. I felt angry. I felt pain because Curt was not on the other end of the phone. Then I slowly watched Johnny look happy, smile, and act like himself, and just as quickly as my bad feelings came, I felt grateful for the "other" grandpa in Iowa.

When Meagan's parents, Jack and Jackie, came to our house right after Curt died, they came with such open arms and love. I told Jack that although Curt was a competitive guy, he never was in competition with the other grandpa. In fact, he saw him as a partner, a teammate, and a truly good influence on Johnny and Norah. He is also an amazing grandpa like Curt was, and I'm thankful Johnny and Norah have him in their lives.

> *If you are in a co-grandparent family, take a minute to think about the good things that the other grandparents do in your kids' lives. Write them a note. Say a prayer of thanks for them, and above all, don't see them as competition. Curt didn't, and that was one of thousands of reasons why he was such a great man.*

June 17

Day 25: The Black Book

Yesterday I drove up to my Omaha office. I'd been having a pretty good day, and was supposed to have a meeting at two with my go-to (manager), Benjamin. As I headed to his office, I walked past Curt's office, which was right next door. I wasn't prepared for how I would react to seeing Curt's office packed up. His office was an empty, ugly shell with plain cardboard boxes stacked neatly, as if they had no awareness of whose valuables they contained. There laid his pictures of bridges—always a symbol to him. I stood in the doorway and cried. I resented that empty room and what it stood for.

Lovingly, Shari, Luann, Gaylene, and Jose helped me take those pictures and boxes to my car. As we loaded all that stuff, I again felt sick to my stomach and full of dark reality, but I still had that meeting with Benjamin. As I went into his office, he hugged me and then he just listened for about forty-five minutes. And offered Kleenex. When I was finally about ready to leave, he handed me a black book, simply entitled, *Curt Liesveld: A Life Well Lived.*

Inside were beautiful tributes to Curt written by so many of our colleagues. And pictures. And Curt's quotes. I tenderly turned each page and cried softly this time, looking up occasionally to smile at Benjamin. I drove home in what felt like a hearse carrying boxes that reminded me of a coffin. The drive was miserable and long.

When I got home, I carried ten heavy boxes from the car to Curt's home office. With each step, I tried to thank God for something. I thanked Him for Shari and Michelle who lovingly packed up that messy office. I thanked Him for a place to work where they care about one's soul as much as one's role. And for the physical strength to move the boxes, and a black book that can help Curt's children, and grandchildren, and great grandchildren know his impact.

> **Think about a book that might be made about you someday and start living out that life.**

June 18

Day 26: An RV

It's hard to pinpoint when and why I miss Curt most, but Johnny's baseball games are a good start. Curt was Johnny's biggest cheerleader at any game, so going to these without him is brutal. Every time Johnny's bat pings the ball, my heart has a little stab of angst that Curt didn't see the hit.

But this year, Johnny's cousin is playing too, so guess who shows up at the games? Most of the Kats family some nights. Last night, Doug and Jane took their RV out to the ball park, and we tailgated before the game. Now, who tailgates before a ten-year-old's game? Well, Curt would have thought it was so fun, especially since he pretty much thought Johnny was the next Alex Gordon. (If you don't know Alex Gordon, go read about Husker/Royals baseball.)

Maybe this summer you can do something to support the kids in your extended family. I hope it's something that includes hot dogs and a ball.

Johnny and his cousin, Teagan

June 19

Day 27: Breathe

Yesterday I felt so aimless and empty. I hadn't slept very well the night before, so I was physically tired. Then I got overwhelmed again with all I need to do yet because of this death thing. I have so much to organize in Curt's office and the garage, and the thought of all of that sometimes makes me a bit crazy. Many thank-you cards still need to be written. Writing isn't hard—finding addresses sometimes is. Marlene has come to help address envelopes and sit with me many times as I write.

Then hell hour came—5:00 p.m. I hate that time of day. It's when my dad used to do chores and Mom was always busy making dinner. As a kid, I just remember it always felt messy, darkish, and a bit cranky during that time of day. Not exactly happy hour. Then I received a text from dear friends, Deb and Craig, with a picture of their new grandson. I felt like maybe my sorrow could be better if I entered into their joy a little. So, I invited them over for a glass of wine.

We sat out on the patio on a beautiful night and ended up talking a lot about Curt. Then we talked about the Brown's grandson. Life and death. Beginning and end. Alpha and omega. And suddenly, I could breathe again.

What's your challenge for today? Find a baby and squeeze her cheeks. Or cuddle him. Or change a diaper to help a tired mom. And know that life and death are both a part of God's bigger plan.

Day 28: Ames vs. The Alps

Curt and I would have been in Switzerland today. Lucerne, I believe. Instead I'm in Ames, Iowa. Not where I thought I'd be on this dreaded Father's Day weekend, but Jane invited me to go along to visit with her daughter and son-in-law, Liz and Jeremy.

Liz is in Vet School, so we got to see the rather impressive vet hospital at Iowa State University. Then we just sat on their porch, talked, cried a little, and ate. Curt officiated Liz and Jeremy's wedding and took a selfie during the ceremony. After he took it, he said, "Now that's the last time I want you to talk about self for a while since marriage is really about a union of two selves."

I am not in Switzerland, but I am with loved ones who let me be myself even though I'm not the life of the party.

> As you go about this weekend and it doesn't quite go as you planned, try to be grateful for what is happening. Sometimes Ames, Iowa, can almost be as good as Switzerland when you are with the right people.

The wedding selfie

June 21

Day 29: Father's Day

My dread of this Father's Day has some light in it. Thank you, Cindy Lange-Kubick of the *Lincoln Journal Star* newspaper, for healing a little part of my heart on this day with your perfectly written article about John and Curt. As always, I hope everyone today can walk proud in their father's steps.

From the *Lincoln Journal Star*:

JACK MITCHELL WALKING HIS FATHER'S WALK
BY CINDY LANGE-KUBICK

On the day before his father died, John Liesveld went for a walk.

It was a Friday in mid-May, cool and turning cloudy. He started from 44th and O streets, the Broadcast House, where he works as a morning host on KLIN radio as Jack Mitchell.

He headed east, the first steps in a 20-mile fundraising trek…

His dad had hurried home from work in Omaha, driving his red convertible from their east Lincoln home to downtown, dropping his wife, Rosanne, off so he could park the Sebring when they spotted their son making his way to Memorial Stadium.

Then the 64-year-old joined them for a picture, John in the middle, all of them grinning…

"It was a very celebratory feeling," John said. "He thought this (annual) walk was one of the very best things I did."

…On the day of his father's funeral, John Liesveld stood in front of the mourners…

He spoke in a voice like his dad's. A son with his father's stocky build, his strong features, his love of Husker sports and Goodrich frozen chocolate malts and Royals baseball.

Curt traveled the world for his job, teaching others to discover and celebrate their strengths, a model developed by Don Clifton, guru of Gallup.

He lived the model. He loved his work. It was his ministry outside the church.

He preached it to John, who discovered his own strengths and used them, happily…

Growing up, John almost never heard his parents criticize others. Not the slow driver in front of them or an annoying coworker or a nosy neighbor.

It was the way his dad taught, by example, like his own father, led by his faith.

"The biggest thing I want to carry is to see people like my dad did. To see what's right about people."

…His grief is still new.

He's feeling his way through, a dad without his own dad.

"He was like my backstop. It feels like the training wheels are off now."

…This week he unlocked his dad's phone for the first time.

He found the last photos he'd taken the day before he died.

His son, John, the happy radio host at the end of a 20-mile day.

If someone wrote an article about you after you died, what would it be about? What would be the headline?

Curt, John, and Rosanne

June 22

Day 30: Empty Chair

How can one feel so normal and almost good for a while, then feel hopeless and heartbroken to the core soon afterwards? My weekend in Ames was not just okay—it was good. I loved being with family. Some of my favorite people all in one spot.

But something happened en route home. Maybe I was just overly tired, or don't like scenic Interstate 80 (that's a joke), or maybe I dreaded seeing the black empty chair in our house. We have two chairs that are exactly alike. Comfy black leather chairs. Curt loved his. The imprint of his bottom is there on the seat. I always teased him that I gave him the best chair—closest to the TV, table on right-hand side for the beverage, etc. When he died, I could have taken that chair, but I haven't.

When I walked in the door yesterday, my house felt lifeless and barren with that black chair staring at me. Then I picked up the print copy of the *Lincoln Journal Star*. The article about John and Curt was big, front and center on the first page. It took our breath away. I was so proud of John, and I missed Curt with all my being.

Tears again—the kind that come from my chest, the kind that make me gag, the kind that won't quit. John and Meagan came to my rescue and suggested the movie *Inside Out* since Norah wanted to see it. Well, I thought I was going to a kids' movie. Nope. They made that movie for grieving and hurting people. The theme? Sadness must be an ally in order to get to joy again. Wow.

Thank you, Walt Disney. You gave me a bit of hope tonight. Not joy, but realistic hope.

> *Go see this movie. It's not just a kids' movie. It's a movie for real people with animated figures telling a parable. I kind of think it was God-ordained.*

June 23

Day 31: A Hug

Yesterday I left to visit my good friend Maika in North Carolina. She could be my daughter, since she's only twenty-nine, but she is a wise young woman and like a soulmate to me. We work together at Gallup and have spent many hours on the road. She is one of the smartest, most interesting, and authentic people I know.

Before I even got to the Lincoln airport, I was getting e-mail updates that O'Hare was a mess because of weather. Great! My grief said, "Why are you doing this? You should just stay home and cry there." But as I landed in Raleigh (only twenty minutes late), I texted Maika like I've done dozens of times at airports asking where I should go to be picked up. The text she sent back read, "You look beautiful." I looked up and there she was, right in front of my eyes.

No one gets picked up inside the airport anymore. And no one has called me beautiful since Curt died. A tiny bit of Curt's love hugged me there in the Raleigh airport, and it was good.

> *Even if you are sixty-three, look for some young friends. They may give you life like Maika gives me. But mostly, don't ever let fear keep you from being with loved ones. It's the closest thing to heaven I know right now.*

June 24

Day 32: Lost and Found

Do you believe there is an Evil One? I do, and he or she was on overtime yesterday. After a wonderful first half of the day in North Carolina, we went to the ocean. To avoid a painfully long post with unnecessary details, let me just say that the day turned miserable when someone stole my iPhone.

We quickly contacted John and asked him to use the Find My Phone app and send us a screen shot of the phone's location. Sure enough, the app could pin point the area where the phone was. The area, however, was a beach crowded with people. We tried texting the phone and offering a reward. We walked in the sand and wind for an hour and a half, using different tactics to try to locate the phone. Finally, the thief was smart enough to turn it off, and we knew the hunt was over.

That was only the start of my misery.

We were running out of time before the Sprint store closed. On top of that, the phone was contracted under Curt's name, and I couldn't get anything changed on the contract without a copy of the death certificate. Maika took over as if she was the mom of this clueless child, and John got on Facebook to alert our friends. Then John's friend Justin helped us reach an executive at Sprint. John used his skills on that phone call to get many workarounds that normally wouldn't have happened. By 10:30 this morning, an amazing Sprint manager had me walking out the door with a new upgraded phone and paying four dollars less a month.

My heroes were an A Team of John, Maika, Justin, the Sprint manager, and Maika's mom, Marcia, who was a calm and steady partner. So, yes, it often feels like an Evil One is warring with the Great One during this time of grief, but I will lean into God's promises and rely on God's A Team.

> *Please do the same. Forgive the thief, have a team that fights battles for you, and above all, believe that you can be victorious over evil. (Oh, and download any app that helps track your phone!)*

June 25

Day 33: "Good"

Most common question asked of me: "How are you doing?"

Most common answer in the last few weeks: "Okay right now."

I never know how to answer, especially if I am being 100 percent honest. Nobody wants me to say words like horrible, hopeless, or angry. When I'm traveling and every plane attendant, person at the register, or gate agent asks, "How are you?" I doubt they really care since they don't know me. And if I told them, "I am not worth a damn right now because my husband just died," they'd be so horrified.

So, this week, when these well-meaning strangers asked how I'm doing, on a few occasions, I said, "Good." It shocked me when I said that word. "Good." Well, I'm not great, but I was good in a few moments, and saying I was good made me believe that some behavior can change how you think and feel.

Curt and I had an ongoing discussion about whether a behavioral or humanistic approach had the most impact on change. Today, I'm going with behavioral (his argument). Saying I was good seemed to change my feelings a tiny bit.

> *Today, try to change some of your words that aren't helping you be better. You may be surprised how much difference it makes.*

June 26

Day 34: Faithfulness

Coming home last night from my short trip was bittersweet. I went directly to the kids' house and was engulfed with hugs and stories. I felt loved. But as the time to go back to my house drew closer, the anxiety grew. Walking alone into the house that I love at night still makes me tense. Sleep came hard, and the night was restless. I needed some beauty and a message that calmed me.

I walked outside just now to feel the calm morning air and saw some beauty. Curt would be all over my flowers with his camera. Now, my phone camera is a humble substitute. The colors, the shapes, the uniqueness of my flowers brought me some peace. I'm so grateful God chose to calm me with a recipe of larkspur, daisies, rudbeckia, and Mexican sunflower. Most of those flowers are perennial and come back each year by reseeding or from their original planting.

Great is thy faithfulness. Morning and evening. Day after day.

Maybe you can come take pictures of my flowers since Curt can't. Or, if not, go buy a perennial and watch the beauty repeat itself as does God's grace.

One of Rosanne's summer pots

Day 35: Relational Depth

Curt would have thought today was a top-ten day. Our dear friends from seminary days, Steve and Martha, came to visit from Michigan. They were planning to come this summer to see us… but still came to see just me.

We had a wonderful day at the Farmers Market in Lincoln. Then I went to a family member's wedding, one Curt was supposed to officiate. Curt's family was there and full of love. After the wedding, Steve and Martha joined me and other dear friends at a winery. How was it that these two groups of friends that represented such different times of our lives seemed like they had all been friends forever?

The evening was full of sweet and deep relationships. But oh, how I kept thinking of Curt and how he would have loved the interplay of human integration and relational depth. The day was both beautiful *and* incomplete. The genius and the pain of the "and."

I'm so sad you weren't with me tonight, Curt. But you would be so happy that our friends have surrounded me with the kind of love that you gave me. Love that is not ordinary. Love that is unending. Love that is not exactly like your love was, but was like a small slice of you for me today.

Friends, invest in relationships. They matter most—both in life and death.

Day 36: Walk Across the Aisle

Sunday. Church. And a message about marriage and husbands. It wasn't easy. I wanted to beg God for just five more minutes with Curt so I could tell him he was the best husband in the world. And then the last song, "Sweetly Broken." The lyrics:

> *At the cross You beckon me*
> *You draw me gently to my knees*
> *And I am lost for words*
> *So lost in love*
> *I'm sweetly broken*
> *Wholly surrendered*

And the tears came. I tried to stop them, but I just couldn't. Suddenly, I felt someone standing beside me. My friend Ann walked across the aisle, stood beside me while the song finished, crying with me, and holding my hand. She was like Jesus in the flesh at that moment. I felt such empathy and deep care. She stayed with me until after church. We just sat there talking. She didn't try to fix anything, but she did show me her unadulterated love and affection—like Curt had done so often for me. Such grief. Such gratitude for her.

Thanks, Ann. Curt would be proud of the way you were using your number-one strength of Empathy.

If you see someone right in the middle of a church service who needs your attention, walk across that aisle and be with them. If you can't find that kind of love in church, where do you find it?

June 29

Day 37: A Song for Curt

It's Monday morning, and it's my day to work on thank-you notes. Some of the people I most want to thank are those who participated in Curt's funeral, including our pastor. Tim provided the perfect introduction to the service.

Following his words, I played the piano as we sang, "Great is Thy Faithfulness."

> *Great is Thy faithfulness, oh God my father;*
> *There is no shadow of turning with Thee;*
> *Thou changest not, Thy compassions they fail not;*
> *As Thou hast been, Thou forever wilt be.*

> *Great is Thy faithfulness! Great is Thy faithfulness!*
> *Morning by morning new mercies I see.*
> *All I have needed Thy hand hath provided;*
> *Great is Thy faithfulness, Lord unto me.*

> *Summer and winter and springtime and harvest,*
> *Sun, moon, and stars in their courses above*
> *Join with all nature in manifold witness*
> *to Thy great faithfulness, mercy and love.*

I played for several reasons: First, I knew it would calm me down to put my fingers on the ivories. Second, I love to play the piano, and this is my favorite hymn. Third, Curt loved to hear me play. He'd often secretly videotape me playing the piano—something which I thought was weird, but now think is so endearing. He gave me our black baby grand piano along with a sweet note. I will never forget those words he wrote about how my willingness to share my musical talent helped him so much in ministry when he was a pastor.

I will miss him not sitting in his chair listening to me play. And honestly, I will miss him telling me he loved to hear me play the piano. But I did get to play for his very important funeral in honor of the man who loved a passionate pianist.

Music heals the soul. Turn on your radio. Pop in a CD
(I know, that's old-school.), plunk out a tune on a piano,
or listen to a great old hymn that Curt loved.

Johnny and Rosanne at the piano

June 30

Day 38: Swing Batter

Energy. I lack it today. Not sure why I feel more tired than usual. Maybe just the busyness of each day. Perhaps the grief…

Who am I kidding? It's a constant bombardment of things to do, memories of the past, and fears of the future that engulf me.

I had no idea how tiring grief can be and how my physical body would respond. The first three weeks after Curt died, I had such a weak, raspy voice. In fact, I felt like I was losing my voice completely right before his funeral. That thought alone sent me into a land of anxiety. I hate not feeling physically well most days. I rush around trying to get everything done that two people used to do, try to work a little part-time, while still dealing with death issues like insurance, bills, thank-you notes, etc., etc. Then I run across something like the old, dirty fishing rag that Curt always wiped his hands on, laying on the bench outside. And I fall apart.

Last night at Johnny's game, I found myself yelling those phrases Curt would often yell like "Rock and fire, Johnny," "Way to go," and yes, even, "Swing, batter." It kind of surprised me. I was shocked that I could elicit that much sound. And I was even more surprised that I felt like yelling for my grandson and his team. So, a weak voice is getting stronger each day—physically and emotionally. But, don't kid yourself, I'm still exhausted all the time.

Today, find your voice. Use it in a powerful but kind way. Speak the truth but in love. Don't comment on everything, but speak up when you can make a difference in this world and make someone else healthier and happier.

July 1

Day 39: Generations

Part of my grief is knowing how others so very close to Curt are grieving. One of those is his mom. She lost a husband twenty-four hours before Curt's funeral. He was ninety-two, and we were ready for him to pass to heaven. Even at that, she lost her precious husband *and* her precious son who cared for his parents so responsibly.

So, yesterday, when John took his daughter, Norah, down to her house, he sent pictures of the three of them. What sweetness and what love. Three generations that love each other in sickness and health, and in life and death. John is like his dad in so many ways, but certainly in how he cares deeply for the same women nowadays. Women named Henrietta and Rosanne.

Grandkids, please visit your grandparents. Or pick up the phone. Or pick some beans with them. It's all good.

Johnny and Norah with Curt's parents, Henrietta and Owen

July 2

Day 40: The Group

The small group of men that Curt met with weekly was of tremendous meaning to him. Each of them are unique and capable of discussing deep spiritual topics, and laughing raucously about some inane story. I grieve for the men in this group because they loved Curt so much. I knew I wanted one of them to speak at Curt's funeral. They all were best friends.

I asked Jeff. It just seemed right. His talk was short, but spot on.

"The men of the group had a tradition, if you will, of meeting every Friday morning early for coffee, and fellowship, and to share the Word of God. Every Friday we would go around the table and each of us in turn would have a chance to share what was happening in our life that week…

"We shared everything. We shared the good and the bad. We shared our wins and our losses…We shared a lot of joy and laughter, and as you all know, Curt's laughter was pretty infectious. Sometimes we were kind of disruptive at the coffee shop because of that.

"But we also shared a lot of hurt and sorrow and pain, fears and tears… Another topic we seemed to hit on quite a bit was how do you maintain your faith and trust in God when life seems to be so darn unfair. It was during these discussions, these moments, that Curt's light shined the most brightly for me. His loving, caring, compassionate nature, his ability to articulate and speak of Christ's love and grace, always reassured me that it was God who was talking to me through Curt."

Is there a group that is so important in your life that you hate missing any of the get-togethers? If you don't have a group, ask at your church. Or just form one of your own. Someday, one of them might be the person to speak at your funeral too.

July 3

Day 41: A Good Conversation

I really miss not talking with Curt. He was a great listener. He often teased me because I would list off the things I had gotten done that day. He simply would listen to me talk passionately about my latest opinion or new idea. Even when one of us was gone at night, we always talked on the phone.

When I got home last night, I just wanted to tell him that I went to a pool party hosted by friends Carrie, Dick, and Kathy, and that it was so fun to see Johnny and Norah playing with John's friends' kids. He would have enjoyed the generational friendship. And that everyone at the party was so kind. And that I got to know some people better whom I've always admired. I wanted to tell him the perennials in the front of our house are at the peak. He would be taking lots of pictures of them. And that Johnny and Norah stayed overnight and both slept in my queen bed last night. Yes, it was cozy. And that I have a very busy day today—a long list of to-dos. He would say, "That doesn't surprise me."

What can I be grateful for? That even though I can't talk to Curt, I still have things that give me some joy. I have friends who include me in their activities, and who treat the widow so kindly and lovingly. That my flowers still look good after being neglected much of this summer. That Johnny and Norah live five minutes away and can sleep over anytime. And that I have a bed they can sleep in with me. And someday, when we get to heaven together, Curt will be waiting for me ready for us to talk through a lot of good things.

Today, have a good conversation. Or be a good listener.
Communication makes life richer.

Day 42: Fireworks

We loved throwing a Fourth of July party. For twenty-nine years, we have hosted a party that featured favorites like water balloons, fireworks, hot dogs, and fishing.

Curt was not usually the life of the party (or even the instigator), but on this holiday, he could have given Uncle Sam a run for his money. I don't know if it was his roots as a kid growing up in small Holland, Nebraska, where the Sunday School put on one heck of a picnic, or just because it was a totally fun holiday where all ages and types of people could gather and celebrate our awesome country.

I've dreaded this day. I woke up this morning with half of the bed empty and felt a weight of dread and grief. Fireworks sounded more like threatening bombs to me. Curt won't be joining in the fun this year. He won't be my party partner.

A week ago, John asked, "What will we do if we don't host the party? We won't have anything to do, and that will be worse." So, we created some new normal. I hosted a come-one, come-all brunch this morning. With a host of help, (Thank you, Ron and Marlene, Jane and Doug) the fishing poles were ready, the patio was clean, and there was an abundance of food. People who have touched our lives from so many different walks of life came together like a beautiful tapestry. Kids ran around, adults renewed old friendships and met new people—something that spells future to me.

Tonight, we'll gather at John and Meagan's. They will host, and John, like his dad, will make the Fourth a holiday that celebrates a country of people who are blessed to be a blessing.

I missed you so much today, Curt. You would be so grateful for how people helped me. You would be so proud of John and Meagan walking in your footsteps. You would have loved to be here. But Norah reminded me again that she is sure Poppo can see everything from heaven—especially the big fireworks.

> *Today, be thankful for the country that we call America. Today, when you hear the fireworks, think of Curt and how he loved to make people happy on this holiday. Today, invite someone to your party who needs a place to go. That's what Curt always did.*

July 5

Day 43: Single Grandparent

This morning at church, Johnny sang as part of the worship team. When I looked up and saw him standing there, he looked just like a ten-year-old Curt.

You see, I knew Curt my whole life. I knew him as a freckle-faced ten-year-old who always knew the answers first in Sunday School. Looking up at Johnny singing, I wanted so much for Curt to stand beside me and squeeze my hand as if to say, "These grandkids are, at least in part, a result of our passionate love for each other."

After Johnny sang, we all turned around to greet each other in church. Behind me was Johnny's amazing Sunday School teacher, LaLanne. She said, "Did you see how Johnny looked to you for strength when he got up there?"

Why, yes, I did notice. So, I will be the best grandparent I can be—working to teach, support, and cheerlead.

> *If you are a single grandparent, know you still count to your precious grandkids. And if you are blessed to be a grandparent team, squeeze each other's hands tightly while watching your precious grandkids. It feels so good.*

Johnny and Rosanne singing

July 6

Day 44: A Plaid Shirt

Yesterday was tough. Sundays are the worst. And I was tired. And trying to be two people again. Plus, my social responsibility wears me out now. That's a phrase Curt used about me: social responsibility. Maybe it's a combination of Relator and Significance talents, but it causes me to always try to make other people comfortable, happy, feel good about themselves, etc. I even do it with my family.

Before May 16th, I did that quite naturally, but now, sometimes I get worn out. By the end of the day yesterday, the weariness, the work at being both Poppo and Grammy, the garbage Curt usually collected on Sunday, the good church that can be so hard to attend these days, and the reality of death came down hard on me. A not-ripe watermelon finally made me break down. I cried and cried, then decided I might as well add more hurt, and try to finally clean up more in Curt's office.

The boxes from work were still there, along with about ten pieces of clothing no one had claimed. Slowly, I went through all that stuff again. The final piece was a plaid shirt Curt wore. Nothing special. One he probably got on sale. But he wore it often, and no one wanted it. Except me. I cried into it for two hours. Not just weeping, but crying from my stomach in a way that makes me feel sick.

After that, I can't find much to feel grateful for today, so I'm asking each of you to pray for me today. I need to find some light. I guess I can be grateful for the fact that I have praying people in my life who will be my intercessors when I can't find a way to pray anymore. Please pray for me. Pray with confidence. And pray with humility.

> *Who needs your prayers right now?*

July 7

Day 45: Labels

Thank you for the outpouring of prayers and love after yesterday's post. I found it profoundly moving and healing. I woke up this morning with less of a scarred heart—at least for the moment.

I have used the word "widow" often in these writings. I've never loved my name, Rosanne. I prefer to be called Rose or Rosey, as I was in high school, college, and seminary days. I'm not a stranger to having a label that I didn't love. I have loved the labels of teacher, pastor's wife, gardener, friend, Mom, Grammy, sister, aunt, musician, hostess, believer, and co-worker, to name just a few. But *widow* I never anticipated. It's a word that gives me negative connotations. It goes with things like "black widow spider," "lonely widow," and "old widow." Real nice, huh?

But I will learn to embrace it—or maybe I won't. But what other word can I use to describe my new role? "No longer married to an amazing man?" "Single now and not happy about it?" Maybe no label at all. Maybe a conversation instead of a label. Maybe someone can just listen to me describe my new state. I know that's not practical or easy, but maybe we'd have fewer problems in the world if we used fewer labels that the labelee (I know that's not a word, but it worked for me) really doesn't appreciate. What would happen if we just took time to talk with people and let them describe themselves the way they want to be described?

> *Labels are usually not very individualized, and Curt hated that. He wanted to know your story, know your uniqueness, and know your strengths. Maybe you can try to drop some labels from your vocabulary and instead just have a conversation. Know that people are more than labels. Especially widows.*

July 8

Day 46: Wait

When I wake up in the morning, my first thoughts are always that Curt is not sleeping in bed with me. He is no longer alive. When I went to bed last night, trying to find sleep, a picture of his hand with his wedding ring kept popping into my mind. I sometimes wonder how long those things will happen.

Everything—yes, every little thing—reminds me of Curt. I can do something as insignificant as go grocery shopping, and I think about what kind of food he'd want me to get. Or I turn off the air conditioner and wonder if he would not want me to. Or a topic comes up in a conversation, and I am more driven to say what his opinion was than mine. I am afraid it will be this way a long, long time before this kind of thing stops. And then I wonder, should I want it to stop? The fear of living in grief for an eternity is sometimes more than the grief of Curt's death. Does that make sense? Like the Psalmist says, "How long, Lord?"

Most research says the first year is the hardest, but that it takes two years to get over a spouse's death. Seriously? In some ways that seems like an intolerably long time when I think of the mornings I wake up to the almost-new news that Curt is gone. But in other ways, I don't see why or how I would ever NOT beware of Curt's life every minute of the day. So, watching seconds, minutes, days and months go by is hard.

Curt's word for the year was *light*. My word was *wait*. So, I guess I will wait, and that's not easy for me to do with Activator as one of my primary talents. But I will wait… and I will, in some weird way, try to enjoy the waiting, knowing it still brings me close to Curt each minute of the day. I didn't mind the picture of his hand with his wedding ring on. It felt good.

So, wait, Rosey. Wait on the Lord with all your strength. How well do you wait? Is there something in life for which you need more patience? Is there someone in your world who needs you to wait better? Even if just for today?

Day 47: Facebook

Some of you have asked me how long I plan to post the grief and gratitude posts. The answer is I have no idea. I started this writing out of a tremendous sense of frustration. I felt inadequate in knowing how to thank people for how much they had done for me in that first week. Facebook was a friend to me even in those early days of grief because I could read and feel so many beautiful words of sympathy. And Curt loved Facebook.

I wrote the first post just for John to thank him for his ongoing and powerful support during those days. And after my fingers left the keys, I felt slightly relieved—even buoyed—having talked about the grief, but also the gratitude. I decided day one would turn into day two. And day two turned into day three. And so on and so forth. Many of you have suggested I shouldn't feel pressured to keep posting. I get that, but honestly, it's the equivalent to taking a Xanax right before having an honest talk with God accompanied by floods of tears. It makes me relax. It makes me think more clearly. I can be honest. I can feel more like I can do this. I can talk about faith and its impact on me. And mostly, I can find something to be grateful for—even though some days, it's nearly impossible.

Don't worry—I will stop this sometime. You won't have to read these long posts forever. For now, suffice it to say, my grief has not lessened. It has changed from shock to realism. Some days I beg God for five more minutes with Curt. On those days, I try so hard to find the light—the light Curt would want me to find.

The light for me today is all of you who take the time to just comment on my posts in a way that makes me feel loved. I sometimes intentionally don't read Facebook during the day so I can hoard it and look forward to reading it in the evening. Mark Zuckerberg, thanks. I bet you didn't know you would help this grief-stricken woman.

July 10

Day 48: 10,000 Steps

I've not had much stamina since Curt died. I'm not used to wearing out physically. I feel so sluggish and that makes me feel like I'm abnormal. And weak. And lazy. And worthless. I just had no idea how much grief would manifest itself in my physical body. It's impossible to explain or describe. I've never experienced anything so physically demanding.

Today I was helping a friend with moving and I happened to look at the number of steps the fitness app on my phone had recorded. It said 10,000. That made me feel a little better and made me think about needing to intentionally get some basic exercise starting tomorrow. Just walking for now. I think it may give me a second wind both physically and emotionally.

What's your favorite way to exercise? Maybe join me in starting over with some physical well-being. Want to go for a walk?

Day 49: Glazed Berry

Since Curt died, so many things in my life seem shallow. Unnecessary. Frivolous. I didn't feel right riding in our convertible anymore. Or eating dessert. And putting on makeup seemed so out of sync with my feelings. The first morning after Curt died, Norah was laying in my lap. She said, "Grammy, you forgot to put that black stuff on your eyes." Yup, not much desire to put on mascara. And the first time I put on lipstick was for the funeral, I felt conflicted. I can't really explain how I felt and still feel. I can only come up with the word "frivolous" when I think about how I feel or how I don't want to be seen.

Last week, I had lunch with my good friends from work, Melissa and Allison. They made me feel a bit normal. They were oh-so-tolerant, even as I recited the same details about my grief. At the end of lunch, I complimented Melissa on her lipstick. I felt weird talking about something so frivolous. In my mail today was a tiny box from a well-known store. Inside it was a tube of lipstick—Clinique Glazed Berry, the color I'd admired on Melissa's lips. The card read, "Rosey, I hope you can find joy in some of life's frivolous gifts."

I went into the bathroom, wiped away the tears, and applied the lipstick. It still feels frivolous, but Curt very much liked my frivolous side. He always told me he liked how I looked, as recently as the night before he died. I'm trying to do some things without feeling like I'm asynchronous with my deep loss.

It's weird. But maybe you need to occasionally have a little glazed berry in your life too. Or at least some friends who take you to lunch and make you feel normal, even if you are a widow wearing lipstick.

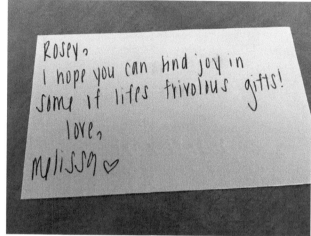

Rosey,
I hope you can find joy in
some of lifes trivolous gifts!
love,
Melissa ♡

A gift of lipstick

July 12

Day 50: Handwriting

Today I decided I had to tackle Curt's office—actually, the drawers of his office. They were rather unorganized. About twenty-five percent of it was Gallup-related stuff, about twenty-five percent church related. Another twenty-five percent of it related to photography (mostly photographs he took that he didn't deem good enough), ten percent a million different cords to who knows what, another ten percent random things like the horn he used during the Fourth of July balloon toss, and five percent tax returns. (Is it still standard that you only need to keep tax returns for seven years?)

Anyway, it took me about four hours. Most of it wasn't too hard emotionally, except when I'd see Curt's handwriting. Then I wanted him back so badly. I didn't know how much I loved his handwriting, and how much it reflected his thinking. Lots of little notes and conceptual ideas—Intellectual combined with Belief as well as Analytical and spiritual. Complicated yet simple, which is such an apt description of how Curt lived and believed.

His handwriting did me in today, but what a privilege that I have so much of his thinking documented in sermon notes, Gallup books, and of course, cards he wrote to me. Below are some random pieces of his writing I found stuffed in the drawers. The top one is a note from Don Clifton. He wrote it early in Curt's career at Gallup. Curt did study champions and thereby became a champion himself.

> *Who is your champion? Who can you champion? And what does your handwriting reflect about you?*

Handwritten notes

July 13

Day 51: Spoiled

When I went through Curt's office I found a notebook that was several years old. Under one tab it said *Gift Ideas*, and had the list of gifts below. Yes, he was an amazing gift-giver. And generous. Never a significant day went by without me receiving a gift he had thought about oh-so-carefully. And flowers. I also found three different florist's numbers in that book so he could send me flowers on just any old day.

I was spoiled, and I will miss that. I felt loved and special when he gave me those gifts. I have tokens of his affection that will last me for the rest of my life. I can count thirteen rings alone Curt gave me. I'm truly thankful. I have a lot of symbols of his love I treasure with all my being.

> *If you are married to the love of your life like I was, bring home a token of that love. Maybe one of those five-dollar flower bouquets you get at the grocery store. Or maybe a pretty ring. Or a good book. Or a paper towel holder. It's always the thought that counts.*

Curt's gift list

Day 52: The Garage

This morning I tried tackling some of the garage. It's the area I dread so much. I don't know how to "do" a garage without Curt. And it's messy. And full of stuff I don't know what to do with. I didn't have much claim to it, so it smacks of him over and over.

The insulated overall I gave him for Christmas may have been one of his favorite gifts. And gloves that covered his hands as he scooped lots of snow off the pond. And hooded sweatshirts. And dirty boots. He wore those to clean off the spillway—one of the outside jobs he seemed to enjoy, oddly enough.

It was a top-ten day when he got out in his winter clothes. He was like a little kid when it snowed. We both loved winter on the pond. Today it is hot outside, and I am angry about the heat. I just want Curt back with these goofy clothes on working and playing outside in the snow.

Yeah, I'm digging deep for gratitude today. Memories? Right now, they aren't enough to overpower the grief. Maybe I should be glad I have a garage. I'm sure there are quite a few people who would find that a luxury. Americans are spoiled. Anyway, I'm hoping I can find some gratitude yet as I plod through this foreign country called the garage.

> *Do you have a garage? If so, be thankful for it.*
> *Or maybe clean it this weekend and think of Curt. Or find a*
> *pair of dirty boots and think of them as a real treasure.*

July 15

Day 53: Processing

I woke up this morning feeling tired again. Sleep wouldn't come last night until 2:00 a.m. I probably was over-stimulated—in a good way.

Two good friends, Jillene and Shari, came to see me last night. We went out to dinner, and the three of us talked for four hours. You see, they knew Curt and loved him too. Yesterday, I was feeling like I wasn't getting to talk about him much. I still think about him 100 percent of my day, but I don't get to talk about those thoughts and feelings often anymore. Sometimes, the time and place just aren't right, and, truthfully, who wants to hear me talk about Curt constantly and then deal with all those tears? I cried a bucket last night. Just ask Shari and Jillene. But I liked that they asked me meaningful questions and listened with such intensity and love. It was a good night because I got down to the depth of my soul again.

Curt said some people think to process and others talk to process. Well, he was the thinker, and I was the talker. But the problem is, now I think more than I get to talk, so it is hard to feel like I get to work through things. I got to emotionally process with people last night, and they understood. They told me things like, "He looked at you like you were his new bride every day." And "He always told stories about you in all his classes and used your strengths as examples." And "Everyone at Gallup admired your marriage." And the best, "Your love story was evident to everyone you were around."

Their words mixed with my words equaled power—power of love, power of relationship, and power of gratitude. I am so thankful for friends who still want to talk for hours about Curt. Just so you know, I'm not done with it yet by any stretch.

Consider whether you need to let someone talk until their heart feels a little stronger. Or consider whether you should open up and talk more when you need to expose your real self. Whether you are the talker or the listener, just do it. Get from behind your wall of isolation and use your words and your ears for good.

Day 54: Theme Thursday

Curt was known around the world for his work around strengths theory and practice. The night of his death, I received an e-mail from one of his colleagues in Asia that said, "As the sun is setting over Asia tonight, our country has gone even darker because our friend and colleague Curt Liesveld has died."

One of the things Curt did was interview individuals on one of their Signature Strengths to create an online video series called "Theme Thursday." He was so good at it. He and his colleague Jim did a masterful job. I believe Curt had completed twenty-four of the thirty-four strength themes. He loved that part of his job, and these broadcasts were followed by thousands. Watching these videos is so hard and yet so good.

Next Thursday, John will be the guest on the first webcast since Curt's death. John will be interviewed by one of my best friends, Maika, and his featured strength will be Significance—a theme I share with him. People who have Significance are independent and want to be viewed as important in the eyes of others. I can't wait to hear what we learn about John and this strength.

After John's webcast, I wrote down some of the significant things he said:

"Significance: The goal is to have the biggest impact on as many people as possible."

"Recognition isn't the end game… It's about putting the fuel into making something big happen down the road."

"Significance is the fuel to get to the goal of impact."

"You aren't bashful about letting other people know you are proud of them."

"At his funeral, when I spoke… I got to have a captive audience… I wanted the people there to be inspired by what my dad was about."

"You want someone in your life who is not afraid of the big stage when it comes along."

> *What are your strengths? Can you tell me? Do you use them for good? Wear them with responsibility and confidence for Curt today. Actually, every day. Actually, for eternity.*

John on "Theme Thursday"

July 17

Day 55: Thank-You Notes

I've finished writing all the formal thank-you notes to people who gave memorial gift money, food, flowers, and helped with the funeral. I believe I've written more than two hundred notes. Marlene came to my house faithfully for several days and spent hours addressing the envelopes. Believe me, it's not always easy to find addresses, and she was a sleuth. The bonus was that Ron would come, wander around the house and yard, and find something he could fix. Unbelievable help.

The thank-yous were a great example of grief and gratitude. At the end of writing sometimes twenty-five or thirty notes, I would be emotionally exhausted after thinking about each of the people, of how they loved Curt, and how they gave so generously. Sometimes I was just shocked at the generosity. It always felt good to write the notes. I felt connected. I felt thankful for this congregation of Curt and Rosanne's life-giving friends and relatives.

Curt would have been amazed too. I still carry the frustration that I probably missed many people whom I should have formally thanked. I had wonderful scribes writing down the people and their contributions, but you know things fall through the cracks.

So, here is my sincere thank you to those I missed: You did the work of angels. You hovered over me and my family during our darkest days. You were Mary and you were Martha. Thank you. I hope someday I can pay you back.

> **Folks, showing up is half the battle. If you can, take someone a casserole or Kleenex, or make a memorial contribution to a great cause (like Curt's grandchildren's education). It is the highest calling.**

Marlene and Rosanne

July 18

Day 56: Poppo

Today is another of those difficult firsts. Norah turns five today. I worry so much that she won't remember Curt, better known as Poppo. Although just the other day when she was doing a dot-to-dot, she said rather matter-of-factly, "Poppo told me to draw to the dots, not just the numbers." Important stuff, you know!

When I think of Curt at his best, I think of his moments with the grandkids. I can see so clearly how he'd tuck his chin into his chest and crinkle up his nose in laughter at Norah's commentary or antics. He'd say, "What a little twerp," "Isn't she just something else?" or "What a cutie!"

Norah thinks she is a teacher and has us pretty much convinced she will be one someday. But she also says she wants to become a doctor. I'm thankful she has Curt's DNA running through her. I miss him so much by my side today. We were perhaps most madly in love with each other when we watched our grandkids. This day hurts. But when I need a shot of positivity, I just listen to Norah give her rendition of heaven. She is convinced Poppo's enjoying seeing everything from up there and that it's a pretty cool place. I'm grateful Curt got to show her how to fish, take her on tons of bike rides, and agreed to be her student when she was playing teacher. And I'm glad he took hundreds of pictures of her.

Happy birthday, Norah. Your Poppo loves you.

Remember birthdays are a big deal. Go all out and celebrate yours when it comes around. Or celebrate someone who might be alone or lonely. Buy a card. Bake a cake. Buy a gift. And today, please say a prayer for all of us as we go through another first.

Curt and Norah

Day 57: Almost Perfect

I am thinking more and more about our marriage and how it was almost perfect. Not perfect—but almost. I love how our dear friend Rick eulogized Curt. He talked of him in the present tense. He talked about how we should always think of him as being in the next room. But the part I loved the most was when he talked about our marriage. Here is part of what he shared:

> "It's just impossible, really, to say everything that you want in five minutes. It's the tip of the iceberg. And I'm going to do something odd today. I'm going to speak in the present tense, just because Curt's here with us in ways. I think those of you who know his strengths work know that strengths don't go away.

> "Curt, I promise you, is one out of a hundred… He's filled with knowledge and possibilities, and genuinely enjoys contributing to the welfare of others. He's complicated so he can understand the complexities of others… He shifts from solitude and concentration to reaching out to others… He gives approval… and, I think, liked approval as well.

> "He's a warm and enthusiastic man… He's a man who enjoyed sensual things…

> "And that brings me to his relationship with Rosanne…many people have remarked about what an inspiration they are as a couple.

> "Listen to what Curt writes in his anniversary card to Rosanne this last year. Men, listen to it. Curt says, 'When I think of all that I have and all that I have done in my life, our marriage is by far my greatest possession and my greatest accomplishment. I thank God for giving me you, and I thank you for being the perfect marriage partner.' Think about that really. Greatest possession and greatest accomplishment. How many of us men think about our marriages in that way and take ownership and action?

"He also e-mailed Rosanne as they built their home in The Preserve: 'Together we've done some wonderful and amazing things. I love you. I trust and admire your instincts and motives. My life has been bigger and better because of you and your desire for more for yourself and others.'"

You see, I asked Rick to speak because I've always admired his marriage with his wife Diane. It was much like ours. When Rick talked about Curt, the husband, it was authentic and oh-so-accurate.

Yes, ours was a marriage to be proud of. I never imagined that our marriage would have so much impact on both me and those around us. Curt was my perfect husband most days, most months, and every year. I had a marriage for almost forty-four years that most people don't experience ever in their lifetime.

Lately, I am grieving more deeply than you can ever imagine. I am also grateful for having a man who made me a woman who could live her life to the fullest. Perhaps one day in the future, that same love will help me live to my fullest potential once again.

> *Please be grateful for your spouse. Encourage them. Honor them. Help him or her live to the fullest.*

July 20

Day 58: A Good Question

After Curt's death, I asked to be relieved of most of my work duties until after Labor Day. I did commit about twenty-five percent of my time to some mentoring, and today, I am teaching for the first time since early May.

The trip to Phoenix went fine. I got to sit on the plane next to one of my best friends at Gallup, JerLene. We talked about teaching fifty teachers how they can teach with their strengths, so I was in my wheelhouse. Then I reached our conference center, which happens to be a beautiful resort. All I could remember was that the last time I was here I wasn't a widow. I kept wanting to text or call Curt and tell him about my trip and day.

I was greeted almost immediately by my other great colleagues, Nancy and Tim. During dinner, we planned and talked; they listened and didn't make me feel bad for crying in public. Nancy asked me a great question: "What has comforted you the most?" Her question helped me focus on something positive. It took me a while to think about, but here are my thoughts:

- ❀ Other people who have gone through grief and now have full and meaningful lives.

- ❀ That I have no regrets concerning my life with Curt and would not do anything differently.

- ❀ My grandchildren—especially Johnny, as he is the easiest person I can talk with about our loss. He is wise beyond his years.

- ❀ Faith. I do believe in heaven and I do believe Curt is now in a place that we can't even imagine.

In about an hour, I will stand in front of some of the most important people in our world—teachers. And I get to teach, challenge, and create hope for an even better future. I hope I don't fall apart at some point. But I may, so keep me in your prayers today.

> *Ask someone a good question like I was asked last night.*
> *Focus that question on something that helps them study their success.*
> *It will be a game-changer for someone.*

July 21

Day 59: Cheerleaders

Last night while I was away on my first work trip, Johnny played in a baseball tournament. They won their first game 3-2. Johnny pitched the last two innings, and struck out four players, including the last batter. (I'm sure Curt would have embellished on that quite a bit more.) I was so disappointed I missed his big game. All I could think of was how wildly excited Curt would have been to see that game. Yes, I know it's only ten-year-olds, but Curt thought it was the major leagues when Johnny played.

When I called back home to talk to Johnny, I learned that there were twenty-two family members there to watch him and his cousin play. They were standing in the gap for Curt last night. Even Johnny's Great Grandma Liesveld was there, and, at ninety-two, had a pretty fun night, as I understand. Thank you to my family and Curt's family for cheering on not only Johnny, but all of us who still ache for Curt to be in the stands. You showed up. And once again, that was everything. I'm so proud of Johnny, but I'm also grateful and proud of our families.

> *Do you like baseball? Do you like dancing? Do you like piano recitals?*
> *Do you like plays? Well, maybe not, but if you love your family,*
> *show up at the things they are involved in once in a while.*
> *That's what families do. At least our family does.*

Johnny on the mound

July 22

Day 60: Ask

Last night I had dinner with a great friend from our seminary days. He lost his wife several years ago and much too early. As we talked, I felt understood and cared for perhaps more than ever in the days since Curt's death.

He was realistic and yet provided healing hope. My grief was realizing I hadn't supported him more at the time of his loss. I've found that the best comforters are those who have lost loved ones too. They just seem like they know what to say as much as what not to say. I'm probably not a good grief support group person, but I do have my own private grief group. I love and respect those friends who also call themselves widows and widowers. It's not a club I had aspired to be a part of, but it works for me right now.

If you need someone, go find them. Ask them out for dinner. Don't wait to be found. Ask for help. Ask for a friend.

July 23

Day 61: The Ivories

Music has always been a huge part of my life. My undergraduate degree was in vocal and piano. I love to play the piano, especially the black baby grand piano Curt gave me for Christmas.

I haven't put my fingers on the ivories since the day of Curt's funeral, but last night, for some reason, I sat down at the piano. The first song I opened to was the classic, "I Will Always Love You," made famous first by Dolly Parton and later by Whitney Houston. I gave Whitney Houston's album to Curt for Valentine's Day many years ago, and I remember perfectly how we loved listening to it and loved how it made us feel. He was quite the romantic at heart whenever you put on the right music.

I'm not sure why I thought it was a good idea to start playing that song last night, but nowadays I do a lot of things that don't make sense. My tears and my fingers were soon in perfect rhythm. I imagined dancing with Curt. I imagined him watching me play, then slowly moving over to the piano to be close to me. I imagined a lot of beautiful things too personal for this public audience. I don't know when I will ever be able to listen to some songs without feeling a deep sense of sadness. I didn't have much gratitude except knowing that those who grieve deeply, loved deeply.

I don't think I'll play a song like that for a while. The pain is too great. I need to pull out Bach or Rachmaninoff so I can pound out more neutral emotions. And I can do that because I have such a beautiful piano right in my house. I love that piano. And I love that Curt loved me playing the piano. Such powerful memories. I am determined to use the piano as a source of healing rather than pain. I'm sure it won't be a smooth road, but then, neither was learning a first hard song to play. It was usually clunky, had a bad sense of timing, and often sounded off-key. In time, I think I will be okay with playing most anything on the piano, even difficult songs, both as a musician and as a woman who lost her first and only love.

> *Do you have a piano? Do you like piano music? Play the piano, even if it's sometimes clunky. Or give piano lessons to your kids and grandkids. Or just buy an album to listen to some peaceful, soul-filling, and healing piano music. And know that "I Will Always Love You"—each of you who has helped me during these most difficult days of my life.*

Day 62: Legacy

Legacy. That word was used a lot during the days following Curt's death. The song sung at his funeral was named, "Legacy." I had always loved that song and remember well the first time Curt and I heard it at a church conference. We both had tears streaming down our faces listening to the powerful words. Just this morning, our good friend Laura had a post on Facebook about legacy relative to Curt's life.

Curt and I always shared a passion about each other's work and almost saw each other as equal partners around our work. We talked work, and concepts, and purpose, and responsibility as much as some people talk about their travel plans or vacations. That's who Curt was from early in his high school years, and I loved that about him. I loved that I got to catch his fever of purpose-driven living. Yesterday, when John was featured on Gallup's "Theme Thursday" online video program, I saw a comment from a person in Nairobi who couldn't wait to hear from Curt's son. Curt had a pretty awesome impact around the globe.

I feel less complete now without his life to add to mine in terms of that missional impact. I know it's just me now, but I didn't lose my calling completely. I read one author who wrote, "At the end I decided that I didn't want my legacy to be all about grief." Right now, it's hard to see the impact of just my single life, but I want to leave a legacy too, which means I need to worry less about myself and more about others. What a simple concept that is so hard to live out, perhaps now more than ever. A legacy doesn't have to look like Curt's life, but it does mean living for more than just yourself as he did so beautifully.

> *What will your legacy be? Your children? Your generous sharing of your resources? Teaching someone to read? Offering to help someone who is weak or sad or who lacks resources? Helping a neighbor and loving them as yourself? Curt would say that his life was well-lived. I would say he left a legacy.*

July 25

Day 63: Vacations

It's the time of year for family vacations. We have taken quite a few trips with our whole family over the years. San Francisco, Chicago, Black Hills, Colorado, and this year, Kansas City. Our plan was to see a Royals baseball game since Curt, John, and Johnny are big fans. This weekend we are all in Kansas City. I don't know if we would have gone except that Jane and Doug said they'd go with us, which made it easier for another first.

Yes, things keep reminding me of Curt. In the pool last night, the kids would have been jumping into his arms instead of mine. He would have had his camera out often capturing the joy of his grandkids. Tonight, he would have made sure we were at the ballpark early to see batting practice.

My head and heart are distracted this weekend. It's been different, but it's been good. I got Norah an American Girl Doll and it was a pretty fun Grammy spoil time. I played in the pool with her just like Curt would have. Tonight, we will cheer on Curt's Royals without him, but we will be happy for the family that we have. I'm grateful that family fills in so many spaces Curt left. Maybe it's not quite the same, but it's much, much better than solitude for me.

Weekend trips are good. Vacations are great. Including someone who may feel left out is saintly. I'm so grateful for my family and how they step up to keep life moving toward new and good possibilities.

> *What are your favorite vacation spots? You don't have to travel the world to find special places. Are you making the kind of memories that will last forever?*

July 26

Day 64: Overnight Guests

I'm going home again. After a pain-healing weekend with family, I must face the fact that I'm going home alone. I miss Curt winding down the day sitting beside me in his chair. I miss going to bed at the same time. I miss having a partner to discuss the upcoming week with when I get home.

The first nights after Curt died are pretty much a blur, but I do remember that the first three nights someone stayed overnight with me. John and his family along with Anne stayed that first horrible, gut-wrenching night. Then the next two nights, some of my best friends stayed: Linda, Rita, and my sister Jane. Although I didn't have overnight support after those first three nights, I had others who stayed with me late into the night until I thought I could maybe sleep.

I don't know how I would have survived those nights staying alone in my house. I've heard of widows who went weeks before they could stay alone. Maybe it helped that both Curt and I traveled so much and were often solo at night. Who am I kidding? I knew he was eventually coming home, but now it's forever. I still hate going home alone, or having a long evening alone. I wasn't cut out for that.

The folks who stayed with me during those first few nights gave me the security and care I needed so, so badly.

The truth is, for weeks I was afraid of my house. I am no longer afraid, even though I'm still empty and sad. John told me early on when I said how I hated going home, "Mom, it's sad, but it's not dark."

> *If you know someone who is afraid, give them some of your courage. Maybe have some guests in your home in times of joy before you go through hell and need guests when you face some awful adversity. Overnight guests are best. They were my lifeline.*

July 27

Day 65: 24 Hours

I often think about what I'd do or say if I had twenty-four more hours with Curt. I have envisioned a romantic dinner, sitting outside on our patio, watching whatever game he was watching. I envision an overnight with our grandkids, and Curt carrying them up to their beds after they fall asleep in my arms. I envision how he'd say I look nice and then kiss me. I envision how he'd be taking pictures of some big event, or of some of the latest flowers blooming. I envision him coming home from work and talking to me about what a good week he had with his students. I envision going to something for the grandkids and he and I exchanging knowing looks. I envision us doing something fun with friends or relatives and him smiling as they told their stories and he listened.

Well, that was very much like his last twenty-four hours. I just happened to review it in my head yesterday and I believe it was a perfect last twenty-four hours for him. At noon, twenty-four hours before he died, he was finishing up a week-long strengths coach class in Omaha. He loved teaching strengths. He had a great week with those students. He walked in with his suit coat draped over his index finger and said, "Man, I'm glad to be home." Then we scurried off to see John on the last few miles of his walk across Lincoln. He had his camera of course, and took a picture of John, him, and me in front of Memorial Stadium.

I remember how Curt smiled the whole time while we celebrated John's successful walk and how he kept taking pictures. He was so proud of John and his dedication to this city and a great cause. Then we rushed home to get changed for Johnny's concert. When I came out of the bathroom dressed up for the concert, he said, "Wow, you look great. I like your face." Isn't that a funny comment? When we got to the concert, he took a picture of Norah and me just because he liked the way we looked that night. At the concert, he was tired but oh-so-proud of his grandson. Tears came down both of our faces on that last song called "River in Judea."

Finally, off to John and Meagan's for a family dinner before heading home to his easy chair where he watched sports for just a little while.

Saturday morning, off to the farmer's market where we were with many of my family members, drinking coffee in the Haymarket. I remember how he smiled when my brother-in-law said he'd met someone who knew Curt, and that "Curt was an international expert on strengths."

Then we went home to do our Saturday morning chores around the yard. He wanted to get some things done and then planned to run over to see his mom and his dad. He had the usual list I'd created for us to get done on Saturday, but he added more to it that day. He cut branches, he cleaned up around some of the yard, and he really wanted to get the lawn mowed. The last thing I said to him is, "Wow, the lawn really looks good." I remember he looked so happy mowing. Not one sign of distress even just a couple of minutes before he went down.

So, that was a good twenty-four hours.

No, it was a great twenty-four hours. He was a happy man. I know he died happy. I think if he could have another twenty-four hours, we would plan the same kind of day. That is a blessing. That is huge. That gives me some peace.

If you died in twenty-four hours, what would you have done today? No regrets? Curt didn't have to do anything big on most days to have joy. He lived each day with purpose and joy and gratitude. He embraced the everyday pleasures. What a good last twenty-four hours he had. Thank you, God.

Curt teaching about strengths

Day 66: Love Notes

Last night, after more than sixty nights of having something to do since Curt died, I had my first full and long night all alone at home. I spent too much time wandering around in the grocery store figuring out what I could eat. I don't like to cook, which doesn't bode well for a single person. I ended up with a frozen meal and wine. Nice combo, huh?

I was doing pretty well, just catching up on work and reading a bit, until I happened to walk by the big basket of cards, letters, and e-mails. I opened a manila envelope with the e-mails from Gallup associates—many of which came within twenty-four hours of my difficult new reality. As I read them, I saw recurring themes:

1. Shock. Total shock since Curt had no signs of ill health.

2. How much everyone respected and loved Curt and his work.

3. How he made such a difference for people all over the globe.

4. How he always talked about me and our family to others, even in his classes.

I was doing pretty well (Why does not crying equal "pretty well"?) until I read an e-mail from one of Curt's regular teaching partners, Al. One paragraph read: "He loved you and his family. Whenever we led together, he would speak of you and your talents in such an admiring way. He thought the world of you, and it showed. And he was so proud of your children, and loved his grandchildren. He spent his last days doing what he loved: teaching a small group (only five) of coaches by day, and watching his grandson play baseball at night. (He drove home twice late from Omaha for Johnny's games that week). He was truly a deeply happy man who made a huge difference in the lives of thousands. That is no small feat." Then the tears came.

I realized this morning that I made it through the long evening by myself. It is not what I enjoy, but I made it, even though the emotional reading of those e-mails was hard. But once again, they gave me so much awareness of who Curt was and how I was loved by no ordinary man.

> *Thank you for your cards and e-mails. They give me strength. Send someone a card today. It may lighten someone's grief.*

July 29

Day 67: Helpers

Today was one of the biggest days of gratitude I've had since May 16th.

I don't know if you've ever completely cleaned your garage, but it is a huge job. All the Christmas decorations in the attic came down, along with many other things only Curt and I could get down in tandem.

Curt loved analogies of marriage. He believed two were more than the sum of one and one. Now, with him gone, I cannot even do half the work we used to do together. Cleaning out the attic and garage was overwhelming for this new widow. Physically, I could not get the things even cleaned out of the attic by myself. Mentally, I'm not the sharpest tack when it comes to tools and what I need for what. And emotionally, of course, the hardest of all. Looking again at the special shovel he used to clear the pond of snow. Looking at his bike. Looking at his coveralls, which I've kept for anyone who will help me clear the ice rink next winter. Looking at his tackle box. Looking at his things and missing him with all my being.

But my angels and heroes—Jane and Doug, Ron and Marlene, and Johnny—worked hard for almost eight hours to help me. They were sensitive and sensible—what a perfect combination for a tough job.

I thank God today for these unbelievable family members. Curt would hate that they had to do all that work because he is gone, but I know he would also be grateful that they stepped in to help. Thank you, dear sisters and brothers-in-law, from both Curt and me. You made a difference too big for words.

> *Please remember that doing hard work for grieving people is sure to get you some extra jewels in your crown. But even if it doesn't, it will be worth diamonds and rubies to the person you help.*

Jane, Ron, Doug, Rosanne, and Marlene

July 30

Day 68: Hello, Sky

Curt and I have had a convertible for about fourteen years. As with many things, I wanted one first. I had found an older, green Sebring that was on sale just down the street from us. I told Curt about it, and there wasn't much of a reaction, so I forgot about it—but not really. I was mad at him for not moving fast enough and giving me the green light to buy it. So, we had a fight. He basically said, "I could care less if we get it. If you want it, I just figured you'd get it." Then he said what he always said: "I trust you. You always want things first, and then I'm better off in the end."

But the damage was done, and I felt so bad the next day for being a jerk of a wife. At work, I told my good friend Mark about my guilty feelings, and the frustration that I would never find another car like that again. He laughed and said, "Nobody buys cars like that now. Just get on the internet and look for one." So, I did and I found the very same car at a better price in a city about 100 miles from us. I called the dealer and asked if we could see it. He said, "You can, but some guy from a Gallup number just asked to come see it today too." Yup, Curt moved faster than me on that one. We went that night and bought the convertible.

We were hooked. We loved driving around. We were sure we could smell all the good things—like lilacs and grilled steaks—better in our convertible! Then that car went to car heaven, and he found a used red Sebring convertible. This time Curt was all over it. He loved that car. He loved to take Norah and Johnny for rides. Norah would ride in it, look up, and say, "Hello, sky!" When Curt died, I could hardly look at that car. And I certainly don't need two cars. I can't get rid of it, but I can't bear to drive it either. Too many memories.

Yesterday we needed to back it out of the garage and realized the battery was dead. After some checking, the mechanic said, "You just need to drive this car more to keep the battery up." Okay, then. Just drive it. I felt like someone who knew nothing about my loss helped me take a step forward.

So, today I will drive the convertible. It will be hard at first, but I will remember our good days in that red convertible that Curt loved. And it will be one more baby step in my new life.

> *What's the message for today? Listen for total strangers who can help you know what is good for you sometimes. They are objective. God may be speaking through them. Listen for the little messages that come from unusual places like a car mechanic. Don't let things rust out. Use them, and love them, and be grateful for them.*

Day 69: Just Wait

I've learned that when your heart is broken, it can make you less of a person. One of the things Curt used to say was, "Hurting people hurt people." Their less-than-perfect self comes from a place of pain. In other words, give hurting people a break if they hurt you. Sounds a bit like grace to me.

Since Curt died, there have been times I've found myself jealous, cynical, or angry at people. (Well, I did that before too, but I feel worse about it now). You'd think I wouldn't have any more room for bad feelings since grief seems to have taken up so much of my life. The good news is, I am realizing grief can cause some extra sensitivity, appreciation, and tenderness on my part.

Or it can cause some jealousy and anger. More than one of my new widow friends have warned me about that. In my worst hours, I think something like, "Just wait, everyone. This will happen to you too. If you think your life is so perfect... just wait."

For the most part, I think that is true. Curt always knew a lot more about people's issues than most, especially in his role as a pastor. He often said to me, "If people think difficult things aren't going to happen to them, they just haven't lived long enough." He was realistic. So much for positivity, huh? So much for gratitude, huh?

This is where I fight hard not to lose the battle. I am already trying to reframe things so I will not be jealous, angry, or bitter.

It's still not all clear to me how I can do this, but it's in my head all the time, and if it eventually goes to my heart, I will win the battle on most days. So, if I'm less-than-kind to you or less-than-happy for you, please extend me grace. I am hurting and I will hurt people. And when I perceive you as being pious or gloating, I will remember that I am the person who loses by thinking that way.

Be careful if you think you have it made it the shade, but also, don't live in fear. We didn't do that, and neither should you. Remember to be sensitive to hurting people, no matter their lot. It could be you someday. And most important, work to soften your heart. Soft is better than hard when it comes to the heart.

August 1

Day 70: Money

I think a lot about money since Curt died. Sounds callous, doesn't it? It's just that everything financial changed with his death. The cost of death and dying is more than I ever imagined. One person doesn't cut the cost of living in half.

Interestingly, Curt spent little time thinking about money—how to make it, how to conserve it, or how to spend it. It wasn't that he didn't care at all about having money—he probably did—but it never, ever drove his life in any way. His careers were not chosen because of money. He never said no to a dream because of it. And he never worried about every little penny that he could save. But, he also mostly bought clothes on sale and had very few man toys. On the other hand, he regularly gave me and our family very generous gifts. He pretty much never questioned the way we spent money or worried about it running out. I honestly think it was a spiritual thing for him. He believed that if people tried to hold on too hard to money, they would live in fear and constant discontent.

Curt often talked about "conservatives." He was not talking about a political perspective, but a worldview that caused people to worry about running out of money, or time, or resources, and limit their generosity for others and themselves. One of his sermons that always drew rave reviews (people have even told me it changed their lives) was called, "Living and Giving Lavishly." It was based on the story in the Bible of Mary pouring expensive perfume on Jesus's feet. If you don't know the story, you should check it out.

Anyway, we were a good pair with money. I liked making it more than he did, and he liked us using it without fear, while not making poor choices.

Back to reality. I now have half of the salary we had and I happened to cancel a large insurance policy just before Curt died. (Yes, bad timing.) For a while, I was feeling that "be careful about giving or spending too much" fear emerge, which both of us disdained.

I'm not worried my money will run out. I spent two hours with my financial consultants this week and I felt pretty secure when leaving their office. I'll be fine. In fact, I am starting to remember again how living in fear about one's future, whether it be money or other things like death, does not pay off. It just makes one weird and crabby and in my opinion, rather un-Christ like.

> *So, pour the nard on the feet of Jesus, send a check to your favorite charity, work hard, but don't let money drive your work. Buy your kids something just for fun. Maybe use a good financial consultant. Remember to be thankful for generous people in your life, and live like someone else is in control of your future and your money. If you don't think that's true, just walk in my steps for a while, and I bet you will change your mind.*

August 2

Day 71: Show It

Sympathy is not overrated. Kindness is not overrated. Sensitivity is not overrated. I've had a lot of these things and I still need more.

My tears and moans today seem relentless. Most of the time, people are sensitive. Once in a while, they aren't. I don't think they try to be insensitive—they just don't know how to be sensitive. Does that make sense? They just don't seem to get that I'm so tired and so sad and so hopeless. I almost want to say to them, "Do you have any idea what I'm going through?" And when that happens, I feel like my life would be better done too. I know I appear strong to a lot of people, but know that I'm really so, so weak. Maybe now more than ever since Curt's death.

Gratitude? I can't even begin to tell you how much it means when those who show tenderness and kindness and sensitivity appear in my life. They are the people who feel like Jesus to me. They get it. They show it. They heal me. Curt would say, "Even if Empathy isn't your strength, it's not an excuse not to figure out how to be sensitive."

> *Figure out how to show your own brand of empathy, and show is the operative word. Be kind. Go the second mile. It would be what Curt would want you to do for me. That I know, and I'm positive that's what Curt would do for you.*

August 3

Day 72: Waves

Whomever coined the phrase, "waves of grief" was a conceptual genius. As you could tell by yesterday's post, it was one of the three worst days for me since May 16th. Funny how I used to be aware of the three best days of the year, and now I'm only aware of the worst days. As I look back on yesterday, I don't know why grief crashed over me like a wave. Part of it is always physical. I've said it before, but the emotional exhaustion from grief along with the new reality of more work on my plate just finally does me in. I'm trying to do so many things around the house that are new, hard, and unlovely. Like picking up a dead bird. Or dragging all the garbage out. Or cleaning off the patio. These jobs aren't physically taxing, but I didn't have to do them before.

Yesterday was also Sunday, which is never easy. Church seemed like an enemy to me yesterday—no fault of the people there. The grandkids stayed the night before, and it's still so hard for me as I try to entertain them both and do things like carry a sleeping five-year-old up the steps to bed. Curt was much better at that carrying thing.

I literally cried all afternoon. I read through all the sympathy cards and boxed them up. I thought about what I had with Curt that is now gone forever. I went beyond tears to desperate moans. But late afternoon, Anne, John, Meagan, and kids came over for dinner and to stay the night since their air conditioner was not working. We had a family dinner—chicken, corn, fruit, asparagus, and potatoes. Comfort food. They all helped get it on the table. I believe it was the first time we sat down to a Sunday meal—something we did regularly before May 16th.

The wave seemed to be coming down. Dinner time was good. It was even fun, and it got better when they stayed the evening, and we could all be together. The wave had crashed hard and then it got so calm. I prefer calm. But I don't always get what I want. Today I feel better. I got to wake up with the grandkids and Meagan in the house. It was like God having compassion on me after yesterday's hell. Grief and gratitude. Waves of grief. Waves of gratitude. it's not always a perfect duo, but if I wait long enough, I find something good again.

> *So, wait. Wait when you are going through hard stuff. Don't be so mired in your bad stuff that you can't find the good.*

Day 73: Friends

Last night I spent the evening with a good friend. Deb is famous for her interior design work, but she is also famous to me for being a thriver rather than a survivor.

Curt and I came to know Deb and her husband, Dick, when they were in our small group. During that time, Dick became ill with cancer and died very quickly. Curt eulogized Dick at his memorial, talking about his strengths as a focal part of that powerful talk. Our roots are intertwined deeply through life and death.

Deb is a fast talker. She can say a lot in a short amount of time. And she cuts to the chase about things. More importantly, she is real and she is hopeful. I listened to her advice. She had so many good things to say, I wish I had taken notes. One of the things she said was, "You are a strong woman. It's just that this isn't how you would have wanted to show how strong you are." Wow, is that ever the truth. She encouraged me about going back to work. She told me to make new friends. She suggested making some new memories sooner rather than later. She said, "Rather than trying to be two grandparents in what you do, just try to love the kids for both you and Curt." Then Deb said, "You are a teacher at heart. I can't wait to see how you will teach others about your new role and new chapter in life." Somehow, that felt good.

Deb, I think you were the good teacher last night. You were real, and you gave me so much air to breathe. You helped with practical things, but you also encouraged me to embrace a full life. Plus, you make a darn good Moscow mule and Thai food.

Friends matter. Deb says they can be like flowers—some perennial, always there. Some are volunteers; they show up when you least expect. And some are annuals. They aren't there forever, but their beauty is strong for a season. For me, friends are everything.

> *Choose your friends wisely. Be open to new ones in your life, then invest. Be real with them. Take time for them. They will show up when you need them most if you invest in them before a crisis. I'm glad I have done that over the years. Friends have come back to bless me in big ways.*

Day 74: Filled Bucket

It's the day before our anniversary, and I have three wonderful women who are taking me away for a couple of nights. It's good because it hit me so hard yesterday. I wonder if our anniversary will always be one of the hardest days to face.

I have this habit when I'm feeling bad to just dive in and make myself miserable. When I was thinking about August 6th coming up, I went into my closet and pulled out this big box of cards I have received from Curt over the years. Oh, my goodness. He was a master at finding the right card. He was a great writer and he clearly saved his best writing for me in those cards. I was trying to find the one from last year, but then ended up reading several random anniversary cards. One of my favorites said on the front, "I wonder where the years have gone. But never how else I could have spent them." Then inside, in his one-of-a-kind handwriting, it said, "I have always known that you were the perfect and only woman for me. It has made me go through life with confidence and absolutely no regrets. What a great way to live life; with a perfect partner and friend."

Yes, Curt filled my bucket every August 6th, and honestly, that was no exception. He was my personal daily bucket filler. His words were always so passionate and so full of appreciation and love for our marriage. I know tomorrow is coming (Hmmm… now that's profound!), and I know it will be hard.

I'm thankful for Curt's words on those cards. I'm thankful for friends who will distract me today and tomorrow. I'm thankful for all those years, and anniversaries, and flowers, and love, and passion. I did have an amazing marriage.

> *Words on cards matter. Write them knowing the difference they can make—now and, perhaps, years down the road.*

Day 75: Happy Anniversary

Happy anniversary, Curt. We didn't quite make it to forty-four years. No card today from you. No perfect gift. No "I love you." No special dinner. And no sweet embrace. But you will be with me forever in my heart. I miss you more than you could ever imagine.

No, I'm not getting along just fine like you always said I would if you died first. Life isn't the same, but the kids are still something we can both we proud of. Johnny and Norah light up my eyes just like they did yours. And we talk about you often. Our friends and family have been the closest thing to you, possibly because they love both you and me.

Thank you for treating me like I was the best person in the world for you. I never doubted you loved me more than life itself. I promise to live in a way that would make you proud of me. I will work hard, and take care of our family. I will stay faithful to our God. I will share our home. I will live and give abundantly. I will use my strengths and I will honor you and keep the good life we had together alive until we see each other again. You were heaven to me until I someday experience it with you.

Love,

Rosanne

Write a note to someone you love today. Say the things you'll wish you had said more often after they are gone.

Curt and Rosanne, wedding and fortieth anniversary

Day 76: Sons

Our son's birthday. He was born on a Sunday, and Curt managed to not miss preaching in church that day. We named him after my dad and Curt's Grandpa Liesveld. It was not an easy birth. The OB doctor told me, "Twenty years ago, one of you wouldn't have lived through that."

I remember Curt taking a call on a wall phone in the delivery room from a parishioner whose daughter was being flown to Minneapolis because she was so near death. Even then, Curt's life was always full of the demands of life-and-death care. The girl lived. And John lived—and thrived.

He is the kind of son every parent would want. Caring, loving, responsible, fun, smart, centered, and always, always respectful of his parents. The worst thing he did was bring hordes of kids over to our house after his curfew (midnight) but before theirs (1:00 a.m.). They would play cards and make noise in the basement until Curt had to pound on the floor of our bedroom to get them to be quieter.

Today, both John and I are missing his dad. Curt always knew how to advise John and love him through each phase. I sometimes would try to teach John through words, but Curt taught by example. I'm so grateful Curt died knowing his son was a success. The night before Curt died, he got to watch John do a benefit walk of twenty-one miles across Lincoln. The smile on Curt's face couldn't have been bigger that evening.

Through my tears today, I'm grateful for a son who told me, just minutes after his dad died, "Mom, you will never be alone. I will always be there for you." Much love to you, John. We will celebrate you tonight. Thanks for being a son with no regrets on anyone's part.

Sons and daughters, will you have no regrets when your parents are gone?

Curt, Johnny, and John

August 8

Day 77: New Eyes

Nowadays the mail is either a comfort or a distress. I hate the bills. I hate the envelopes that have Curt's name on them. I hate advertisements for vacations. But I love cards and notes, and occasionally, a letter from a place that makes me smile. That letter came yesterday from the organ donation center.

We had a call shortly after Curt died and were told how they were able to use his long bones. I was in such a fog; I don't remember feeling much at the time. But the letter yesterday talked about how two people had received corneal transplants from Curt's eyes, restoring their eyesight. I showed the letter to Johnny. He smiled big. Then we hugged and cried a little.

Going through that grueling interview with the organ donor organization just minutes after I knew I had lost Curt was perhaps the hardest thing I did in those first hours of my new reality. If John hadn't helped me answer all those personal questions, I would have walked out of the room. But that letter yesterday made it all worth it. New eyes!

We all need new eyes from time to time. Maybe to see the good around us, maybe to sense and react to someone's hurt, maybe to see God's handiwork. Maybe just to see our own lives with hope.

> *Close your eyes for a minute and think of what you are grateful for right now. Then open them and see clearly, just like two people are doing today as they see through Curt's eyes. I hope they not only received visual clarity with Curt's eyes, but also his clarity about life and what counts.*

August 9

Day 78: Rita's Deck

Last night, I invited my friend Rita to join me and my family for the evening. I also invited my friend Mark, who is staying with me for a few days. We ended up at Rita's house on her awesome deck with pizza, wine, and sparkling water. It was a thrown together, eclectic group, but the party didn't break up for more than four hours.

The talk was varied from strengths, (Mark is the new Executive Director of the Clifton Strengths Institute at the University of Nebraska), to starting a business (Rita is an admired entrepreneur), to running a non-profit (Meagan has a significant leadership role at Cedars, an organization for abused and neglected children), to being grateful for what we've been given. I thought so many times how Curt would have loved to sit around the table with our talk of strengths, young people, and ideas.

Just as I was getting a bit sad that Curt was not by my side, Johnny joined the conversation. He sounds like a ten-year-old Curt when he talks. His understanding of strengths and how to use them is not ordinary for anyone, much less a kid. He said he wants to write about strengths "like a kid would talk about them." All of a sudden, I thought how he and Curt could have written a whole new lexicon for strengths descriptions.

It was so fun to watch and listen to this group of people, thrown together rather randomly on a Saturday night, talking, laughing, thinking, and being grateful together for the strengths we have, for our work, and mostly, for friends. It was a good night. I do think Johnny has just a few of his Poppo's genes because I felt like Curt was there last night with me in a ten-year-old body.

> *I'd recommend ordering a pizza and inviting some folks over. Take a risk and put together some people who may not even know each other well. Maybe throw in a kid or two, then just let the topics flow, without having to have the last word, or be right about everything, and without judging. It feels good.*

August 10

Day 79: Stormy Mornings

Each morning I wake up and have to remember again that I'm now a widow. It's difficult to even explain how disheartening that is day after day. And then I get up and try to figure out why I need to still be here without Curt.

Some days I feel the bit of light that forces me to put one foot in front of another. But most days, it's like going into an awful storm. Yesterday my friend Kim brought me a basket of sweet and comforting items with a card. Her writing inside was so profound and full of depth. After reading it, I felt like I had a picture of getting through those stormy mornings. You see, Kim and her husband, Jim, know grief too. It was their son, much, much, much too early in life. She knows grief and she can also write about life now, so I hang onto her words. This quote was on the front of her card:

Storms can be intimidating.

Stand strong in the rain,

let it germinate and grow the seed of hope deep within you.

I so appreciate the kind gestures from people. It just feels good.

If you have any kind of grief in your life, check out Kim Berg's book, Schema of a Soul. It's powerful. Or maybe find a sweet little basket and fill it with goodies for an aching soul. It makes one's soul feel cared for and loved. And they may be able to face their storm a bit easier the next morning.

Kim's card

Day 80: Seasons

I love the change of seasons. I've always loved the newness, the feel, and the forward-looking nature of the emerging season. I also like re-seasoning the look of my house. Yesterday I had that feeling that late summer was here. My house—with its bright, cottage feel—seemed a bit off, so I thought I'd pull out the pictures and rugs and arrangements that have more of the late-summer look and feel. Sunflowers muted the bright yellows of high summer, and the brilliant orange of summer needed to be toned down a bit.

I started to pull out a few things and suddenly had that sick-to-the-gut feeling when I realized I was not all that excited about the changing of seasons now that I'm alone. I was faced again with the hard reality that my love of future anticipation is pretty much crushed now. But I plodded on, as I've learned to do, dutifully making some changes in the way the house looks. I was doing okay until I pulled out two of the pictures I usually put up this time of year. One is of a house with shutters that Curt took when we were on the French Riviera. The other is of a Paris bistro that we'd visited a few times, taken on a rainy night.

Suddenly, I felt so intensely sad about the prospect of never going to those beautiful spots again with my best travel partner. For a minute, I thought about not putting up those pictures, but then I did—just making myself do the right thing.

One of my favorite verses in the Bible exclaims, "to everything there is a season." I had forgotten that part of that passage says there is "a time to live and a time to die." I wanted to tell God the last part of that was not one of His best ideas. But it's true. I need to work on falling in love with the seasons again—both the seasons that come with the calendar changing, and those that come with life changing.

> *Curt had his season. I will have my season. And you will have your season. Enjoy each one. Maybe buy some peaches today. Or put up a picture of sunflowers. Or buy a candle that smells like late summer to you. "To everything there is a season, and a time to every purpose under the heaven." Ecclesiastes 3:1.*

Day 81: First Day of School

Today is the first day of school in our great city. For most of my life, I have worked in education. I was a teacher in three different states for ten years and have worked at Gallup in education for the past twenty-nine years.

When it's the first morning of school, I still miss not showing up either as a student or a teacher. Since Curt has been gone, I struggle so much with my identity. Although I was definitely an independent woman in most ways, I was always so proud of the identity and value I had because of our marriage. I now often wonder if I've ever really made a difference all by myself, or if it was always (and will always be) because of Curt.

Then I received a letter from Rick and Valerie, one of the young couples who were part of the church Curt pastored in Mitchell, South Dakota. In Rick's words, "Curt's teaching and preaching helped me to begin to understand the need for a relationship with Christ." Rick wasn't just a parishioner. He was also my principal at Whittier Elementary. He was young—Whitter was a new school for him—but he won me over in the first staff meeting when he said in a rather emotional voice, "I wanted to be at this school. It has the toughest, neediest kids in the city. We will make a difference here." I watched this young man lead a school with wisdom, care, and determination not ordinary to most principals.

Then I read the next paragraph in his letter and I felt a moment of knowing my life had made a difference there too. "You also played an important role in my early leadership development. I was eager, but green. It was a real learning time for me, and your patience and professionalism were of tremendous help to me. You were one of the best teachers that I have ever seen in front of students. I can remember a couple conversations when I benefitted from your wisdom and support."

I won't lie. It felt good to read those words after having felt insignificant since May 16th. Rick and Valerie both wrote words that make me know I had value in my past life as an individual—and made me hope that I still will.

I received a second note from another friend just a few days ago. It said, "I want to encourage you. I know you are an accomplished woman with an abundance of talent. My prayer for you is that you can find a new song to sing, and, in time, be a blessing to others around you."

Take a minute to tell someone they made a difference in your life. When people take time to tell others they count, it may make them feel like a whole and worthwhile person again. Just do it. Please.

Day 82: The Death Certificate

I need to clean out my purse. It gets messy, and I hate digging in it to find things. I also need to take out the white envelope marked "death certificate" that I hide in the very bottom so that I won't see it each time I look for something in my purse.

I was told one must have a lot of these death certificates. I remember the day the big envelope came in the mail with the return address: Nebraska Department of Records. Because I've often needed a copy, I put one in a plain envelope in my purse. I hate looking at it all the time. The neatly typed words that are so sterile and callous. Date of birth. Date of death. Cause of death: Cardiac Arrest or Other.

We are not 100 percent sure what caused Curt's death. The physician told us they treated it like cardiac arrest, but it could have been a clot to the lung or even something else. No autopsy—I asked John, and he didn't want that. Just two months before he died, Curt had a physical and his numbers were perfect; he never, ever had one symptom indicating physical distress in his life, including the minutes before he died.

So, I don't know for sure the cause of Curt's death. I do know it was sudden. I was sure he was gone as soon as I saw him shortly after he went down. It was fast—very, very fast. No possibility of reviving him. The lead EMT on the scene told me the same thing—no suffering, just gone.

Every day I see that white envelope in my purse. I think I will take it out today. But every day, in my mind, I also see Curt laying there, gone—the way I found him. I can't take that out of mind as easily as I can take the envelope out of my purse.

Gratitude—of course—that Curt didn't suffer or even know about his impending death, but that's not enough gratitude to conquer the grief. For Curt's sake, though, I am grateful for his swift entrance into heaven. Lesson today? Gosh, I don't know. Maybe know death can come quickly. The last thing I said to Curt was, "Wow, the lawn looks great where you mowed." He looked very happy and smiled about that.

> **Death doesn't always give you warning. Live like Curt did. Mow the lawn and smile because you enjoy it so much. And be ready to meet your Maker.**

August 14

Day 83: Don't Go Away

My posts have been too long lately. I apologize. I know most people don't need to know all the details that are inside me, screaming to get out. I hate that Curt had to die for me to write these. I'd rather be posting about our trip to some lovely spot, or getting to have the grandkids overnight with him. Instead, I talk to all of you in order to make myself sane some days.

But I know it can be too much. I'm less-than-happy I had to have my husband die to have a reason to write these kinds of posts. I'm glad for the people who have encouraged, been responsive, and made it easier for me to keep up with everyone because it means I don't have to repeat my truthful responses to "How are you?" so many times. I've had so many people invite me for coffee, happy hour (well, kind of happy), meals, etc. and show me the kind of support and tenderness needed by someone who still is so heartbroken.

So, thank you. I'm sure I have not said that enough even though that was the impetus for these daily posts. Please know I have appreciated every kind word, gift, meal, and cup of coffee. I know it isn't fun to walk with someone in grief, so you are doing heroic work when you spend time with me. It is the work of angels. When people asked me early on what I needed, I just said, "Don't go away." And I still mean that.

I worry that my widow status will take me out of some social circles, so I absolutely appreciate all of you who have stuck with me day after day. I believe it has helped me face life and death with more reality—and more hope.

> *Keep it up. Not just for me, but for others too. Be sure your calendar has some openings in it for helping others. I know I didn't have enough of that. The truth is, we all need each other. Don't we?*

August 15

Day 84: Questions

Lately, I feel like each day is getting harder. I realize how lonely I am at certain points of the day. Waking up alone is tough. Being with couples is tough. Being around places we were always together is tough. Being with people who are happy is sometimes tough. And, of course, any time home alone at night is tough.

I know from reading that this point in grief is when most people want you to be "normal" again, but sometimes I feel less normal than ever now. It's a new normal. Aren't you supposed to gravitate to that new normal? I'm trying. I'm trying so hard, but it's not what I expected—to be a widow at age sixty-three with no lead-up time to prepare mentally and emotionally. Yesterday, I just wanted to say to God, "Why wasn't my prayer answered?" I hear people talking about their prayers being answered all the time. Why did I get the big "NO"? I know there were many people praying for Curt to live. Why weren't all those prayers answered? I will never understand that.

Theologically, a lot of pious people think they know everything about faith when things like this happen. I won't lie when I say this hasn't been easy on my faith, but I dutifully put one foot in front of the other, spiritually now too. I wish I could say my faith is stronger than ever, but I can't. Maybe someday… but not now. Please don't give "spiritual" answers that frankly don't make sense to most people. God reveals Himself through your heart more than your words most days. Your heart of love and grace and kindness will always be the biggest clue that God exists and is real for me.

> *Having said all of that, I honestly still covet your prayers. I'm not sure if they will be answered—just the way our pleading prayers for Curt to live were not answered. Please don't use the line, "Your prayer was answered—just not the way you wanted." That doesn't help. I still say, "pray without ceasing." That doesn't mean your head needs to be bowed every second, but it does mean that your living and acting and talking and thinking is prayerful. Do both today please, for me and for yourself: Bow your head and pray and lift up your head and hands and heart minute by minute and live in a prayer-filled way.*

August 16

Day 85: First Quarter Report

August 16th. May 16th. Three months ago today, Curt left this world as we know it. I cannot believe what I have gone through in these past three months. Nothing, nothing in my life previously comes close to these three months.

Three months is a quarter of the year, so in many ways, it is my new first quarter. Having been in a revenue-producing role for many years, I knew how important the first quarter performance was in business. It predicted in a big way how we could end the year—either successfully meeting our goals or falling short. I knew forecasting was important, and the first quarter performance enabled me to do that for the rest of the year. My CFO once said, "If the first quarter is bad, it is pretty hard to ever catch up." Wow. I wonder if that is true for grief too? I'd say this first quarter has been... bad. But maybe grief is different. Maybe you can catch up throughout the next quarters. I hope so. I so want to end strong.

My first theme on the Clifton StrengthsFinder is Futuristic. That theme has been a huge part of my life for as long as I remember. I can get pictures in my head almost too quickly of what something will be or can be. They are often vivid and always positive. They sometimes include all the senses, so I can see, feel, hear, touch, and even smell the positive future ahead. Now that all feels like one heck of a bad joke. Almost all my future pictures had Curt in them. As I look to second quarter, third quarter, fourth quarter, and then into the years ahead, I need to reframe most of my visions. I didn't do very well with that this first quarter.

But last night, I was with my small group, and they jump-started me with a picture of the future me. It took their visions to give me a bit of a picture of the God-ordained me. They blessed me and gave me hope in a deep and powerful way.

So, here I go into second quarter. Shock isn't there every day, but reality is. How can I use my Futuristic talent to eventually create a more positive reality? I don't know yet, but I'm trying and I'm thinking. I do know Curt will always be a part of my past and my future. He made me so much of who I am today and he will continue to impact me in the future.

> *I encourage you to have a good second quarter too. Start now to live intentionally and with the end in mind. It may impact your story of success.*

August 17

Day 86: Reminders

I've said before how tired I am. Although it's a little better, it still shocks me how exhausted I can become. I also notice how fuzzy my thinking is at times. I forget so many things. I'm sure it's partially because almost every minute of every day something makes me think of Curt. It's like my brain is constantly crammed with extra thoughts and memories—and most of them take up emotional real estate.

I take a shower and when I wipe down the glass doors, I think of how meticulously Curt did that. I put on a top and remember how he would say, "That looks nice on you." I go to get a cup of coffee and see his favorite mug—red, of course. I try to use the remote and switch something on the stupid TV and remember how he could always figure out the remote when I couldn't. I look in the garage fridge, and there sits the beer he liked. I look at the car and see when the oil was last changed and realize he changed it just five days before he died. I get the mail, and there are always envelopes with his name on them. I go to church and remember how he often quoted a thought from the message and put it on Facebook. I put on a necklace and remember I can't fasten it without him helping me. I get up in the morning and reach over to touch him before remembering he's not there. I watch Johnny play football and envision Curt chatting up everyone he could about how good Johnny was doing as a ten-year-old quarterback. I walk into work and walk past his office and the empty place he leaves there too. I want to print off one of his photographs and think of how he did that all for me before.

And at the end of the day, I keep thinking I hear the door open and Curt walking through the door. It goes on and on and on. So, the constant reminders of Curt and the weariness of emotional trauma sets in. It just takes up tons of space in my heart and mind. People say these things will bring a smile to me at some point, but they don't yet. I hold on to the promise that they will in time.

So maybe my gratitude is for the reminders and memories I will have in the future. Curt's fingerprints are all over my world, and someday maybe they won't cause me exhaustion, but joy.

> If you have a spouse, or good friend, or significant other, notice how many times you are reminded of them. If your reminders are not always positive, see if you can turn those thoughts into positives. Focus on what your partner does right. Curt was so good at that, and our lives together were better because of it.

August 18

Day 87: Strengths in Grief

Curt and I were huge advocates of strengths-based living (based on Don Clifton's research and philosophy), and knowing one's strengths so that they can be maximized. I've tried so hard to figure out how to use my strengths in this season of grief. My strengths are: Futuristic, Activator, Relator, Significance, and Command. I don't know that anyone has written about grief and strengths. I wish Curt had written or talked about this specific scenario. I sure could use his wisdom now.

None of my strengths seem to be popping much for me right now. I've mentioned before my Futuristic strength. That one is the hardest. I did some writing on the plane today about it, but it's still so blurry and almost seems impossible to embrace right now. I think I can see my Activator and even Command at work at times, but not in the way I would like to use them.

But my Relator strength—that one seems to be my friend both before and after Curt's death. Relators like close, intimate relationships with people. They want to go deep. I want to go deep. I want you to know about me and I want to know about you. Curt had that strength too, so the two of us loved deep, meaningful relationships, and those relationships grew more and more meaningful over time. I'm so grateful for that right now. Investing heavily in people has led to people investing a lot in me lately, which means so much to me. I can hardly fathom the number of people willing to hang out with me even when I'm not that much fun. In fact, I'm not fun at all, but I can still embrace my Relator amid grief and see it as a strength.

> **If you haven't learned your strengths, go to http://www.GallupStrengthsCenter.com and learn how you, too, can fully live out who you were meant to be. It may change how you see yourself and make your future something bright and hopeful.**

August 19

Day 88: Pronouns

Pronouns. I can't quit saying "our," "we," and "us." I am clumsy when I try to say "my house" or any of those phrases where I am now supposed to use the singular. It sounds foreign to me. For a long time, the plural worked for me and now, out of the blue, I need to change my pronouns. Singular sounds so, well… single.

I'm trying to use the right pronouns. I had a mom who insisted on good grammar, but I don't think she was thinking of this situation. She would have understood when I say the wrong thing. I don't like switching to the singular, but I will try. In many ways, I know plural is still the right form to use. Our kids. Our home. Our memories. So, please, give me some grace around grammar.

I will need grace on many levels as I move to this new normal. I'm thankful for good grammar, but I'm even more thankful for good memories around us, our, and we.

> *No matter what your pronoun—singular or plural, know grammar is less important than feeling like you are significant no matter your identity. I'm trying to believe that in my heart of hearts as I move to the singular.*

August 20

Day 89: Tears

This morning when I woke up in my hotel, I realized yesterday was the first day since Curt's death that I hadn't cried. That's almost one hundred days of crying before I had a day without tears. I don't know how to feel about that. At first I felt kind of like I had made some progress—only to quickly feel bad for not crying.

Maybe I didn't cry because I was with people all day in client meetings and busy with work. But I was alone after 5:00 p.m. and spent a fair amount of time alone in my hotel room last night. I do remember feeling like I needed to call Curt—like I always did on the road—then remembering I had no one to call. At that point, I could have cried. Instead, I picked up my phone and texted John and Meagan as well as Anne to see how they were. I got to FaceTime with Johnny and Norah, and they seemed happy to see and hear me.

I know I could have cried if I had done the things that tip off tears, like look at pictures of Curt and me or Curt and the kids on my phone. Or listen to our songs.

Or even just remember all the many nights we spent on trips together in the same hotel chain. I can guarantee I could have cried, but I didn't work at it, as my tears have always come whether I want them to or not.

As I sat alone, a thousand miles away from home, I preferred not to encourage the grief and pain. I know tears are a good thing. I've had every form of them over the last one hundred days—sobs, wailing, gentle tears, moaning tears, and even tears that made me physically sick—all of them coming by surprise and never controllable. So, yesterday seemed like a day I'd never see.

But I'm no fool. I know that after a good day, I often crash with a vengeance and have a serious crying session. Maybe tonight. Maybe tomorrow. Who knows?

When Johnny was little, he would sometimes see tears in my eyes and wonder if I was okay. I'd tell him, "Yes, people cry when something feels good to them too, like hearing great music, or tender words, or seeing someone succeed, or watching a God-inspired act of love." So, tears can come from many places. I'm waiting for mine to come from someplace again that feels good, and moving, and powerful, instead of flowing from sadness and grief.

> *Please don't deny your tears, but let them flow out of appreciation, awe, and joy as much as, if not more than, sorrow. I'm working on that too.*

Day 90: What If…

Curt and I didn't talk much about what we'd do if one of us died. The exception to that was a discussion we had about the house, for some reason. I think it had to do with insurance, as all important life discussions seem to involve insurance. I said I'd want to stay in our house. It would give me, the kids, and grandkids comfort. He said, and I quote, "If you die first, I will sell the house as fast as I can, rent an apartment, pull down the shades, and watch sports all day."

I don't think he would have done that, but he said the house had my fingerprints all over it and he would not be able to stand living here if I was not here too. When people ask if I'll stay in this house, I'm always slightly taken aback. This house gives me comfort and respite now more than ever. And yes, I know it will be a lot of work. And yes, I still love to share it for good.

Yesterday after I got home from work, I saw three ducks sitting on the edge of the pond. They were beautiful. And not to sound too goofy, but the white one was like a symbol to me of peace in this dark time of life. I'm grateful for my home even though I now work twice as hard to keep it up. Curt would want me here. He knew I would be here. As much as I wish it had been me who went so swiftly, I'm equally glad Curt is not sitting in a dark apartment watching sports all day—odd feelings to be sure.

Open your drapes today. Let the sun in or even the clouds. Fall in love again with your space. Ordain your space. It may heal you one day.

Day 91: A Stack of Books

Books. This stack of books beside my chair tells a story of my life right now. Three of the books were given to me. The one on *Second Firsts* is quite good. And the book by John Eldredge, *The Journey of Desire*, I took out of Curt's office when I cleaned it up. He had so many books. An entire wall in his office holds the books I kept after donating dozens of others. Curt always said I'd like this book about desire. I had a lot of desires before Curt's death and even a few now.

Books don't help me like a human contact and conversation does, but they do make me think about life and death and purpose. At this point in life, I need lots of important and encouraging thoughts, and these books have become a little like good friends to me.

> **What are you reading? What's the best book to help you through a difficult time? Think about reading a good book today.**

The books beside my chair

Day 92: Amen and Amen

Family. Curt's family. Last night I asked fourteen of Curt's family members over for dinner. I have wanted so much to keep "his side" of the family "our side," and now in some ways, it's truly "my side" of the family too. I decided on shish kabobs.

Midway through the day, I was reminded again that I'm not a good cook and that entertaining by myself is less-than-easy. But John showed up just when I needed him. He cut up tons of onions, peppers, pineapple, and mushrooms. Johnny stacked them neatly on the skewers. I felt ready, until minutes before the guests arrived. I spilled two cups of dry rice and water all over the floor, only to be out-done by the weather. It started raining just as everyone came, and we had to haul things in.

The family came through big time to help. Everyone brought food. The guys grilled in the rain. Claude fixed my rice cooker. Cherise washed a lot of dishes. Everyone stood in for the person that was all-too-obviously missing—their brother, their son, their uncle, their dad, their Poppo. If I thought I couldn't handle this physically at times, the emotional part of having Curt's family over without him there was almost unbearable at one point. But as we sat down around the tables, hands clasped, and heads bowed, John said a prayer that caused us to say a spontaneous "Amen!" through our collective tears.

The prayer centered me and made me proud of John's capacity to stand in his dad's shoes. We talked. We laughed. We ate. We cried. We prayed. We hugged. We loved. And even though there seemed to be an empty seat at the table, we found peace and love, watching the rain come down gently on the pond and knowing God's grace is sufficient for all.

I love Curt's family. They are my family. I thank them for loving me as one of their own, despite losing the blood connection.

> *Are there people you can call family, even though they don't share your DNA? Can you reach out and hold their hand, hug them, eat with them, or pray with them? Don't wait too long to figure out how to love your "other family." In time, you will find that family means the world to you when you need them most.*

August 24

Day 93: Mitchell

Yesterday, four amazing friends I've known for more than forty years came to see me. They drove six hours to spend time with me. Their visit took effort and time.

These were our best friends when we were a young pastor and wife in our first church in Mitchell, South Dakota. One of them walked the floors with John when he had his colicky evenings. One of them babysat John when I taught school. Three of them had babies the same years our kids were born, so we had hundreds of coffees, kid playdates, and days working in church together.

When we arrived at that church, there were literally no babies or even little kids. A year after John was born, Curt baptized ten babies. The church grew and flourished, and young couples serving in that church became the norm. During this visit, I learned that before Curt became pastor, the church was ready to offer the position to another person. After a long talk with Curt on the phone, they postponed their meeting to vote on the current candidates until they could have us come for an interview. After that, it was a done deal.

We moved to Mitchell and started a life that was almost idyllic. What a God thing that was. We spent ten years there with people who loved us into leadership. Never, ever did someone complain about Curt's or my work in that church. Instead, they just kept giving us grace and love, even though I know we must have made many mistakes.

Last night, as we sat out on our patio on a perfect evening, we talked about the past. And we talked about how life had taken us on many different paths. One of the women lost her son in an accident when he was just a young teenager. Let me tell you, she knows grief too. So, we cut through the crap. We talked about real things, but we laughed and cried—sometimes in the same minute.

I'm so grateful for friends—old friends who made such an amazing effort to just come be with me. It meant the world to me. Thank you, Glad, Janet, Wyonne, and Mavis. You gave me great joy and great love.

> *Today, think about reaching out to old friends or maybe loving someone young into leadership. You'd be surprised how they can be some of the best friends of your life. Pick up the phone or even drive six hours to go see them. Rekindle the joy of matured friendships. I promise it will feel good.*

August 25

Day 94: What Was God Thinking?

After my company left yesterday, I had a quiet house for a while. I basked in the high of having had visitors and the first good Sunday with my kids since May 16th, but Monday afternoon, those other feelings emerged. Not as crashing as some waves, but another wave. (Maybe from only eighty feet instead of one hundred this time.) It was one of those times when I was overwhelmed with thoughts of, "Is this really true? Have I really lost Curt forever?" "What on earth was God thinking?"

I decided to be proactive and see if the grandkids could come over. We sat and talked and tried to figure out exactly what species that white duck is that has made our home his home. Then Johnny got stung by a wasp. It hurt, and he demonstrated his pain with tears and moans. Norah looked at Johnny and me and said, "My teachers tell you to just think in your head it doesn't hurt, and then it will be better. But, actually, that doesn't really work."

We laughed at her wisdom. Her statement was profound. Sometimes I try hard to say in my head that I'm okay, but Norah's right. It doesn't work.

I went to bed and worried I wouldn't sleep since I was feeling this eighty-foot wave of grief. So, I prayed and asked God what I had done wrong to deserve this. Now having a pretty good theological background, and having been schooled by a mom who constantly emphasized grace over works, I should have known better. But, honestly, that's how I felt last night. What did I do that God decided to punish me with Curt's death?

I fell asleep before God responded. Or maybe He put me to sleep, hovering gently over me and granting me some peace and calm. I'm grateful I grew up understanding God's grace and mercy because I can sometimes "think in my head" that God didn't punish me by causing Curt's death, but that thought doesn't always reach my heart. Sorry for the theological discourse—simple as it is—but it was my experience of grace, grief, and gratitude yesterday.

Do you know what grace is? Have you read a good theologian lately? Or have you prayed before falling asleep, telling God your woes, much like the Psalmist David? I'd recommit to doing that. You may fall asleep, waking up to grace instead of guilt.

Day 95: Photographing Joy

Last night I went to Denver Botanical Gardens with Curt's sisters and brother-in-law. It was a beautiful summer night. Curt and I went to dozens of botanical gardens all over the country and even visited the Chelsea Flower Show in England. He loved photography, and I loved flowers. It was a perfect match.

Curt's sister, Cori, is an accomplished photographer much like her brother. Last night, as I walked among the beautiful gardens, I saw Curt in his sister over and over again with the camera being their common prized possession. So many things Cori did reminded me of Curt. The way she crouched down with her camera. The way she shook her head at a picture that wasn't good enough. The way she talked about how the light wasn't quite right. And mostly, the way her eye found just the right view for each beautiful flower in the garden.

I miss Curt the photographer, but what a joy to know that Cori was there with me and filling in much like Curt.

Who's the photographer in your life? Pictures seem to have an impact on emotion only equaled by music. Find your favorite picture. Frame it. Remember the good times that it represents. And love the photographer who took it too.

Day 96: Lovely In-Laws

Yesterday I was in the Rocky Mountains with Curt's sisters. Curt and I spent so much time together in this God country. We skied here; we worked here; we hiked here; and we brought our family here several times. Being in these sweet mountain towns and smelling the mountain air was both sad and reviving.

I hadn't felt like I'd really been on a little vacation this summer. Even though this wasn't like those vacations of my former life, it felt special. Curt loved the mountains. Being with his sisters, who are in their own unique times of grief, was good. They didn't flinch when I'd mention his name. They could talk about him with ease, and they were so kind and authentic. I know I've said this often, but I am so grateful for all of Curt's family.

Today we will go to Lake Dillon where I remember Curt stopping last February to take some smashing pictures. It will make me miss him horribly, so I will lean into the beauty of this area and even more into the beauty of his sisters, Sandy and Cori .

> *My best advice to young wives is to learn to love your in-laws.*
> *My advice to all of you is to visit the mountains. Maybe go on a*
> *trip there with your family, or even your in-laws. It will make*
> *for precious memories if you invest and give and love.*

Curt the photographer in Colorado

August 28

Day 97: *"Metaphorically Speaking"*

The grief I carry is often a result of taking on the grief of others who were close to Curt. One of those is Johnny. I can't even begin to tell you how hard it was to watch his wretched sadness. It was the deepest sadness I've ever seen.

Johnny learned so much from his Poppo, and Curt's best days were when he could be with Johnny. The night before the funeral, we had a sharing time with close friends and relatives. Johnny told me he wanted to get up and say something. I was afraid he'd be unable to talk without being uncontrollably emotional, so I suggested he ask his mom if it was okay. Soon he was up there talking about when he learned to ride his bike without training wheels. He told us he got discouraged when he fell down on the sidewalk, but Curt kept telling him, "Keep between the lines. Stay focused. And don't give up." Then Johnny said, "Metaphorically speaking, I think what Poppo said will stay with me as good advice for life." Then he sat down.

Just like that. We were all a little stunned. Most ten-year-old kids don't know much about metaphors, much less use them in such a meaningful way. Yup, he's his Poppo's grandson. I hate, hate, hate that Johnny doesn't have Poppo around anymore, but I know Johnny will remember often to "Keep between the lines. Stay focused. And don't give up."

I'd say that's good advice for all of us today.

> **What's your metaphor for life?**

August 29

Day 98: DIL

Coming home after being gone is always hard. It seems like the longer I'm gone, the harder it is to walk in the house.

Today when we got home after five days in Colorado, Curt's sister walked in the house with me. "This has got to be so hard coming home alone to your house," she said. I saw the empathy and sadness in her eyes. When she left, I had that hard cry I needed to have after feeling slightly normal for a while. I just wanted so badly to have Curt greet me when I got home. I wanted to know he'd be there in the bed tonight with me. I just wanted him back—even if for a little while. But I know this is not just a bad nightmare, and I'm trying so hard to be strong and find my way.

I'm so glad I have a girl's night planned with Meagan and Norah. The thought of time with my daughter-in-law and granddaughter gives me some light—just a splinter of light, but light.

One of Curt's greatest joys was that I had such a sweet relationship with Meagan. He would say, "You both are lucky to have each other." But the truth is, I gained more in her than I ever deserved. She welcomes me with open arms—more like she is my own daughter than one by marriage. She is an amazing woman in so many ways and has her own amazing mother. I don't try to be her mother, but I do love her as a daughter.

So today, I had that punched-in-the-gut feeling when I got home. That "can this really be true?" feeling. That "someone please wake me from this nightmare" feeling. But I also can't wait to go out with Meagan tonight because I love her. We will shop and find things we both like. We will eat together. We will talk. And I will hug her because she is my light, not just today, but every day.

> *It's so important to figure out how to treat those people who are family by marriage with the same love as you do your blood relatives. Curt loved our daughter-in-law and he loved watching the two of us do life together. I hope you work at having someone you can do life with too. It brings light.*

Meagan and Rosanne

Day 99: Neighborhood

Our neighborhood is very close. We loved living in a small area where everyone knows each other and we're good friends.

Last night we had a small dinner at our neighbor's house. The dinner invitation read, "Let's wrap our arms of love around Rosanne." My neighbors have kept up with me, so there was no need to go over things from the past, which is sometimes hard. I missed Curt sitting beside me with the other couples. I missed him laughing at the guys' jokes. I missed us walking over there and back home together. I was alone once again, and that is a reality that doesn't go away.

I'm so glad I have people who live in such close emotional and literal proximity that they can feel my pain and help me toward healing. Before I left, they gave me a group hug. Middle-aged men and loving women literally wrapped their arms around me. It wasn't even awkward. It was a group of neighbors doing what they do best. If that wasn't enough, when I got home, I found a card from Bob and Holly, who had been our neighbors more than twenty-five years ago. They now live in Colorado, but she had stopped by and left a beautiful bracelet for me, with the initials C and R on it. After all those years, she still showed up to show she cared.

Neighbors—old and new—matter in life. Both give me joy.

> *Do you know your neighbors? Can you count on them to know you well enough to walk through grief with you if necessary? Or share boundless joy? Do you know their garage code and cell phone numbers? Maybe you should. Would you do a group hug with them or show up after twenty-five years, bringing a sweet gift? It's an honor to have a neighbor—and a responsibility to be a good one.*

Day 100: A Century of Days

One hundred is a lot of days—at least it is when I try to match some gratitude to the grief with whom I've become best friends. I suppose someday I'll look back and think I may have been crazy to do this—that I am putting too much pressure on myself, or just allowing people into my private world too much. Both are reactions others may have to these posts now, and I may have someday.

Right now, I don't care.

When my fingers hit the keys of the computer or phone or iPad, it is kind of like they are hitting the keys on the piano when I sit down to play. I often don't have any idea what will come out for a melody. When I am finished with the song, I always feel better when I walk away from the piano. So I do it. And even though one hundred days of penning thoughts seems like a lot, I know my awareness of what is left in my world that is still good is piqued when I finish a post. There must be a word for one hundred days. Whatever it is, that word today means one thing: I will probably do 101 because I need to. At least for now. Someday, I hope to be done. Someday, I hope the gratitude has more words in my posts than the grief. Someday is probably a long time off. Until then, I will work to find something to be grateful for each day.

Today, I am thankful for this computer technology and Facebook. Weird? Yup. But it has brought me some healing. And mostly, it's brought me people who care—a lot of people who care—in ways I would have never imagined. And that is immeasurable.

I hope you use technology for good. It really can be a good, God thing.

September 1

Day 101: Balm

Friends are the balm for my wounds. Today, I spent time with my longtime friend Linda . We drove out to her lake house and had conversation about common life events. Linda lost her husband, Tom, more than ten years ago to the awful disease ALS. We often compare what is worse—living for two years like she did, knowing her husband would die soon, or my situation of such sudden shock. We have decided neither is best. In fact, neither is good. In fact, both situations are horrible, but Linda is another example of how to have a thriving life despite terrible loss. She is quick to tell me how hellish those first months and years were, so I know she didn't arrive at thriving easily.

Having good models like Linda makes it easier for me. She isn't afraid to talk about her life in a way that helps me deal with mine. I listen with great admiration and appreciation. She is a lot like me in many ways, so I'm able to project a little and have hope for the future. Now, please, understand what I am writing, but know the other truth too. I am so disappointed and sad yet. My future is not secure, but neither is anyone's. I sometimes feel like the voice of negativity when I say that, but it's the god-awful truth. That's why I try so hard to listen and learn and love my friend Linda, and so many who have paved a path for me with their own grief.

Maybe there's a friend you can walk with and talk to about tough stuff. I promise, your investment in the together time will help you. Be a friend. Find a friend. Invest in a friend. It pays off in big ways.

September 2

Day 102: A Divine Plan?

So many firsts take my energy and strength away. An unexpected one was when I went to our family physician a few days ago. He was also Curt's physician. As I sat waiting, I got more and more emotional. Those exam tables don't exactly make one relaxed. When the doc came in and asked, "How are you?" with a knowing look, the tears started.

The doctor asked me to describe in my own words what had happened the day Curt died. He told me how he'd immediately reviewed Curt's records to see if there was anything they had missed. There wasn't. I knew that. I had seen the printout of all the numbers and data myself. Then my doc said, "You know, it's so hard to understand this kind of thing. I hope you believe he is in a better place."

"Do you believe there is a heaven?" I kind of surprised myself by asking such a direct question. He didn't hesitate. "I really do. It influences my practice every day." He went on to say how his job was to save lives, but he knew there were divine plans unknown to any of us.

Divine plan? It didn't feel so divine to me. But I did listen to this wise physician who talked about the difference between people who wouldn't want to suffer or be less of who they are, and those who want to live as long as possible no matter what. I told him that without a doubt, Curt went out at the top of his game in many ways, and that Curt had a brilliant mind, and I was so glad it wasn't compromised in any way.

I had gone in for a blood pressure check and came out of a therapy session.

Choose your physician wisely. Maybe ask him or her what they believe. Know that they have a tough job, and although we want them to be God, they aren't. Work at being healthy, but know that you aren't in complete control of your life. Make an appointment for an exam, and, if possible, make a friend of your physician.

Day 103: Despise Not Thy Youth

I miss Curt's profound thinking, concepts, and clarity of belief. One thing he valued is young people, and I do too. I love working with younger people and seeing them grow and develop. When you are sixty-three, young is a little older than it used to be. Curt often quoted the verse in the Bible, "Despise not thy youth." In other words, don't think being young is a problem.

People who help me in my grief come from all walks in life, all places, and all ages. Last night, my niece Danielle came over with dinner and offered to watch a movie with me. She called and reached out. She is twenty-six. I am as old as dirt to someone like her. We only got halfway through the movie because we found out we both just wanted to talk, so we did. For a long time.

We talked about her strengths. We talked about our mutual family. We talked about our work. We talked about her friends. We talked about Curt. We talked about the future. She has the strength of Empathy, and we talked about how there is a raw side and a more mature side to every strength, and how each strength needs to stretch and grow. Empathy, not used to its fullest potential, may just be feelings without appropriate and helpful response. But last night, Danielle modeled the mature side of Empathy. You see, she didn't just feel for me deeply, she put legs, hands, and voice to her Empathy. She did something with it. She showed up with Chinese food and she was a kind and generous soul. I had the privilege of being ministered to by a young person who has never been in my shoes, but knew how to be with me in my grief.

> *Despise not thy youth. If you are young, know you can start being the best of who you already are right now. Move from the world of me to the world out there that needs you. Your youth is not a deficit; it's a huge advantage. It can change someone's world if you start to own your successes and do more of what you are already doing well.*

September 4

Day 104: Purpose

I sometimes almost torture myself by trying to think what I miss most about not having Curt with me anymore. I have a long list, but very close to the top is having someone I can talk with about things that are happening in my life. There are just things I wouldn't go on and on about with others because they are too personal, or frankly, because I get too excited and know other people would get sick of listening to me.

Yesterday was one of those days. I had my first meeting of the school year with the sixteen-year-old woman I mentor through the TeamMates program. I love that girl, and yesterday as we sat outside her high school, she asked if I needed a hug. Maybe that's against the rules, but at that point, I didn't care. Yes, I did need her to hug me. I wanted to come home and tell Curt how she is doing well, studying hard, and anxious to move into a new home.

Last night, I was asked by my good friends Cindy and Tosca to host the non-profit Center for Legal Immigration Assistance, as they shared their mission and purpose with a group of about twenty. I didn't realize they would also have two of the refugee families come to talk about the journeys from their countries to Lincoln, Nebraska. One family had escaped the Syrian atrocities, and the other woman and her three children were from Uganda, also escaping horrible conditions.

As they told their stories of courage, hope, and faith, I kept looking around the room for Curt to catch his eye with my own eye, all teared up from the experience. I wanted the two of us to experience the power of the evening together. I wanted him to hear the stories of how Lincoln is the best place in the world because "people are respectful and helpful."

I missed debriefing with him afterwards and having him listen to my excitement about going to see Ugandan Deborah and her three children move into their new Habitat for Humanity house in a few weeks. I miss so much getting excited about things with Curt. He always fed my eager conversation about topics I care about deeply. He always encouraged me. He always understood me.

But I'm grateful I have the kind of friends who introduce me to exciting opportunities and wonderful people. I'm glad my house can still host a holy evening like we had last night. I'm glad I can still be a part of something bigger than myself.

> *If you've never heard a refugee's story, try reading or hearing about their journeys. If you haven't ever given to a non-profit cause that makes a difference, think about doing that. And most of all, be kind to people of all colors and backgrounds. I kind of think they are the real heroes in this country.*

September 5

Day 105: Game Day

It's Husker game day. This was a day Curt always loved. Most people who knew Curt knew he loved all sports, but Husker football was when he became a rather fanatical fan. I loved sharing life with him when he became a bit of an alter ego on game days. The mild-mannered, thoughtful, level-headed man I knew became opinionated ("What a horrible call!") and competitive ("I can't stand those…"). He used words he normally didn't use, as in, "What a stupid play!" I do believe he was known to let a few rarely used adjectives slip when describing what he perceived as a bad call. I can hear him say, "Oh, come on!!!!" when he got frustrated.

You may think I'm shallow when I miss him today for the first football game, but I can't help it. I will miss entertaining with him at our house. I will miss sitting at our favorite sports bar watching the game. I will miss him when I buy the grandkids their annual Husker shirts. I got them the best Husker outfits I could find this season because he would want me to.

I will have some friends over to watch the game, and I will listen to my son sound a lot like his dad when he cheers on our team and be thankful for the similarity.

Do you have a team you follow fanatically? If you don't, I'm sure Curt would invite you to be a Husker fan. Be a good fan. And remember—even good guys like Curt can be crazy and competitive fans.

Curt and Rosanne

Day 106: Regret

I sometimes think I'm feeling sorrier for myself than I should. I often feel cheated now when I have to be the one to do everything around the house and yard, and anything in between. When something breaks—like my lock on the door, or the hose outside for the umpteenth time—or when I need to put out the garbage or do some other chore Curt used to do, I want to throw up my arms and say, "Why did he have to die?" I can quickly find myself discouraged, tired, bitter, and frustrated about the day-to-day reality.

Millions of women around the world live singly and manage those things. I know they do. So why do I feel so frustrated and discouraged? I guess I just had it too good before. The sad fact is I didn't appreciate all that Curt did around the house. That's the only thing I regret.

I regret that I didn't appreciate enough of the things he did for me. Maybe it was because he didn't necessarily like doing things around the house. Fixing things that were broken wasn't one of his strengths. Quite frankly, he didn't like household upkeep in general, but he had great Responsibility and did what he thought he should do to make our home enjoyable. Mostly, he did it for me. He wanted to make me happy. I know that now more than before his death.

I miss the help and I feel guilty for feeling sorry for myself. So, I will take out the garbage, call to have the lock fixed, go get the oil changed, try to remember how to run the sprinkler system, and change the light bulbs in the ceiling. Now if I can figure out how to get that wasp nest knocked down from the highest peak of the house…

Thanks, Curt, for all you did for me. I didn't say it enough.

> *If someone is your help around the house—even hired help—thank them before it is too late.*

Day 107: Brotherly Love

Yesterday, my brother David came to see me. These days I think anyone who is willing to spend one-on-one time with me has a lot of courage or tons of responsibility. I know it can't be easy or a lot of laughs, but he dared to spend the night with me.

We had dinner and then we just sat and talked until it was time for him to go upstairs to the guest bedroom for the night. He helped me think about my future without dismissing my past. He encouraged me to keep an eye on the new possibilities in my life. If other people said what he said, it would feel like they didn't know my pain. But not my brother. His words gave me some hope. Some focus. Some future. This came from someone who knew and loved and admired Curt as much as anyone I know.

Relationships allow us to be honest and caring at the same time. I could hear and value what my brother said because he does care—because he has proven himself over and over with his generosity. Because he has been there. Although I wish the night could have included Curt (He always thought the world of David too), it was a boost for me. Curt would have appreciated David working with me on that Futuristic strength of mine.

> *Do you have a brother or sister who is full of love and support for you? Thank them. Maybe you are meant to be that kind of difference maker for one of your siblings. Brothers and sisters, sisters and sisters, brothers and brothers, make your parents proud.*

Day 108: Love of Labor

Today I go back to work full-time. Work has been a big part of my life. I worked full-time for almost thirty years, and ten years before that, I taught school off and on. I have been able to work part-time since Curt's death, and that has been a huge blessing.

I don't know how people can go back to work quickly after a loss like mine. I had so much to do, so much to take care of. I was so tired—exhausted some days—and I had little focus or motivation. I did go to the office once a week to keep somewhat engaged in work while taking care of all the challenges that came with my new reality.

I'm grateful to go back to work full-time. I love my colleagues. I love my job. I love the mission of what I do. I love my clients. And, hard as it might be at times, I love that I get to be around people who knew the bigness Curt brought to Gallup.

Today I know clearly what I am grateful for—it is for my employer and the people at work who are also a second family to me. They have been so good to me in so many ways. I can't even begin to thank everyone at Gallup enough. I look forward to the opportunities I'll have to make some impact on our clients. I think I will be a different person going back—a better person. I know that I can speak more than ever to what counts in life.

So here I go. No more lunches with friends, no more happy hours, no more coffees any time, any day. They were so healing, but now I'm ready to work. Thank you, God, for work.

> *Does your work feed you? Do you have great relationships with your co-workers? Love your work. Love your co-workers. Love your boss. And work hard—be amazing at what you do.*

September 9

Day 109: Mercy

Last night was one of those tough nights. It was beautiful outside, and the joy of the seasonal change seemed to fight with my memories of starting each season with Curt. I wanted to sit outside with him, eat dinner on the patio, watch whatever game he was watching at this time of year, and enjoy the beauty of the outdoors together. Instead, I stayed inside and missed my companion. I had a hard time not thinking of either every good thing we enjoyed together or of the initial horror of his death. So I tried laying it out to God.

Now, I am not the most model pray-er. I am sporadic and unfocused in my prayers, but I knew what I was throwing up to God last night. I was asking for mercy and healing. I just wanted to find some light. I have such a love/hate relationship with prayer, but I still do it. By the time I went to bed, I was sad, but not dark. I'm ready to be less sad. I'm not trying to be sad. It just happens.

Early today I plan to ask God to keep me focused and reasonably happy. Is that too much—to give me some peace, some picture of what can be? To give me mercy?

Blessed are the merciful, for they shall obtain mercy.

> *Mercy. In Hebrew, mercy might be translated as compassion. It's something we should expect from decent human beings. Even more, we probably should give mercy to some indecent human beings. It's a word not used often, but I think that we all know when we need it or should give it. Have some mercy. Give some mercy.*

Day 110: Kindred Souls

Just two days ago, it would have been my mom's ninety-seventh birthday. Most years, I thought a lot about her on her birthday, but this year, I thought of her and the relationship she had with Curt.

Mom and Dad always treated Curt, and all their sons- or daughters-in-law, with total love and acceptance. Because Curt was also a pastor to my mom, she appreciated his theological opinion and pastoral ways. She often—yes, often—asked him all those difficult theological questions.

The night before she died, she called and asked if Curt was home. He was out riding his bike, so we talked about her day, which was a Sunday. She seemed a little slower. She couldn't remember some things about her day, but overall, it was an ordinary conversation. Then Curt walked in and I told her he was home and could talk to her. "No, that's all right," she said. "I feel better now that I've talked to you." That night she died.

I will always remember how patient, loving, and kind Curt was with Mom. He admired her. He was amazed by her. He appreciated her. The feelings were mutual. Mom depended on Curt. She always felt better after he gave his best explanation of things like predestination. Or grace. Or the one she thought about most, "I'm not good enough for…" He was so good at helping her know she was better than good enough. That's what he did so well.

So, Mom and Curt—kindred souls in some ways—are both gone now. I miss Mom. She was kind of crazy smart, both in the book way and in conceptual ways. She called a spade a spade, but preached grace. I miss Curt. He was crazy smart too, both in facts but also in profound concepts.

Mom liked good grammar, so I will try to get those commas and apostrophes right, and spell the words correctly in these posts, but if I don't, just try to understand the content, please.

September 11

Day 111: Not Surprised

I'm constantly caught off guard by how grief affects my thinking. One of the things I often instinctively wonder now is what Curt would think about what I'm doing, what I just said, what I feel, who I'm with, where I'm going, and on and on. It's like a guessing game, wondering what he would say and, more importantly, wanting him to be proud of me.

Mostly I imagine him reacting to my new world and telling me what he thinks about it. I sometimes think he'd be surprised at how much I miss him or how I'd do anything to have him back. Or how I know more than ever that our marriage was not ordinary in any sense. But mostly, I think he'd say, "I'm not surprised."

He wouldn't be surprised at how we celebrated his life at his funeral. He'd be embarrassed, but not surprised, since he knew both John and I would want a service fitting of his greatness. He'd not be surprised at our families. He knew how they would rally. He might be a little amazed at the amount of help I've received, but would say, "I'm not surprised. I knew they all loved you." And I don't think he'd be surprised that I'm keeping up pretty well with the Lottage (the name I gave our house—a combination of lodge in winter and cottage in summer). He would say he's not surprised at how many people I've shared my grief with both in person and via Facebook.

He would be impressed (and a little surprised) that, with my brother-in-law Ron's help, I jumped the battery in my car this morning. (I am pretty sure I can do that by myself next time, after Ron's excellent teaching.) Curt wouldn't be surprised that I'm going back to work. He knew how I loved my work. He wouldn't be surprised at how John, Meagan, Johnny, Norah, and Anne have stayed near me to love me into healing.

He may be impressed, but not surprised, with how I managed to call for the air conditioner to be fixed (he always did that), how I can clean off the patio off pretty well now without his help, how I can work the remote (usually), how I can run the sprinkler system now, how I can remember to put out the garbage, and a few other things he always did for us.

When I think about what Curt would think or say about how I'm doing, I mostly want him to be proud of me. How odd is that? That's one of the more logical thoughts I have. The others, if I told you, would make you think I'm totally crazy.

> *What does your thinking say about you? Are there things you think that make you feel like you are a little crazy? You probably aren't, but it doesn't hurt to share some of that thinking. Whom do you want to be proud of you? It's okay to name that person. Wanting to make someone proud may be one of the highest compliments you can pay that person.*

September 12

Day 112: So Hard—Again

It's been a hard last few days, and today is no exception. I always loved coming home on Saturday morning from coffee or the Farmer's Market and working in the yard, partly because Curt and I always did that together. The day he died, that's exactly what we were doing. Now, Saturdays in the yard are so hard. I feel so lonely without him there to talk with or help me with those little things that I can't quite do myself.

I don't know why this week has been so hard. Maybe it's the challenges of so many things going wrong in the house or with car. Or maybe it's the beautiful weather that heralds the next season of my new, alone self. Maybe it's just reality setting in again. I woke up this morning thinking of too many things I just won't do or have much of (if any) with Curt gone now. Vacations with him. Sleeping with him. Surprise gifts from him. Compliments from him. Meals with him. Games with him. Holidays with him. Talks with him.

So here, almost four months later, I'm feeling as discouraged as ever. Crying is the only thing I can do that helps—and that's not exactly satisfying. Gratitude is too hard to find today. I am reaching deep for some to hang on to. I'm trying hard to "give thanks in all things." I am going outside to work now and I will try so hard to be grateful for what we had—even if it wasn't nearly long enough.

> *Maybe sometimes we just have to say thank you without knowing specifically what we are grateful for. Does that make sense? I hope you can find gratitude more easily than I can today.*

September 13

Day 113: Kids and Cupboards

I should probably let you know how the rest of the day went yesterday. After working outside and not feeling any relief from the grief, I decided to go see Johnny and Norah. We went to Barnes and Noble, then to their favorite lunch spot. Back at their house, I helped John and Meagan reorganize some kitchen cupboards. Oddly enough, that helped me start to turn the corner. Somehow dealing with inanimate objects like bowls and dinnerware felt good. Maybe it was that it didn't evoke emotion, but maybe it was just because I was helping someone else.

Later, I went to Rita's house to watch the Husker football game with some other close friends from our small group. Each one greeted me with a hug. I responded with tears, but as we sat around the table on her deck, having tailgate food and wine, watching Curt's team blow out their opposition, I felt a little life come back. Maybe it was because they weren't afraid to mention his name as we talked about football. Maybe it was because it was a safe group of humans who know me pretty intimately and know how to make things feel better for me. Maybe it was the prayer they said for me that gave me peace. Heck, it might have been the wine.

At the end of the day, I was still a widow, but I felt a little bit of strength come back. What helped? Grandchildren, because when I hug them, it's the most like hugging Curt. Maybe some honest, mindless labor, because it distracted my mind, and I felt like I accomplished something tangible. Maybe it was good friends who just take me as I come—a bit broken, but loved. Or maybe it was the Husker win. That never hurts. I am not naïve about this grief thing. I know it ebbs and flows. Waves. I hope I get down to a fifty-foot wave someday. In the meantime, I will try to be honest, not a burden, and perhaps, even make a difference in some unexpected way.

> *So, what's the lesson? If it isn't your best day, find some kids. They help. Find some menial labor, like cleaning out a drawer. That may help. And, for sure, accept those invites for social times with friends. Even when you want to hide inside and cry or deny your reality, take the step toward people. I would say it almost always pays off with a win.*

September 14

Day 114: Impact

I'm in DC starting a week of teaching the strengths course Curt was famous for. I had just become certified to teach this course shortly before Curt died. Leading the class this week is going to be a reminder of his big impact in the world of strengths development.

At Curt's funeral, his go-to at Gallup spoke of Curt's impact and dedication to the strengths philosophy. Benjamin was one of Curt's best sounding boards and a true friend. Here is an excerpt of what he shared:

> "Curt's wisdom was in his ability to see and capture the essence. In his photography, he could capture the essence of a place or a person. In his words, he could capture the essence of a philosophy. With his questions, he could reveal the essence of another human being. All of us at Gallup who worked with him were able to see just the awe that people had when they heard Curt speak and read his words for the first time. He could cut through complexity, and his wisdom was in simplicity and revealing essence.

> "His kindness created a space where you could be yourself—where you could be who you really are. And sharing the space with him, as all of us have and so many other thousands around the world have in his classes, left each person, every interaction, all of us, better—better, freer, stronger because of it. It's incredible the lives he touched...

> "Curt was a learner. Curt, the renowned expert on strengths in the entire world, would be talking to someone new to strengths and asking them about who they are, and so many times I saw him honor them by genuinely saying he'd learned something about them, he'd learned something from them. It was an incredible honor for them, but the magic was that as Curt was learning about others, he was helping them learn about and discover themselves. So many of us

encountered for the first time our authentic selves through Curt, through our interactions with Curt…

"First, he would teach people to love those parts of themselves that they had never loved before because they were told somehow it wasn't right. And Curt would help them see, and love and fall in love with themselves for the first time in many ways. And then, he would help them understand that, in order to help others, they had to love all of the aspects of other people.

"Curt lived his authentic self, and he modeled that for all of us… And he talked about how, in order to be self-actualized, you had to align your soul with your role—who you are with what you do. And there's no one that I know who had done that more beautifully than Curt. His soul and his role were perfectly aligned. He was a man of integrity; every thought, every word, every action was perfectly in sync with his soul and with his passion for what he was doing. And his contribution to the world, and his mission to the world, was to help other people one by one—through coaches that he trained or through his own coaching—to learn and love themselves, and to live their authentic selves. Curt would say, and just this past week he wrote, if we would do this, then the world would be more hopeful, more joyful, more powerful, and more beautiful. And because of Curt, the world is all of those things, and we thank him for his legacy. And Curt, we love you."

What a powerful testament to Curt's passion and his attraction to thousands of his followers. I know I will be quoting Curt often. I pray I can invoke his presence as I teach.

> *If you knew Curt, or someone like him who works to make others better, be grateful. If they are still living, send them a thank-you note. If not, tell their family or colleagues how they impacted your life.*

September 15

Day 115: A Kiss

I will be teaching all week. I attended this same class as a student in February. Curt was the teacher. Yesterday I kept saying things that sounded like they came out of his mouth. Much of the curriculum was his personal work. He just knew how to make the complex simple, so today, I did channel Curt.

One of the participants came up early in the day and asked if I knew Curt. Well, yes, I did. She was one of his regular followers. She was kind and so full of appropriate condolences. I managed to not mention his name all day except for when I once referred to a "giant in the strengths world."

It was a bittersweet day, and I was doing quite well until I was in the hotel ready for bed. I saw a scene on TV where someone kissed their husband on the forehead. All I could do was remember the last time I did that as Curt laid lifeless. It was the last time I saw his body, so that image was in my head very late into the night.

I'm tired this morning. I couldn't shake the image or the feelings I had knowing it was my last kiss, but I'm ready to go into the classroom and be the best teacher I can be in Curt's honor. A kiss on the forehead is a sweet thing, but a kiss on a lifeless forehead is not what I want to remember now.

Go kiss a loved one today. Enjoy the sweetness and love. I'd do anything to get to kiss Curt this morning before I head off to do the transformational work he once did.

Curt and Rosanne on her sixtieth birthday

Day 116: Wise Counsel

I'm staying in the same hotel in DC that Curt and I stayed in last March. I met my good friends Nancy and Connie for dinner last night. I am teaching with Nancy, and her gentleness and flexibility make the long days fly by. Connie has been a great friend and hired me almost thirty years ago at Gallup. We ended up going to the same restaurant as Curt and I had last March. That seems unlikely given the hundreds of restaurants in DC, but it just happened. Walking from the hotel to this awesome restaurant and back reminded me of Curt walking by my side. Curt and I always had such memorable times when we worked together in great cities like DC. We probably had been here twenty-five times.

Connie and I had the last part of the evening to ourselves, sitting outside in the most beautiful weather and talking. She is a counselor at heart. Her questions brought out important feelings. She is one of the only people I know who can honor one's past— my partnership with Curt—while aiming me toward the future. It was an evening of insight and sensitivity. Reality and hope. Memories and future anticipation. Aligning past experience with forward movement. Many people only want to focus on what I've lost and others want to move right to the future, but her approach included both. The genius of the *and* was at play thanks to Connie.

I've not been involved in a formal grief group because I'm surrounded by people who give me wise counsel. People who validate the grief, but also help me see the future help me heal.

> *Who is the wise counsel in your life? Are you a wise counselor for others? Try putting the past and future together in one glorious picture. It's such a gift.*

Day 117: Keeping Myself

Last night after class, Nancy and I went out for a drink. We sat outside again and the night was beautiful. It has been a few days since I've had a really good cry. I've teared up each day, but that's the new normal for me.

As we talked, she somehow knew how to get me to reveal some of my deepest fears, horrible memories, and valleys of grief. She knew that Curt and I had a great partnership because she and her husband Matt have one too. She knew my loss and knew my love, so she let me talk and cried with me—which is always a good thing for me. Toward the end of our conversation, she said, "One thing is sure: you may have lost him, but you haven't lost yourself. You are still the person Curt loved." That got to me. Probably because, in all this grief, I feel like I'm not myself, like I've lost my identity, like I've lost the real me.

It took a good friend to help me know I am still myself—just a bit worn and lot sad most of the time, but I do believe I haven't lost my normal self. Somehow that helps. Losing Curt was enough. Losing myself would be another loss. Thanks, Nancy, for giving me some comfort last night. Thanks for encouraging me. Thanks for crying with me.

> *Do you know who you are? One of Curt's sayings was, "You can't be somebody else, but you can be more of who you already are." How can you be more of who you already are? Can you keep a highlight reel of your best self so you can study it and replicate your best you in the days to come? Can you be more of who you already are? It can be a comfort to find yourself and keep yourself—and maybe love yourself.*

Day 118: Best Days

Curt and I would spend some time each summer reviewing our three best days of the year. It was our way to share with each other and study success. Then we would analyze and think about how we could have more of the best days. We did that for years. I would often write down a day if I thought it had the potential to be on my final list. Curt would go through his photographs to find his best three days. Prior to May 16th, I had started a list of those best days. Since I don't have him to share them with this year, let me share them with you.

The first one was helping Anne move into her new apartment. Second was on our trip to Door County, Wisconsin, when we drove all over and saw magnificent fall scenery and finished the day with an awesome dinner. Day three was the evening we attended Johnny's boys choir concert in December and listened to his amazing solo, "Light a Candle."

I realize how many of the best days included Curt. I wonder what my best three days will look like next year. Will I have three best days or do I need to work at making some good days?

I'm pretty sure I can tell you my worst three days since May 16th, but I really want to be able to report to you next summer what my three best days looked like, felt like, and how they made me a more complete person. So today, I'm starting to document any day that maybe isn't a best day, but a good day. Then, one day, I may see this year as having some best days.

> *What were your best three days of the year? I encourage you to try this exercise. Studying the best will help you do more of what was good.*

September 19

Day 119: Memories

I had a good week in DC. I loved being with both colleagues and the students we had in our coaching class. I was afraid when I started this class that the memories would just bring sadness and give me an ache and make me hate facing the future.

But it was different this week. Teaching the class was filled with many reminders of Curt. His words were on the screen. His mannerisms when he taught kept flashing before my eyes. The way people in the class talked about him with admiration and the way he was a minister in the classroom were in my head and heart all week. But for the first time since he died, the memories didn't hurt. They kind of gave me energy. Only once (maybe twice) did I get teary during class, and that was when Jim Clifton, our CEO, came in and talked. Listening to Jim speak of the power of jobs, of engagement, of strengths, of the Special Olympics using strengths, of his dad, Don Clifton, and on and on, I just felt the power of Curt through him.

The letter Jim sent to the Gallup tribe, as he calls it, following Curt's death was one of the first and most powerful tributes to Curt's legacy.

> "Tribe,
>
> "I am so deeply sorry to let you know that we lost our beloved tribe brother Curt Liesveld yesterday. It is an unexpected and extraordinary loss to Rosanne and his two children. It is an unexpected and extraordinary loss to you and me because he loved us a lot too. To know him and be around him at all was to be in the presence of love, goodness, rare indescribable selflessness, purpose, hard work and fun. Curt lived on earth to seriously improve people.
>
> "When I would see Curt in the Washington building, I had to get my hands on him—I just had to hug him and shake him and see that smile that sort of tucked into his chin. I had to say something funny so I could hear that laugh. I felt better at my job, my life, and

everything in the world when grabbing him—something goes into you when he is around.

"Curt was simply a saint among us.

"You wonder how many lives he impacted in his tribe strengths ministry—he taught thousands and thousands of clients, students, coaches, leaders, of all kinds. Then they go back somewhere and teach what they learned from him to tens of thousands more in their companies and organizations and institutions. He sent huge, serious, spectacular, positive energy throughout our global teaching networks.

"He lived and worked a life that mattered to his family, the tribe, and especially our country and the world. So, he got that done—even though he is leaving a little too early.

"Curt, have a speedy trip to heaven—get some rest—then check in with all our friends who will be there to meet you at the gates. They are going to want a full update of this strengths explosion (especially Don Clifton) that you have been a huge part in triggering..."

Jim

Jim Clifton
Chairman and CEO
Gallup

Even though Curt was all over that classroom, for the first time, that experience felt good to me. I'm grateful for that. I'm hoping that feeling returns in other ways, but I feel like it's a long time out.

> *Whose presence do you need to invoke in order to feel fulfilled and fulfilling? Is there someone from your past you call on who makes your work more powerful? I hope everyone becomes a legacy that gives others emotional strength to go on with life and make a difference.*

Day 120: Real Love

I think I've finally figured out what real love is in a marriage. In all my life, I could never have imagined how much grief I would have when Curt left me. The other day, I had this thought: "I'm glad Curt doesn't have to go through this after losing me. I'm glad it is me who is suffering and not him." I truly would hate to think of him having to suffer the way I am.

So, today is a short post. All I know is that I had no idea how hard this would be (perhaps because I never imagined myself a widow in my sixties). But I also can't bear thinking of Curt being in my place. It kind of reminds me of when I was in labor with my kids. I saw how Curt was so helpless wanting to help me. I was in the most pain I'd ever had in my life, but he was not able to do anything about it. So, weirdly enough, in my distorted grief thinking, I'm glad he doesn't have to be the one to do what I am doing now. I think that might be true love—to want to be the one who suffers. Death may be the penultimate expression of that sentiment.

Kind of morbid. Kind of true. Kind of evidence of a deep love. Not quite gratitude, yet oddly close.

> *I have no idea what lesson this has for you today. Maybe none, except to ask, "What does real love look like in your life?"*

September 21

Day 121: "Death"

I had someone tell me the other day that she shudders when I use the words *died* and *death*, especially with Curt's name in front of them. I get it. I shudder too, but I have never used the less final sounding words like *passed* or *passed away*. I'm not sure why.

I get that those who believe in heaven think of death more as a passing into another life, and that seems to be more palatable for most people. Perhaps more spiritual, too. Yet, the Bible uses the words death and dying all the time. In a lot of things, I've tried not to steer away from a word or experience that might be hard for me. I'm not sure if that's smart or not. Some counselor might advise me not to go headfirst into grief at times, but I feel like I'm not being real if I don't use real words. Curt's death makes our marriage final. Although I'd like to use a softer word, it wouldn't make the grief true to what I am experiencing. I may not make much sense, but I need to face some of these feelings, memories, words, and thoughts with fortitude—knowing they will almost always make me shudder, throw me into dread, and for sure, make me cry.

Last night I read that the people who heal more quickly after loss are those who grieved honestly and deeply. I don't think those people would shy away from using the words, *death* or *died*. I'm grateful I have enough strength to plow through grief most days. It's odd that grief takes strength when you feel weak.

I know. This post is confusing today. I do know words make a difference. And as much as I use real words to describe my grief, I'd like to find real words to find my future.

What are your words? Do they reflect the real you? Do you have a word you are avoiding? Do you have a word that describes your life? A word like "light," for instance? That word said much more than we ever knew when Curt chose it for his word of the year. Maybe yours will, too. Choose your words carefully.

Day 122: Kindness

I've noticed when I'm having a hard day that people who are nice make me feel better. How profound is that? It sounds so simplistic, but I have been touched over and over again by people who are just plain kind.

What is kindness? Well, it's hard to describe, but I know it by the way it makes me feel. When I travel, people who work in airlines and hotels can make me feel better just by being friendly and saying "hello" and "thank you." Kindness is often generosity (and for sure not stinginess) like, "Let me buy that coffee for you." Kindness almost always works for me when people enthusiastically greet me, like "Good morning, Rosey!" Kindness is often people who find something encouraging to say like, "You did really well on that first week back to work." Kindness is volunteering to help even with small things, like "let me take that out of the car for you." Kindness is sometimes physical, like a hug in the middle of the break room, or the touch on my shoulder. Kindness is sometimes initiative, like "Do you feel like doing something tomorrow night?" Kindness is often just asking, "How are you doing today?"

Pretty simple, huh? All I know is I've needed a lot of kindness when I feel discouraged, beat up, and fearful. Here's the gratitude part: I've gotten a lot of kindness, and it has made a difference for me. I hope I can be kinder than before Curt died. It's a goal I have now more than ever.

So, thanks to all of you who have shown that kindness is not overrated.

> *How do you show kindness on a regular basis? Be kind today.*
> *You may make someone's day a lot better.*

September 23

Day 123: Images

Yesterday at work, I was going through some old e-mails and saw one from John with an attachment. I quickly clicked on it to see if it was something I should save. A wonderful picture of Curt appeared on my screen. In a second, my heart raced, and I immediately had tears in my eyes. His features were so strong. His still-dark and full head of hair perfectly framed his face. His eyes were crinkled as he smiled, leaving small slits into his soul. His face was rugged and handsome. I don't think he ever thought of himself as handsome, but he knew I loved the way he looked.

Looking at pictures of Curt is one of the hardest things to do yet, but they help replace pictures I have in my head of the way he looked when I found him lying in the grass, clearly without life. Sometimes I can't delete that image in my head at night before I go to bed. Last night was one of those nights, and I didn't sleep well as a result. So I'm going to try to look more at his handsome face, even though that is a different kind of hard. I want to replace the image of death with an image of life.

How about you? Are there images in your head you need to replace? Things that make you sad or afraid or confused? Maybe you can find some beautiful images and linger on them a while. I know in time my memories will exclude the dark images and be all about light. I'd encourage you to collect your favorite pictures of people, places, and things to create a lasting impression of joy in your life too. Pictures can be worth a thousand words.

Day 124: The Scent

I talked the other day about how pictures of Curt still make me miss him so. I've noticed that scents do too. For a long time, when I opened the door to his closet, I held my breath so I wouldn't smell the scent of his body. At the beginning, I was almost always afraid to go into that closet, partly because I kept thinking he might still be in there. I did a lot of weird thinking in those first weeks.

But yesterday, I went in the closet, and when I got in there, I did something that took me by surprise. I took in a deep breath and smelled Curt. For the first time, I wanted to smell his scent. It was comforting. Then I realized that some of my clothes are in his closet, and they may take on his smell too. That made me even happier. It's very weird how sometimes the thing you dread can kind of turn into a comfort. That isn't happening much yet, but I will take every grief-turned-to-comfort moment I can find. I'm grateful for a small turning point.

Now, don't expect me to have that kind of reaction with most things yet—music, vacation pictures, notes, and Curt's handwriting still make me utterly sad. For now, I will walk into his closet and take a deep breath and bathe in the scent of the man I love.

I hope you find reminders of your loved ones all around you today. I hope your senses can come alive today with or about someone you love. Drink it in. The senses were meant for memories and pleasure.

September 25

Day 125: Futuristic Mojo

As I mentioned earlier, my strengths, as measured on the Clifton StrengthsFinder, are Futuristic, Activator, Relator, Significance and Command. I wish Curt could help me know how to use them after losing him, especially the Futuristic strength. He was amazing at helping me understand what I do best and framing things in a way that made me dive into my strengths full force and use them more and more. Curt would talk about how talent only becomes a strength when it moves from its more immature, raw form to being fully mature and being used for good. Talents are recurring patterns, thoughts, and behavior until they are productively applied, at which time they really are strengths.

I feel like I could use a strengths coach right now to help me figure out how Futuristic could be a strength for me in this season of grief. My future is only a day-to-day thing right now. I do wake up and try to think of something to look forward to each day, but that's not enough. My need is to go much further into the future with pictures, ideas, and experiences. So, yesterday I spent some time journaling about the strength of Futuristic. I don't journal well, so that was not easy, but it did allow me to pen some thoughts about how I might move into the new normal.

Futuristic is a strength that tends to see a positive, compelling future. That's the part I still can't grasp. I wrote about my near future, and my further-out future. My near future had lots of pictures of Curt still in it—although more in the form of celebrating and honoring him. Curt always said I was a promoter, so promoting him is part of my near future. The far future took more work, and it's pretty blurry. It's hard to replace those pictures I had of the two of us doing good things together, working together, loving our grandkids together, and just having a companion for everything I do.

I long to get my Futuristic mojo back in action. I'll take any advice you have. As Curt said, "Strengths are enduring and natural and powerful," so I will keep believing it will work for me in a productive fashion again one day.

September 26

Day 126: The Helpers

I'm still a bit overwhelmed when I have to do the chores Curt did around the house and yard. This week, when I realized I had no idea how to turn off the sprinkler system for the fall, I had help from my nephew Terry. He came over without me asking to show me how to do it. Little things like that matter. They take away some of the grief-related stress that so easily immerses me.

Then it was the outdoor fire pit. Doug went beyond just helping me hook it up to fixing a broken part that I would have no idea what to do with. Then it was the bird feeders this morning. Curt and I loved to watch the birds in our tree-filled area, but he took care of all the bird feeders. I didn't even know if I could reach them, but Doug relocated them for me. The nice thing is, Johnny can also reach them, so he fed the birds this morning. Curt would be so proud of him.

I'm slowly getting better at doing some things around the house, even though I hate the reason I must do them. The help from smart, loving, and helpful people makes all the difference. I won't have to worry about those irrigation pipes freezing. I'm grateful for a fire pit where we can still roast hot dogs. And I won't have to miss seeing the birds eat at the feeders.

I'm grateful for help. I'm grateful for people who teach me how to do things I've never had to do before.

> *Are you a helper? Whom have you helped lately? Are you willing to ask for help when you need it? We all have a role. We all need each other's strengths.*

Goldfinches

Day 127: Bittersweet

Last night I had my precious grandkids overnight. Those evenings are always bittersweet. I wonder if I'm enough for them now. When there were two of us, we could each take one and focus on them. I worry that they get less than they deserve with only me. I can't quit thinking about how Curt and I were a team when taking care of them. I would hold Norah until she fell asleep, and he would pick her up and carry her to her bed. Now I do both. I miss his strong arms lifting her out of mine.

Today Johnny and I shed a few tears together, and I whispered in his ear, "You help me feel like Poppo is still here when I hug you." Grief and gratitude are never such powerful partners as when I am with my grandkids.

Thank you, God, for those precious children.

> *Do you have grandchildren? Are you a grandchild? There's a bond that transcends even death in that generational relationship. What a gift it is, even on the hardest days.*

September 28

Day 128: Cousins

I've said before that those who have been through loss in many ways offer the most understanding, and therefore, the most comfort. Late last week, I received a note and a small gift from Curt's cousin Joyce. Joyce and Curt were Facebook friends, and like so many other family members, got reacquainted via technology. (Thank you, again, Mark Zuckerberg.)

Joyce has been a regular supporter of mine on these grief and gratitude posts, and no wonder. She, too, had a tragic loss in her life more than five years ago. She has been encouraging, kind (Yes, there's that "k" word again.), wise, and spiritually grounded. When I received her profound note, I read every word with anticipation of her wisdom. She particularly alluded to the healing power of giving back.

As I opened her card, I was at a point in the day when I really needed to cry, but couldn't get myself to do it. Her words immediately gave me the energy to cry—and that was a gift. Just knowing her loss, her testimony to the process, and the outcomes made my tears almost like medicine. Amid shared hurts and tears, I made a step forward after reading her note. Thank you, Joyce. You made a difference. Curt would be so grateful to you too.

I hope you find a cousin somewhere who can make a big difference for you. Maybe "friend" them on Facebook. Maybe plan a reunion with them (Joyce is now taking that on with some help from other Liesvelds) or just pray for them. It's all good.

Day 129: A White Handkerchief

It seems very odd what things bring Curt back to me in a moment, like the other day when I saw a white handkerchief. Most young guys don't carry handkerchiefs anymore. I don't think most people have carried a handkerchief since tissues were invented! Maybe Curt wouldn't have carried one his whole life, but he always had problems with allergies and asthma, so it was his constant companion when his nose seemed to be runny, itchy, and bothersome.

From the time I was a little girl in church, I can remember Curt pulling out his white handkerchief and blowing his nose. It had a distinct sound. After we got married, I couldn't believe how many of those white handkerchiefs were in the laundry. But what I remember even more is how he always put them to good use: wiping our kids' and grandkids' faces off when they were dirty, wiping the inside of the windshield off when it got that smeary gunk on it, giving one to me when I teared up in concerts or church or, for sure, at the grandkids' performances. We both always needed a white handkerchief then.

When we cleaned out Curt's closet, we didn't keep the white handkerchiefs. Because they were rather monotone and not unique in any way, we gave them away. I wish I had kept one. Those plain, white pieces of cotton had his name all over them. Not in a monogram way, but in an emotional way. They told the story of a kid grown up to be an amazing man who used even his handkerchief for the benefit of others.

I wish I had one so, when I cry now, I could bury my face in it. I just remembered—literally just now—that there is one in the rag drawer. It has frayed edges, and I thought it might work for cleaning. I can't wait to pull it out. I will have that memento of comfort. A plain, white piece of cloth that still feels like a loving husband.

I know—this is yet another odd thing I'm writing about, but these are the things that give me pause. And grief. And gratitude.

Do you have a real handkerchief? Do you use it? Does it wipe away tears?
Be thankful for that piece of boring, white cloth—and for the tears that
God gives you in times of joy or sorrow.

September 30

Day 130: Touch

One of the things I miss so much is the affection Curt showed for me. Although we were never very publicly affectionate, he was a very intimate and affectionate husband. He showed his affection in so many ways: gifts, notes, words, and touch. I miss all those things.

Maybe most of all, I miss his touch. I miss holding hands so much. I miss how he would not just hug me, but let out a little sigh each time that sounded like pure pleasure to me. I miss putting my feet on him in bed to warm them up. I miss the contact of his physical self. I know that may seem too private, but it's a real part of my grief. I remember how at one point in Curt's ministry, somebody was not happy that Curt had people stand and greet each other at the beginning of the worship service. The man called it "the abominable handshake." Curt responded that he would never quit doing that because he had once heard a widow say she loved that time of the service best because it was the only time she was touched all week.

Curt was a proponent of affection, and I was the benefactor. I'm happy now for hugs. I'll even take a handshake. The best hugs come from the grandkids, but honestly, when I was in the first weeks of this grief, I most needed the hugs from my son. I remember in the middle of that first dark and hellish night after Curt died, John hugged me as we desperately clung to each other for comfort. The comfort for me was that his face felt so much like Curt's. It still makes me cry to think about that moment.

I'm grateful for touch. It will never be the same as Curt's touch, but I will take any good substitute—and not a side hug. A real hug. Or a touch on the hand. Or even eyes connecting that say, "I understand your pain and I love you." I'll take that hug any day knowing it is, in part, a hug from Curt.

> *Find your affection. It doesn't have to be grandiose.*
> *It can even be awkward at first. But do it—do it for the other*
> *person—and soon it will feel good to you too.*

Johnny, Curt, and Norah

October 1

Day 131: Good Job

A year ago today, Anne moved into her new apartment. She had waited a long time for that day. I remember how happy Curt and I were for her. Curt worked hard with John, getting her all moved in, lifting heavy furniture and setting it all up.

So today, I think about how Curt and I would have a moment together being happy and proud of our daughter. I miss those moments with him when no one else can quite take his place. I am so, so grateful Anne got all settled in before he died, and that he saw her happy and successful.

Anne, I bet your dad would say, "Good job!" to you today. I know you miss him every day too. Sometimes it takes a village to help develop and celebrate. Today I appreciate everyone in Anne's village who has contributed in any way to her well-being and success.

What villages are you part of? What role do you play that makes a difference for others?

Anne and Rosanne

October 2

Day 132: Fuel

Yesterday I had lunch with a friend and colleague. Jo Ann and I worked at Gallup for twenty-eight years, and I learned many, many things from here. She taught me a lot about talent. She taught me about the Catholic faith (she is a Catholic sister). She taught me that purpose trumps everything. When we met yesterday, she blessed me with words that could only come from a wise, missional, and caring friend.

We talked and talked, and she was okay with listening to me think aloud about her future endeavors in the strengths world. It felt good to think about someone else's future since I'm not doing so well thinking about my own.

When I got home, I found an e-mail Jo Ann wrote me a few days ago.

"I read your Facebook piece already this morning. You write so much about RELATIONSHIPS. You and Pope Francis are on the same page! Love it. So right, it gives and sustains LIFE! You and Curt have high Relator, I know, and it fuels you. An early action item I read for this theme that spoke so much to me reads: 'No matter how busy you are, stay in contact with your friends. They are your FUEL.'"

Her comparison of me to the Pope made me smile. Today, I wish I could be doing relationships with Curt by my side. I miss that so much, but I'm so grateful for the relationships we both developed over the years. They have sustained me in so many ways over the last few months.

> *I hope you take time to foster relationships.*
> *You may even get compared to the Pope someday.*

Day 133: Telling Pictures

There are some things that are sure to give me an emotional jolt: music, photographs Curt took, gifts he gave me. But pictures of Curt himself are still the hardest, and I have literally dozens of them around the house. There was a time when I purposely looked away when I unexpectedly saw his picture. I know how cowardly and full of avoidance that sounds. What I notice is not just a picture of this man I loved so deeply, but that when I look at him, it seems he is looking directly into my eyes. It's a piercing, but loving look I feel. Sometimes it just takes my breath away.

Yesterday I had that experience and I felt like he was right there in the room as he looked back at me. But it's a trick, just like so many times I've felt tricked by an evil force. As much as it feels like those eyes are living, I quickly realize he is not here. So, I'm trying to look at those pictures and not feel blindsided by the emotion.

Or maybe I should feel the emotion. I can't even begin to tell you how many things like that make me feel conflicted. I am going to try to look into his eyes in those pictures— hard as it may be—to look at him and see his love for me. Look at him and see his honesty. Look at him and see his responsibility. Look at him and see his happiness. Look at him and see his faith. Look at his eyes that seem to still say, "I love you."

I can't imagine what it was like years ago when there weren't many pictures of loved ones who had left this world. I'm thankful for the hundreds of pictures of Curt and I hope that, soon, they won't deliver conflicting emotions, but emotions of peace and love.

I'd suggest taking pictures of your loved ones and filling all the nooks and crannies in your house with them. And look deep in their eyes while they are still with you here on earth.

Curt and Rosanne

Day 134: Morning Routine

I often wonder when I will ever wake up in the morning and not have the first thought in my mind be that Curt is gone forever. Right now, it seems like I will always have that as my greeting as I open my eyes. I can understand how some people might want to stay in bed and not wake up because it is just too hard.

This morning was no exception. I woke up and wanted to have a do-over. I wanted to have Curt back and look forward to a Sunday of fun with him. Just as I sat down to type this, I heard a text come in. It was from John, who asked if I wanted to get coffee before church. Why, yes, I do.

Little things make all the difference. Little things like just asking me if I want to do something. Or just saying, "I am thinking of you." A short post today to say my grief is my morning routine, along with brushing my teeth. My gratitude is my daily response as I look for the good things God has placed in my way.

What are you thankful for today? Can you start your day by centering on those things? Might you text someone today out of the blue and say, "Want to meet me for coffee?" Small acts of kindness can create life-changing days.

October 5

Day 135: In All Things

Yesterday was a day of grief and gratitude. It was a day when I cried and I laughed. It was sad and it was good. I went to get a jacket out of my front closet, and realized I had not taken care of Curt's jackets and coats. My hand touched them one at a time, and I again had that feeling of unadulterated sadness. I pulled them out, put them in a pile and waited for John to come to see if he wanted any of them. When he tried them on, he reached into the pockets of one of them, and pulled out the gloves. Those gloves that kept Curt's hands warm and protected, made all of us break down in tears.

Soon afterwards, Curt's brother Claude came over to help with the leaves in the gutter—one more thing that Curt would have done. After Claude finished, I gave him a few things I'd found in Curt's office that were tokens of a beloved brotherly relationship: an old glass used for their root beer floats and pictures in original, hand-crafted frames. Then we had our turn at tears.

Finally, Johnny went out behind the house to put the firewood in the garage where I can get at it this winter. When I went out to see how he was doing, he burst into tears. You see, he and Poppo always did that together.

But the gratitude emerged amidst the grief. The coats looked so good on John. My gutters are free of leaves—and I have a brother-in-law I love so very much who, once again, filled in for his brother. And Johnny, well, he finished all the firewood and ended the day with a smile as his football team won with him quarterbacking in fine fashion.

The grief was deep yesterday, but the gratitude competed bravely alongside the tears. I'm not sure which one won, but I will continue to look for what I can be thankful for in these hard days.

In all things, give thanks. Can you give that a try today?

Day 136: Leftover Sweaters

Yesterday I went to the dry cleaners and as I was ready to leave, they said, "You have two items to pick up." Sure enough, they were two of Curt's sweaters. Carrying them out to my car was one of the unexpected stab-in-the-heart experiences. I wanted to say to the woman behind the counter, "Don't you know those were my husband's, and he's dead now?" As if it were her fault.

Sometimes I feel angry at people when it isn't their fault at all for not knowing my loss. I'm sure people in positions behind counters, checking out groceries, or mowing lawns get the brunt from people who think they should know everything. In truth, they may be having a bad day too. Try a little grace. Don't always say what you think, even though you may be right. People come wrapped in their own issues. They come wounded and tired and hopeless some days. Sometimes they, like my dry-cleaning person, just don't know what you've gone through and aren't doing anything wrong. They just picked a bad day to give you the clothes of your deceased husband and then ask to be paid for them.

Grace. Patience. A quiet tongue. I need these more than ever since Curt died because I pretty much want to yell at most people about their seeming incompetence—which is really my incompetence.

Give a break to someone today. Go the second mile.
Imagine what might be going on in their lives, smile, and say,
"Thank you." They may need that more than you realize. Trust me, you
won't feel better yourself when you take it out on someone else.

October 7

Day 137: Best-laid Plans

I had a dream that Curt was lost. I spent a lot of my dream searching for him—never to find him. I don't think it takes a dream expert to analyze that one.

I think I've been dealing with realizing the finality of his death. For many of the first weeks after his death, I could only put one foot in front of another. Now I look out a few weeks—occasionally months when it comes to work commitments. I still don't look at the future with any joy. It often feels like an elephant is sitting on my chest as I find it impossible to anticipate the future. I try hard to be positive and grateful, but some days I just have to admit my future is bleak and has no invitational power. I envy those who have plans. My plans don't exist for the most part.

This morning I prayed that God would surprise me in the future with some joy. I usually thought I could control the joy in my life, and now, I know I can't. It's not a fun lesson to learn. Maybe the real lesson is that life isn't about always looking forward to something fun. Maybe it's about sacrifice with joy. Or work with joy. Or waiting for surprises with joy. I'm not in control, except for choosing to be grateful.

Today, once again, I find gratitude hiding—much like Curt was in my dream. So, with Discipline and Belief, I will just say, "Thank you." I will just believe God has a good surprise in my future, and maybe even be thankful for the unknown—the things I can't control.

Are you a person who must know what's happening and wants to plan the future to your specifications? That's cool, but it may be even better to let God surprise you with something greater than you can control. I really don't know, but I'm willing to ask for that bit of favor.

Day 138: The Right Way

I am quite sure I may have some critics for being public about my grief and gratitude, or at least some people who are not comfortable with my posts. Some people just say, "I could never do that," and that's enough for me to question my brand of grief expression.

Many days I feel insecure—whether it is legitimate or not. I guess I took to heart what most widows told me: "Don't let anyone tell you the right way to grieve. Do whatever is right for you." So, even though I may feel bad that some people aren't so sure about my posts, my transparency, my ugliness, my instruction, my public emotion—I feel like it was a bit ordained, I did not plan to do this in any way. The first few posts had no plan to them. I had no initial strategy in my head. I hate to play the G card, but it felt like God was leading me, and it still does.

Curt used to tell people who were going through grief to share it with people who cared about them. In fact, he was very clear they needed to talk to the right people about their disappointments and grief. This circle of humans must be the right people for me. You'll notice I don't have that many friends on Facebook because I've always been a bit choosy.

Thank you for being my friend. Thank you for encouraging me. Thank you for messaging me, taking me out for coffee, commenting on a post, or sending a card. There will never be too many of those things done for me—they hold me up in God-like arms. Thank you for listening and reading. It may be hard for you sometimes, but guess what. It's even harder for me.

It's hard to weep with those who weep. Avoiding pain, as I've learned, is not possible or even healthy. Thanks for entering into the sanctuary of my grief and gratitude. And for not judging. And for supporting me with prayers and words, and even quiet love. Your practice with me will make you even better for the next person who needs your friendship amidst their grief. Know you are making a difference in my life.

October 9

Day 139: Circle of Life

My great niece and her husband, Lauren and Alan, had a baby two days ago. The circle of life goes on. They will be awesome parents, and little Thomas will have the best grandparents ever.

I remember when Curt married Lauren and Alan. They both have Competition in the strengths. In the wedding message, Curt talked about them being competitive about things like who could say thank you the most, or who could give the most compliments to the other. Who could win at being a servant spouse? I bet Curt would say to them now, "Who can be the best support as you enter the world of parenthood?" Curt was such a perfect partner in terms of raising our kids. I think both of our kids saw us as both being in the game of parenthood with our eyes on winning.

Here's to a new baby in our family. Here's to new life. Here's to a child who has a bright future. Curt would be so happy that the union he blessed now includes a new baby.

Who is your most recent family member? How did you welcome him or her to the family? How can you support and help young parents? The circle of life can be made even more beautiful with your involvement and blessing.

Curt officiating at Lauren and Alan's wedding

October 10

Day 140: Happy Hour

Last night I hosted the happy hour our neighborhood has every Friday. Curt and I had hosted the group every year around this time. After all, my neighbors were heroes to me during the time of Curt's death. They were there for me.

After many of the group left, some of the neighbors stayed later, and we ordered pizza. We sat around the fire pit and talked and laughed. I tried not to refer to Curt too much, but they were ready to listen to me brag on my grandkids, talk about my new normal, and reminisce about earlier times we'd had together. And they were ready to hug me and be okay with my tears and broken voice.

When they left, I felt such a combination of gratitude and grief. Gratitude to these precious souls who live so nearby me. Gratitude that these men would gather the plates and load my dishwasher. Gratitude that they would not think I was incomplete and could not still host them in my home. Yet, as I turned off the outdoor lights, the fire pit, and the candles inside, I could only think of Curt's year of light. My tears increased with each light I extinguished.

So, grief and gratitude intermingle on a Friday night with my neighbors and with me missing my precious Curt. Curt always said his well-being was better because of where we lived. And I believe mine is too—now more than ever.

> *Do you have good neighbors, or should you be a good neighbor?*
> *Pizza and brownies are easy and work well on a Friday night for making*
> *good neighbors. Believe me, it's something I'm so grateful for,*
> *even though I wanted Curt to be here for this beautiful*
> *October evening. He would have loved it too.*

October 11

Day 141: Messy Faith

There are many times that I think, "Curt would have loved to see that." Or do that. Or hear that. Or taste that—especially the cake Donna made last night. I do believe that, but then my more rational and spiritual side argues that heaven is better than anything he would experience on earth. More beautiful. More goose bumps. More high fives. More smiles. More magnificent. More ecstasy. And I believe that too.

Faith is hard. It's messy. It's leaning into a lot of mushiness sometimes. It sometimes screams at sophisticated, analytical thinking. Yet, Curt had faith and he was very analytical. I think it takes faith to have faith. While I don't like to be naïve or believe life is perfect with enough faith, I lean into it. Don't ask me to explain it. Faith is believing what you can't see or touch or feel. So, back to heaven, I believe Curt is experiencing more than he ever would on earth. I still wish he was here so I could watch him enjoy life. So, there.

Once again, my grief messes with my faith. And, once again, my gratitude makes my faith real.

> **What do you have faith in? Your health? Your money? Your politics? Your job? Your afterlife? I'm hoping it's the latter.**

October 12

Day 142: Goals

This morning I was flipping through my phone and came across a category I have in an app titled, "Goals." I have written goals for almost thirty-five years, and I believe I can find most of them. I normally categorize them into things such as education, family, physical, financial, spiritual, work, house, social, travel, and then one marked couple.

I wasn't sure I wanted to look at those goals since so many of them included my partnership with Curt. We didn't accomplish that goal of seeing Switzerland. We didn't do seminars together for work. We didn't take the grandkids on another trip. We didn't plan for our retirement. We didn't lead more marriage seminars at church together. And so on and so on.

Now the concept of a goal feels so unnecessary, so blurry. Almost every year there was a goal or two I didn't accomplish, but this year, I won't accomplish most of them. So, what do I do? My brother suggested I write some new goals for the next six months or so, so I tried that. But they look so anemic. So uninviting. So hard. The first few weeks, my goal was just not to fall apart every day, and I didn't accomplish that one.

Many years, my goals took us places and pushed me forward. Through a master's degree, through building a house, through traveling with Curt, through reaching financial goals, through growing spiritually. So, I am thankful for what life has given me as I plodded through those goals. Now, I need to figure out a new life.

Like a predestined act from God, this morning, my wonderful friend Jo Ann Miller sent me a message that included this:

> *"'To destroy is always the first step in any creation,' the poet e.e. cummings wrote. Change is often traumatic, unwanted, unacceptable. Yet, all of them—death, the loss of a job, divorce—do, in the end, free us to begin again, to create our lives anew. Not everybody gets that opportunity."*

The opportunity to create life anew? It was no coincidence I happened to turn to my goals this morning and receive her well-timed message.

What about you? Do you write goals? What do they say about you? I'd love to hear about that. I could use some advice as I consider the profound concept of creation starting with destruction.

Day 143: A Favorite Season

It's October—normally one of my favorite months. It was beautiful last night, but the night was long and lonely. This week I've had less going on than almost any week since May 16th. My guess is that is kind of how it goes. At least that's what I've been told.

I had that deep ache of grief—the kind that feels like a hole in my heart. I know a lot of people care about me, but when I'm having a bad night, I feel so alone. It may just be that kind of week. Memories from past years come rushing into view. Memories of the crisp fall days we loved, memories of fall trips, memories of special days in our October life.

Grief seems unending lately, but today I will work at gratitude again because this ache I've had is both dull and sharp, and I need to find some antidote—some gratitude that can be salve to my wounds. I want to love October once again.

> **What do you love about this month of October?**
> **I hope you can love the autumnal feel. It was Curt's favorite season.**

October 14

Day 144: Birthday

October 14th. My birthday. A year ago I would never have believed I would be a widow when I turned sixty-four. Looking forward to this day has been less-than-happy.

I went back to find last year's birthday card from Curt to see what he had said. His precious, handwritten note simply says, "My greatest joy in life is knowing you and being known by you." So perfect—just like he was for me.

Someone wrote me a note yesterday that said, "Happy Birthday. I hope all your birthday wishes come true." Well, there's just one wish today, and I don't think it's coming true. I will remember the many other birthdays when Curt spoiled me, celebrated me, loved me, and made me feel like this date was the most important one on the calendar.

Thank you in advance for your kind thoughts and words. I know each loving act will help me get through this day.

> *Please enjoy your day today. Enjoy your breath.*
> *Enjoy the weather. Enjoy laughter. Enjoy your friends.*
> *Enjoy your best friend. Enjoy good food. Enjoy your work. Enjoy life.*

Day 145: Moments

My birthday mirrored my last five months of grief and gratitude. Moments of terrible sadness. Moments of fear. Moments of anger. Moments of despair, Moments of hating my life. And then, moments of light. Moments of hope. Moments of love. Moments of determination. And moments to give thanks in all things.

It was tough. I used my best friends, who happen to be my sisters, as safe humans to talk with about my grief. They had to watch me cry and not be able to do anything about it. As they left, I felt guilty for ruining their days too.

Then cards came—many people remembering me in kind and generous ways. About mid-afternoon, my friend Nelda came over with flowers—the kind Curt would have given me. I couldn't hide my tears from her either. The flowers were so beautiful, and it lifted my spirits to know someone took time out of her day just to say, "I'm thinking of you."

As Nelda left, another friend arrived. Shar lost her thirty-four-year-old daughter less than a year ago, and survived and thrived for many years as a single mom to four kids. She talked and listened. It was a small moment of being understood, or at least a safe place for me to talk about the pain of the day.

In the evening, my kids and grandkids came over bearing gifts and cards. A handwritten card read, "In the last several months you have become more important to us than ever, not just because of circumstances, but because of who you are. We love being with you. We love having fun with you. More than ever. And it's not a function of circumstances or pity." My extraordinary daughter-in-law wrote, "I am so grateful for your investment in me, John, and the kids. Your daily investment in our lives makes each of us better and our lives happier." Those words along with hot dogs, s'mores, and a Kansas City Royals victory made me feel like I might find joy again someday in my new life.

Today I'm grateful for this journey. I've never said that before and I might not say it again for a long time, but for a moment this morning, I am a tiny bit grateful for the opportunity to live life in gratitude in the midst of pain and darkness.

> *When is your birthday? What birthday do you remember as the best one ever? Whose birthday is it today, and how can you bless them? Whatever you do, know it will make a difference—one moment at a time.*

October 16

Day 146: Thanks, Mark

One of the benefits of these Facebook posts is that my Facebook friends are up-to-date with my life, and the many daily grief challenges. This morning, I ran into someone who is a friend, but not on Facebook. It was the first time I had seen her since Curt's death five months ago. The questions started, and I felt like I had to bring her up-to-date with how I am now. And I had to recount the circumstances around Curt's death.

It's always hard when I'm not caught up with people. Each time I run into people who don't read my grief and gratitude posts, I have to start over with: "How are you?" "What did Curt die from?" "Did he have symptoms ahead of time?" "How are the kids?" "Are you working now?" And on and on and on. Not much fun.

When I run into Facebook friends, it's easier. We start with the here and now. They know much of the journey. They are sensitive because, in many instances, they know where I was just twenty-four hours ago. This is something to be grateful for today. I have more people who know my grief and gratitude and can be right there with me in the moment.

So, I experienced grief this morning as I reviewed each morbid death detail (They seemed to want to know them all), but gratitude that often I don't need to do that and can instead lean into the moment with people who keep up with me. Again, thanks to Mark Zuckerberg. I doubt if this was what he was thinking with Facebook, but maybe God had a plan he wasn't aware of too. That happens, you know—a plan we aren't aware of.

> *What plans have you noticed that you weren't aware of in your life? How have you reacted to them? Did you hate to relinquish control like I do? It's a deep theological question, but do you think your actions determine your outcome, or is there another Power that has control?*

October 17

Day 147: Favorites

Last night, four of my closest friends came over for a post-birthday dinner. They are friends whom I've "coffeed" with for almost thirty years. It was one of the nights when I could catch my breath and feel some joy. After dinner, we watched my favorite movie, *Chocolat*.

I love that movie for so many reasons. It's set in France, my favorite country. It's about chocolate, my favorite food. It's about church, one of my favorite institutions. It's about celebrations, my favorite thing to do. But mostly it's about grace. A young priest says this in his Easter homily: "I think we can't go around measuring our goodness by what we don't do, by what we deny ourselves, what we resist, and who we exclude. I think we've got to measure goodness by what we embrace, what we create, and who we include."

That reminds me so much of Curt's view of grace. He often said the church (and all within it) should be known more for being FOR something than AGAINST something. I love this quote from author Jo Anne Harris: "Life is what you celebrate. All of it. Even its end." That's what I want on my tombstone.

Today I will work at celebrating even the end of Curt's life. I'm not sure how, but I want to try. His funeral was a wonderful celebration of him. Oddly, it still gives me so much satisfaction when I remember that day. Grace and celebration are good topics for me. Maybe they are for you too.

> *What should you celebrate? Whom should you tolerate?*
> *Are you for more things than you are against?*

October 18

Day 148: Savings

I took a picture today—a picture of Johnny and Norah holding their first savings account for college. Curt's memorial money was used to start this fund.

Curt adored his grandchildren. They were the light of his life. I hope they never forget him or how much he loved them. Last week we roasted hot dogs on our grill for the first time since he did it with us last fall. I put Norah's hot dog on the stick, but she promptly informed me that Poppo put the hot dogs on two at a time and horizontally. I guess she remembers him.

I hope this start of savings makes a dent into the future for Johnny and Norah. What I do know is that Curt's influence will certainly make a dent on their future. His legacy will live on in them.

> *Do you save for college? Do you invest in others in a way that will leave a dent?*

Johnny and Norah with college savings plan

October 19

Day 149: A Sabbath

I'm teaching all week in Atlanta. My travel for vacation seems non-existent anymore, so travel for work allows me to get out of Dodge occasionally. But I still miss the trips Curt and I used to take in the autumn.

A year ago, we traveled to Chicago for a Husker game, then headed to Door County, Wisconsin. It was such a beautiful time together. Curt had so much fun taking pictures of the gorgeous fall color. I remember when we ate dinner at night, we both had that young-in-love feeling. So sweet.

I miss having a retreat. With twenty-three years in ministry, weekends never existed. And later, with both of us working and traveling many hours, we often needed a Sabbath in the form of a few days of vacation. I miss the time with Curt recreating. I need to figure that out, but for now, I will be grateful for work travel. It's not exactly rest or recreation, but it gives me a new view.

Do you take vacations? How do you recharge?
Is there a day of rest for you? What is your Sabbath?

Day 150: Unapologetic

I used a word yesterday while teaching: unapologetic. As in, "Coaches need to have an unapologetic focus on the positive, natural potential of the client." I had written that word in my teaching guide when I first listened to Curt teach a strengths course some time ago. When I said that line, my voice broke momentarily. It took me totally by surprise when that word came out of my mouth and touched my heartstrings. I was suddenly aware of Curt's power with words, not to mention, how he embraced looking at human beings as beautifully created and full of potential.

I love getting to use Curt's words. I love even more carrying on his good work. Even though we are different teachers and coaches, we carry very similar values and beliefs.

> *What would you say you are unapologetic about?*
> *Is it a stepping stone or a stumbling block? Can you put that*
> *unapologetic belief into a sentence and live it out for good?*

Day 151: Mercy Notes

One of the hardest times for me is when I'm in a hotel or restaurant at the end of my out-of-town work day. I have such a big need to call Curt and talk to him. It's an immediate empty feeling when I realize I can't do that. No one to tell about my day. No one to affirm about their day. No one to talk with about what we can do when we're both back home. No one to whine to when I'm feeling sorry for myself.

But last night, the FaceTime ringtone on my phone sounded just when I was feeling alone. It was Johnny. It was good to both see and hear him. He talked about his day for almost thirty minutes. I got to hear about his successes. I even got to help him with his piano lesson. He told me he learned how to play mercy notes. I said "I've never heard of a mercy note." Then he took his phone and showed me his piano book and played that mercy note for me. I held back my laughter a bit and told him it was actually called a grace note. "Oh yeah… grace and mercy seemed like the same thing, so I got mixed up."

I loved it that I got to see and hear him in place of Curt last night. And I loved that he knew about mercy and grace. Yes, in music that delicate embellishment is a grace note, not a mercy note. But yes, Johnny, they are similar gifts in life.

I hope he knows both mercy and grace in his life. And I hope he offers both as well.

> *Do you use technology like FaceTime with your loved ones? Do you keep in touch with your family even when you don't always feel like it? And finally, do you confuse mercy with grace? It's okay if you do—as long as you practice them both. It's all good.*

October 22

Day 152: Why Work?

Work was important for Curt. We would occasionally even get in a fight about how important it was to him. He was always so dedicated to doing his job 100 percent. He used his Responsibility strength largely for the benefit of his employer, whether it was the church he served or his last employer, Gallup.

I love my work too. Curt never aspired to retire. I guess that was because his work had purpose. It gave him identity and mission. Me too. This week, as I teach at a school district thousands of miles from my home, I know how work makes my life more meaningful in the face of grief. The purpose gives me energy when I'm normally drowning in weariness.

Part of my love for work has to do with my colleagues. They are such a source of power to me. My co-teacher, Nancy, has served as an amazing model of great teaching, and I learn from her each day. But she is also my mirror for the future. She helps me sort through the chaos and listens and says the things that give me hope.

Hope. It's so important. I can deal with the crap each day if I just have hope, and some people seem to make hope look real. I'm grateful for work, and for help to hope—hope for a life that still counts, a life that still has joy, a life that is still loved.

> *So, think about hope. What is your hope? Who gives you hope? Can you offer hope to someone who needs to see the light? I hope so.*

October 23

Day 153: Models

I've had models all my life who've influenced and informed my decisions, actions, and future. When I was young, it was often teachers and older girls I thought had it all together. Later, the models took on different characteristics. They still often were teachers, sometimes friends, sometimes other moms and co-workers, but always women I admired and likely imitated in some form. As I get older, I have fewer models. I'm not sure why. Maybe I'm too old to change, or maybe the models have less appeal to me.

At any rate, I noticed the other day how much I admired Kathie Lee Gifford. You may not like her politics, her out-loud faith, or the glass of wine that sits on her desk, but she has always been funny, full of faith, and authentic. When she lost her husband, Frank Gifford, very suddenly, I was curious to watch how she responded. A couple of nights ago, she got an award, and I heard her interview. When asked how she was, she said, "Great. I've got my children. I've got my family. I've got my faith, and I've got a great job." I think she meant it very honestly.

So, I do have a widow model. (I don't think I ever imagined using those two words together in the same sentence.) She does give me a picture of what can be—maybe even of what should be. I'm sure her millions of dollars help her feel comfortable, but she loved her husband, and even money won't change that he is now gone. I admire her, and I think I can learn from her. I wish I could have lunch with her and ask her a lot of questions.

> *Do you have a model? Whom do you admire? Do they know? Whom would you like to be more like? Curt also knew the power of a good model. I think he'd approve of me having a widow model.*

October 24

Day 154: World Series

Curt was a huge Kansas City Royals fan, so last night I stayed up until 11:30 to see if his team would make it to the World Series. I watched the first seven innings with John and family.

After the game, I texted John to say, "Dad would want me to text you like he would have about that game." John replied, "I keep wanting to tell him they won." I simply said, "Go ahead."

Once again, we all miss our Curt when his team makes it to the World Series. I do know Curt is having a Royal time in heaven.

Can I talk you into cheering for the Royals or the Huskers or your hometown team? We need several more fans to take Curt's place.

Rosanne, Norah, and Johnny in Kansas City

October 25

Day 155: I Dreamed a Dream

Last night I went to see my great niece's marching band competition. One of the bands did a program from *Les Misérables*. The music from that production is some of the most passionate I know. The storyline has equal power.

When this high school band started playing "I Dreamed a Dream" under a moonlit, gorgeous night, the tears started. You see, Curt and I saw *Les Misérables* for the first time in London's theatre district many years ago at the theatre where it debuted. We had seats in the very front of this historic theatre and, honestly, didn't know the music or story that well. By the end of this powerful piece of art, both of us had tears streaming down our faces as we rose with the rest of the audience for a well-deserved standing ovation.

I miss Curt's passion. He was emotional and owned it. We both seemed to feel things deeply and that seemed to create a magnificent bond. I missed Curt at a marching band competition last night. In the oddest places, I miss him… day after day.

How do you express emotion? What things do you feel deeply? Can you share that emotion with someone significant? If not, think about sharing some of your feelings with a friend or family member. It's a gift you can offer.

October 26

Day 156: A Good Day

Yesterday was one of those firsts again. Johnny had his first Boys Choir concert of the season. Sitting there listening and watching him sing made my heart ache. I remembered so vividly that the night before Curt died, we went to Johnny's spring concert. We were so crazy proud and touched by our grandson's talent and the power of music.

We asked Curt's mom to go with us last night, and she was more than anxious to go hear Johnny sing. As I sat listening to Johnny and fighting back tears, I looked down the row at Curt's mom. I caught her face in silhouette, and it struck me how much she looks like Curt. All I could think of was that I was so grateful she was there, and that I knew Curt would be so utterly grateful his mom was being loved and taken care of by the family he left behind.

I made it through the concert thanks to the kind touch Meagan gave me. She knows how to touch me on my knee or on my shoulder in a way that makes me heal a bit. As we all sat outside on the patio together after the concert eating our pumpkin dessert, Curt's Mom said, "It's been a good day."

In all my years, I've never heard her make that proclamation. That made it a good day for me too.

> *What makes a good day for you? When you have a good day, can you exclaim it? How can you make a good day for someone else? Goods days are good for you.*

October 27

Day 157: Say His Name

It feels easier and a bit more comforting to talk about Curt lately. For the last five months, I felt like any mention of him either made me fall apart or made other people feel awkward. Now, even with the kids, we talk about Dad a little more, with a little more ease, and occasionally with some sweetness.

Most grief advice says to talk about the person who has died, to not avoid the memories of the person. I will often need to mention Curt—even in rather uneventful situations. Will you assure me you'll talk to me about things you remember or feel about him? I need others to talk about Curt just like I need to do that. I cherish your words about him. I never thought I'd be writing such words as this, but I'm grateful I can usually be honest and authentic in my grief.

Thank you for talking about Curt naturally, with love, and with gratitude for his life. Even if it does make me cry a little, I still want you to talk about him. It makes me feel better in the long run.

> *Sometimes we need to remember. Sometimes we need to remember and verbalize the memories. Sometimes we need to cry and laugh at the same time. And, every time, we need to be authentic.*

October 28

Day 158: Sirens and Flashing Lights

Driving to work yesterday, I heard the sirens on an ambulance that was right behind me. Next, I saw the flashing lights. Suddenly, my head was flooded with memories—not the kind of memories or pictures I want in my head or my heart.

I had this immediate memory of trying desperately give Curt CPR while calling 911 and my son. I remember misdialing as my hands were shaking so much that I couldn't hold my phone. It seemed like forever before the emergency crew got there, although I know they are very close to our house. The sound of that firetruck and ambulance will forever be seared in my mind—how I prayed and hoped, but didn't believe that they could help Curt.

Despite those hard memories and seared-in-the-mind pictures, I'm glad I was with Curt and was the first to find him. I wouldn't want to have been second or third on the scene. At least I know I gave him my best—my best CPR, my best prayers, my best efforts. This is not one of those happy posts, but it is all real stuff in my life. Even after 158 days.

After Curt died, I was trying to locate a set of keys that were never found, and I talked to a person who answered the phone at the fire station. It gave me a chance to say thanks. It's not an easy thing be thankful for on some days, but I am still trying to give thanks in all things. It's a tough job some days. But lots of people have tough jobs, don't they?

> *Thank an emergency crew. Maybe take a plate of cookies to a fire station to show gratitude. Call them and say, "Thanks for being a first responder. Thanks for working hard at saving lives. Thanks for doing a tough job."*

October 29

Day 159: Emotionally Amplified

Today I depart today from my usual post to share part of a post written by John. This reflects his love of his dad and their shared love of sports—especially the Kansas City Royals. You might say he talks about grief and gratitude too.

"I won't post about the connection between the Royals World Series run and my Dad forever because I'm sure it wears on some, and frankly, the games will end soon. And I understand it may appear as a ploy for sympathy, but I really don't need that. There's something oddly warm about those moments when I realize I can't talk to him about whatever just happened, which triggers immediate speculation about what he'd say and how he'd react.

"My dad loved him some Alex Gordon. When I watched games with Dad, and Alex gunned someone down or made a diving catch, Dad would do this thing where he raised his eyebrows, opened his mouth and slowly shook his head. Our conversations and texts about the Royals always veered toward how Alex was doing. I'm sure it started by him being the hometown guy, but it definitely deepened as we saw his ups and downs, position switches, and eventually, his full development into a bona fide star after it looked like it'd fallen apart.

"So, when Alex hit the first game-tying/winning homerun in the ninth inning of a World Series game one since Kirk Gibson, after running across the room, sliding across the floor on my knees with my fists clenched like I had just scored a freaking goal in the World Cup, screaming into my hands, I realized it was going to take some effort not to cry. It's nearly impossible after anything notable happens with Husker football (and soon basketball) and the Royals not to immediately have the impulse that I need to talk to my dad. Then comes the resulting disappointment that it won't happen, but that triggers that combination of speculation and memory, which is… kind of nice.

"Thanks for bearing with me and my Royals posts. If you happen to watch any of the games with me going forward (or see me react here), this is my disclaimer that I'm going to be a little (well, a lot) emotionally amplified."

What stirs your emotions? Make room for those around you to express their emotions—happy, sad, sweet, and poignant.

Day 160: Friday Mornings

One of the hardest things is going to coffee with five of my very good longtime friends. It's a fun group and always full of stories of travel or family, and anticipation of things to come.

But the hard part is on Friday morning. The Scooter's Coffee where we meet was also the place where Curt met with the men from his small group. That was a group he loved, and on Friday mornings, when my friends and I sat in a booth whining or laughing about our lives, he would always walk toward the table and stand there to talk with us. He was so well-acquainted with my friends that we ignored him some mornings and just kept on talking. He always looked happy when he approached our table, maybe because it was Friday, and he'd just had a deep talk with best friends about life and faith, along with a lot of belly laughs. Then we would be spending time together on the weekend—something we both loved so much.

So, Friday mornings sitting at coffee is now hard for me. When the rest of the guys walk out past our booth, I keep thinking Curt will walk out with them. Maybe that's why weekends are so hard for me. They start with Friday morning coffee and memories that now bring me to tears. Grief is relentless. One well-known author who writes about grief is a big proponent of changing the way you do things after loss, yet it's hard to change something like a well-ingrained weekly coffee with close friends.

I'm searching for gratitude today. I am grateful Curt had amazing friends—friends who didn't judge. Friends with open minds. Friends who could study deeply. Friends who could talk about life. Friends who were among the first to be called after Curt died. I'm grateful I have friends too. Friends who ask if it's been a hard week. I so need people to ask me that question. Without it, I would not get to be open with my loss and feelings.

Today, ask a good question of someone, even if you know it won't be easy for them to answer. Today, be honest when people ask you questions. And today, be grateful for Friday mornings and for friends. I know Curt was.

October 31

Day 161: Holiday Dread

A friend asked me to go to an open house at one of our favorite gift and decor shops. I got there early and quickly realized I had been thrown into the first of many holiday grief moments. The place was full of beautiful Christmas decor and was streaming holiday music that unleashed my emotions. Normally those emotions would be anticipation and joy, but yesterday, that same music brought me intense sadness, feelings of dread, and almost fear. Tears filled my eyes as I awkwardly tried to avoid looking at anyone in that store.

Curt was famous for buying me a pre-Christmas gift at the outset of the holidays. He loved doing that, and I loved the new pieces of decor he found for me. His fingerprints are all over our Christmas decorations. My friend Rita arrived, and she knew this was not easy for me. She reminded me how last year, Curt had conspired with her to buy me not only a candle holder we'd both admired, but also the candle, the wreath, and the box they had it staged on. He was kind of like Mary when she poured the perfume on Jesus's feet. Just do it all. She's worth it. He's worth it. So, we had a little laugh.

I hadn't anticipated having those difficult moments about the upcoming holidays so early. I hope that maybe by starting early, I can spread the grief out, and it will be a little less painful. I'll try most anything nowadays to find a way to manage my future grief. I'm sure grief experts would tell me that's not a good thing to do, but I've quit trying to figure out the right thing to do.

Anyway, gratitude? Maybe it's that I won't be all alone for Christmas. I've never wanted anyone to be alone on Christmas, and now I'm glad I have family and friends nearby. I'm grateful that, even yesterday, I had a good friend with me for the first hard experience of holiday grief.

> *So, enough about Christmas, except to ask you if it's too early to think about what you can do for others this year during the holidays. What perfume can you pour on someone's feet? Pour it out until there's none left.*

November 1

Day 162: A Better Version

I've learned that grief can make me less-than-perfect in many ways. There are times I get angry. There are times I feel hurt. There are times I feel jealous. There are times I feel left out. There are times I am resentful. There are times I feel lonely. I had a few of feelings at times before Curt died. Others are rather new for me. Great. On top of everything else, now I worry that I've become less lovely.

The worst feelings are the ones about being left out. I've often heard the woes of single people—how they don't get invited to things, how they don't get the texts that say "We're meeting for breakfast, come join us," etc. I'm pretty sure it doesn't happen as often as they make it sound, but it's probably true some of the time. I've already been overly sensitive to this. "Why didn't they call me?" "Why didn't they text me?" "Why didn't I get invited?" I know it's not really true that I'm not included, but when I'm hurt, sad, and discouraged, negative thoughts erupt easily.

My loss seems very recent, and it feels very early in this new reality, but other people seem to have gone back to normal. I must fight hard not to find my ugly side. As in all these posts, I have worked hard to be honest, so that's my ugly honesty for today. Many people say they are better people after loss. I'm hoping that someday I can say that. My Futuristic strength kicks in a little with that vision occasionally.

Forgive me if I'm not myself. I've had a bad five months. I'm grateful for the second chance at being a better version of myself in the future. I know I will be different and I want that to be a good different.

> *What would you like for your life to reflect? How can you be the best version of what God created? In the meantime, don't leave out the single person. Wear kid gloves around them occasionally when they are still so raw, and never assume they don't covet your love. I'm pretty sure we all do. I hope it doesn't take a death to make you a better version of yourself. It can start today.*

November 2

Day 163: Tulips

Every fall I plant lots of tulips. Correction—Curt and I planted a lot of tulips. Of all the things Curt did in the yard, I most appreciated when he dug beds for more than four hundred bulbs. His Dutch heritage made him partial to tulips, and he also knew that in the spring, he'd have great photography opportunities.

Last July when the bulb catalog came, I did what any grief-stricken Activator would do. I ordered four hundred bulbs, even though I had lost my strong, reliable planting partner. You know me—sometimes it's ready, fire, aim. When the perfectly packed bags of bulbs arrived and sat lonely in the garage, I wondered what the heck I'd been thinking. I entertained the idea of paying someone to plant them, but that went against my Dutch bones.

Then John and Meagan said they'd help. I didn't have to ask. They just knew what would make a difference for me. Other gardening experts joined in, including Anne,

Johnny, and Norah. John grunted just like his dad when he pushed the spade in the hard ground. Meagan worked the other spade despite having a bad sinus headache. Anne raked leaves and was the runner for topsoil and bags. Norah and Johnny learned how to plant tulips with their tips up and evenly spaced. It was a team effort.

Curt must have smiled from above watching his kids and grandkids stand in the gap. I was happier than I've been for a long time. I had hope. I felt renewed. And I have something to look forward to in the spring.

> *How about you? Do you ever plant spring bulbs?*
> *Do you like tulips or daffodils or crocus or hyacinth?*
> *Can you work hard this fall for some joy next spring? I hope so.*

November 3

Day 164: The Mentor

Yesterday I arrived in Houston for work. I love my work and even enjoy the travel most days, except when something brings me back to memories of my former life. Staying at hotels Curt and I frequented for work makes me miss those precious trips we had together. And at the end of the day, I still feel like I need to call him and report how my day went. Even harder is coming home, walking into the house, and knowing he won't be there to greet me at the end of a work trip.

But I still value and appreciate work trips, especially when I get to be with my colleagues. A new colleague I've had the privilege of mentoring has become a good friend. Jenny is the age of my son, but age seems irrelevant when one becomes a good friend. I love watching her talent blossom. I especially love working with young women and helping them to be the best they can be. At dinner last night, Jenny asked, "When do you miss Curt most?" I loved that she dared to ask me hard questions, and that our relationship, although relatively new, is deep. Even though she never knew Curt, she has heard of his work from colleagues and the legacy he left through his writings and teachings. Curt loved watching me work with young people. He loved that I loved them, and he did everything to support me as I maneuvered through life with them and their development.

> *Do you have a mentor? Are you a mentor? Who helped develop you into who you are today? Can you develop someone into a better version of themselves? Maybe today you can start the path to mentorship—as a mentor or as a mentee. Whether it's a formal or informal role, it's an opportunity you won't want to miss.*

November 4

Day 165: Doing and Being

I sometimes think about what my life would be like if Curt hadn't died. To say that my life is different now is rather obvious, but it's also different in ways I didn't expect. Before Curt died, I was always planning ahead, thinking of the next thing to do. I was sometimes less-than in the moment. I was just busy, busy. I'm still busy, in some ways more than ever.

It does feel different. I don't plan as much or get obsessed with the next great trip or next big party. I've learned something about living in the here and now. With my strength of Futuristic, I will always want to be further ahead into the future than most folks, but now I know how much I've benefitted from people who aren't so busy that they can't do something kind or helpful. My grief has given me pause about being available.

Honestly, I'm the kind of person who just didn't have enough open time to do the things I should have for people. I was gone too much. I was working a lot, and my head was always thinking about the next great opportunity. Who knows if I'll be more sensitive to others now. I hope I've learned a bit about needing open time to be able to be there for others. It's difficult for me to be a great friend when I'm not even around, so I hope my awareness of just *being* stays in the forefront as much or more than the *doing* normally does. I've learned from many of you how to be flexible, how to change a schedule to do something for someone else, how to think ahead about someone, how to be present. You've taught me so much already.

Keep up the good work, friends. I've been honored to be the recipient of your presence.

> *Do you have some space in your life to do good?*
> *I know it will be good for you too.*

Day 166: Ordinary Things

I honestly wonder how some people manage their grief. I know I'm a strong person, yet losing Curt so unexpectedly is the hardest thing I could have ever imagined. It must be even more difficult for those who have young children, those who have no faith, or those who have never been fairly independent, or those who have regrets.

I can't even imagine having regrets. I do regret not thanking Curt for helping me with things in the yard more often. I honestly can't think of other regrets, even though I try. Our love was an everyday, ordinary love that evolved into something extraordinary. It didn't depend on our circumstances. Sitting beside each other in our chairs felt as good as some exotic experience. We just liked being together, but we weren't dependent on each other. We had pretty independent lives in a lot of ways, but we loved the ordinariness of our lives too.

My ordinary life is not what it used to be, but I have no regrets. I'm sure I've said that before, but I lean into that for comfort almost daily. Now, here's the deal—having no regrets doesn't mean we got to do everything fun and exciting we could have or wanted to. We didn't. But in the end, that wasn't what mattered. What mattered was having Curt beside me sitting in his black chair, or in church, or in the car, or on the patio, or at our favorite bar, or in bed. Those ordinary things that I miss the most may be why I have no regrets.

> *Today, think about the ordinary things you love—the things that don't cost much and don't take much effort. Embrace the good in the ordinary. Have no regrets.*

November 6

Day 167: A Sacred Spot

Early on I could hardly get near that spot on the edge of the yard where Curt died. I could hardly get near that spot on the edge of the yard without falling apart, but as time has gone on, that spot almost seems a little sacred to me now. I kind of like wandering over there. Yesterday I made some decisions about making that area into a memorial garden.

Some of John's best friends gave me an extremely generous gift certificate to a local garden center. My Futuristic thinking kicked in a bit recently when I envisioned what could be there where Curt took his last breath. Nothing fancy, nothing effusive, but natural and beautiful in its own skin, a lot like Curt was. Yesterday I met with the garden center owner, and listened to him talk about what could be. Dick knows I like horticulture and landscaping, so our conversation was quick, but deep. He was kind and he listened. In just a few weeks, the first efforts will start at making that side of the yard a place to remember. I hope by next May it will be fully developed—simply, naturally, and with a light. A light for Curt. Stay tuned. I hope some healing may take place in the journey.

My grief has not triumphed over my sense of purpose and strength on this one. I'm grateful for good horticulturists like Dick. I'm even more grateful for horticulturists who are caring.

Do you have a place outdoors that is special to you? Can you make a special outdoor place where you can celebrate life?

Day 168: Those Holiday Lights

I've started doing some work on winterizing outside. Most years that meant not just getting the summer/fall things done, but bringing out the winter hardscapes. When I went to look for the hardscapes, I saw the Christmas lights and wanted to cry. Curt always put up the lights himself. He liked it. In fact, his post on Facebook from a little over a year ago talked about putting up the lights in seventy-degree weather. He had it down to a science. And an art.

I knew I couldn't do the outdoor lighting and I briefly considered not doing anything. Then I thought about how depressing that would be for the kids and grandkids, so I got on the computer and Googled companies that might put them up. Up came the name of the gentleman who did our original landscape plans—Dave. I liked Dave and trusted him, so I called him to do an estimate. That company doesn't usually use your own lights, but after he saw how many Curt had carefully put away in containers, he agreed to use them.

Late yesterday afternoon, after feeling crummy with a bad cold and dreading each approaching day toward Christmas, I had a message on my phone. It was Dave, asking if they could put up the lights tomorrow. I called him back, left a message that said, "Thanks, Dave, but I do need to know the cost before I proceed." He returned that call in short order, and said, "You don't have to worry about the cost. The neighbors and I are picking up this year's bill."

Well, I hadn't cried hard for a couple weeks, but the flood gates opened. I cried and thanked God for good human beings who do just the right things to make my life more joyful. What a kind, kind act from people I love dearly. I'm grateful for neighbors, for people who go the second mile, and for Christmas lights.

Are you thinking about putting lights up? Do you like to listen to Christmas music when you hang them? Will you remember Curt when you put up your Christmas lights this year? Please and thank you.

November 8

Day 169: A Good Saturday

Another Saturday and I missed Curt like I always do on the weekends. I had the grandkids here for a couple hours yesterday, and they helped me dump some pots and clean up the yard, and even though it probably took more time to get these things done with them around, they were awesome company. It's still hard when

Saturday meets me in the morning, but yesterday was good. The day was beautiful, and John came later to help me finish the work we started.

The kids and I took a walk through the neighborhood at the end of the afternoon and went down a semi-steep sidewalk in the neighborhood. Norah told us how Poppo used to take her on his bike in the cart and how he'd take her up that hill. Then Johnny talked about bike rides with Poppo and how Poppo told him, "You can do that big hill. Keep pushing."

At night, John made dinner while we watched the Huskers have an awesome win. After they won, John, Johnny, Anne, and I jumped around and hugged each other. I think we were not only celebrating a win, but also the joy of having each other—even without their dad and the love of my life. Then my favorite part—they stayed overnight. I love that. It's so good to have someone in the house with me. It's kind of like Curt is still here with me when I go to bed.

So, yesterday was a Saturday, and I don't believe I cried or even teared up. That may be a first. It doesn't mean I didn't miss Curt; it just means my emotions of joy were bigger than the grief for once. I've learned the pattern. I'll probably have a bad day coming up soon, but for those twenty-four hours, it felt like a good Saturday.

What is your favorite day of the week? How do you spend it? Be sure part of it is with some loved ones. That is the icing on the cake. People make the difference.

November 9

Day 170: Convoluted Thinking

Lately I've had moments of convoluted, grief-weird thinking. It's almost embarrassing to realize what I am thinking sometimes. For instance, sometimes I think, "Wow, I'm glad I had this awful thing happen to me. Now it's over, and I don't have to think about it happening in the future." I bet a counselor would have a heyday with that one. It amazes me how my mind plays with my logic and emotions to come up with some of these weird thoughts.

Along with my heart being broken, I think my head has been broken too. Logic and memory seem to have taken a vacation for the past five months. I've forgotten so many things that happened in the first few weeks of Curt's death. Most of that time is a blur. Maybe that's the way God helps you heal, but it kind of makes me a little crazy when I realize how much I can't remember. Yesterday I tried to find something I know I dealt with soon after Curt died. Normally I can find anything, but now it's like a big eraser has erased parts of my brain.

So, if you did something or said something to me that I didn't respond to "normally," please forgive me. And if I said something out of place or forgot something I should have remembered, please forgive me for that too. I think this is a real lesson that your heart and head are closely intertwined

How about you? Have you noticed that your heart affects your head? Or how your head affects your heart? If you have some clues on how to get them working at top form, let me know. I could use the help.

Day 171: Morning

I've had a cold for about a week now. It's the first time I've been sick in my new state. It's super easy to get tired and discouraged. Frankly, I miss having someone to complain to about how bad I feel and I miss Curt being a bit of a nursemaid. The worst was last night. I was so tired and just wanted to sit in front of the TV and let my body heal. I made the mistake of turning on a TV show where a doctor was explaining how to tell people that their loved one had died.

You know, yesterday I said I didn't remember a lot about the first week or two after Curt died, but I do remember being at the hospital and being told he did not make it. I already knew in my head and heart that he was gone, but that scene is not one I like to remember. Last night, my brain couldn't turn it off as I lay in bed, coughing myself into a frenzy. It was not a good night.

Now that it's morning, I still feel crummy and have little-to-no voice, but that scene isn't haunting me. I'm thinking more rationally. One thing I'm grateful for in that awful nightmare is that I didn't get my hopes up at the hospital. Unlike the rest of the family there, I wasn't surprised when the doctor told us he was gone. That's very little to be thankful for, but I have to take what I can from the bad memory.

The lessons here? No. 1: Don't watch shows before you go to bed that will keep you from sleep. No. 2: Appreciate it when someone takes care of you when you don't feel well. No. 3: Know that the morning makes things a little better (usually). Does joy come in the morning? Well, for me it isn't quite joy, but it's usually better than the night when I'm sick and tired of being sick and tired and alone. Be grateful for mornings.

November 11

Day 172: Top of His Game

As much I wish Curt would have lived for many, many more years, at times I honestly believe he got to go in a way, and even at a time, that may have been just right for him. Who am I to know that or even speculate? But I think about it often.

Maybe I should have been more aware when he said often in the past year, "I don't aspire to live to be ninety-two." I know he wouldn't have wanted to be less than 100 percent, and I'm sure Curt, like all of us, wouldn't choose to suffer. On my worst days, I try to be grateful he went so quickly, and in many ways at the peak of his life. Maximizer was one of his signature strengths. He only wanted to work with good and get to excellence. One of Curt's best friends and colleagues said, "Leave it up to a Maximizer to leave at the top of his game." In some ways, I believe God allowed for what we see as his premature death. Maybe it wasn't premature. Maybe it was the right time, or at least a time when Curt didn't have to anticipate sickness or have a less-than-productive life. He didn't have to worry about bothering anyone else with taking care of him. He would have hated that.

So, once again, there is grief and gratitude. Grief is winning out, as it usually does on this one, but I let gratitude peek in once in a while to give me a sense of the bigger God-controlled life. I'm not sure what the life lesson is for today—maybe that we can't control everything in our lives—or our deaths. Maybe that God may know best. That sounds a little too spiritually syrupy for me, but I do believe it. I really do.

So, control what you can. Don't think you can figure it all out. Relinquish control with grace and have faith that someone knows more than you.

Day 173: The Kiss

It was thirteen years ago today that we bought the lot for our house. I remember so well going to sign for it. We were sitting in a rather formal office around a table with the realtor. We signed a ton of papers, then the realtor left the room for a minute. Curt leaned across the table and gave me a kiss. Then he sat back down in his chair with a big smile on his face.

His spontaneity took me by surprise because we ordinarily didn't show public affection—especially in a realtor's office in the middle of the day. Later I asked him why he did that. He said, "I was happy and realized again how much I love you." For some reason, that kiss was sealed in my mind. We recalled that kiss often as the years passed. Curt was never as quick as I am to jump into things, but over the years, we figured out how to trust each other's strengths as we navigated life and enjoyed the adventures. I would see a picture of what could be and jump ahead too quickly. He would analyze the possibilities and think of our responsibilities. Then we'd both use our love for each other and come together to do a lot of great and small things.

Today my heart aches for him to lean across the table again and kiss me. And smile. And say, "You always saw and wanted things before I did, but then after we did them, I realized I wanted them too."

Trust was perhaps our hallmark as a couple. We trusted each other and knew that we would gain the most when we leaned into each other's strengths and values. I'm grateful we had that for forty-four years. Some people may never have that.

If you have a spouse or significant other, do you trust them for big things and small things? Do you kiss each other in unusual locations when you feel spontaneous joy? Do you lean into each other's strengths so that you complete each other? I hope so.

Rosanne the day Curt and she bought the lot for their home

November 13

Day 174: Adjustments

We're getting new neighbors to our west. The rafters for the roof are going up on their house today. For years, it was an empty lot, so it's different to see a house next to ours now.

It makes me think about adjustments. There are many things in my life I didn't really cherish as they were happening. Change sometimes brings about anxiety. I'm always amazed that after I've gotten used to something, it often wasn't as big a deal as I thought it was going to be. I'm hoping it is that way with the new house next door. I'm hoping soon it seems normal. Actually, I'm hoping the neighbors will become my friends and that the relationship trumps everything.

I'm trying to draw some parallels to the other adjustments in my life. Right now, I don't cherish the changes I've been forced into. Life seems foreign and out of sync and brutally unplanned. I'm hoping that it will all seem more normal in time. I'm not sure normal is what I should aspire to, but it is better than abnormal. My mom used to say, "You can get used to doing anything if you do it long enough." Really? This was the same woman who always told me, "It could have been worse." when something bad happened.

I know a new house next to me or a new life means change, and change takes a while to get used to for sure. Soon, the new normal may be a good normal. I sound like I'm pretty positive today. I'm really not, but I'm working on finding the positives as much as possible—on finding the gratitude.

> *Have you had change in your life you didn't expect? Did you get used to the new normal? Did it become a good normal? If so, I will take any encouragement on the topic. I prefer positive to negative words, just so you know.*

November 14

Day 175: Brave?

Last night I went to a birthday party for a good friend. I'm still fighting a bit of a cold, and my voice isn't very strong, so I knew socializing would be difficult. When I walked into the house, I didn't see anyone I knew. For a Relator, that's not easy. For a new widow, it's hard. Plus, everyone was part of a couple. Everyone. But I went in, put on a smile, and grabbed a glass of wine.

Within a few minutes, the host greeted me and told me how brave it was for me to come to the party. I honestly didn't think of it as brave—maybe desperation to feel normal, and a need to show gratitude to these friends for their thoughtfulness of including me. Soon, other good friends showed up. They were so kind and kept saying things that made me feel good. Things like, "You look great," (I really didn't) and, again, "You are brave." And they talked naturally about Curt.

In the end, I felt buoyed by loving relationships and a bit by the fact that, yes, I did venture out to do something that wasn't easy. People used the word brave for me, and that so isn't true. I just do what I think I should do, and what Curt would want me to do. And God. Those are the forces that push me forward. Whether it was brave or desperate or responsible, I'm glad I went through some uncertainty and pain first, to experience an evening of satisfaction and a little joy.

> *When are you most brave? When do you do hard things just because you think you should? Has it paid off? Are you better for doing those things?*

November 15

Day 176: Outward

Today at church, our pastor, Tim, was honored along with his wife, Karron, for their fifteen years of service. My appreciation for what it's like to be a pastor and pastor's wife was at the forefront of my mind. Curt and I had two different churches over twenty-three years where we were also honored with love and appreciation on multiple occasions. I had a hard time not going down memory lane and reliving some of the biggest highlights of our life. Curt always said that being a pastor brought him some of the highest highs and the lowest lows.

About the middle of the celebration I decided to turn my eyes toward the honorees and not focus on my loss. Tim was the most amazing person in the world when

Curt died. Always sensitive, always honoring, and always selfless. When John got up for his part in the service honoring Tim, he told Tim, in a choked-up voice, what he meant to him. Then Meagan led the congregation in prayer as the entire church blessed Tim and Karron for the future. I felt a deep sense of gratitude that I have our children, who know and love the church—the church universal and the church local. Curt would be so proud of their commitments. And Anne's too. She volunteers for so many things in her church and is a regular supporter of its causes.

Today I learned I can turn my sometimes-inward focus outward and find peace. Thank you, Tim, for your sensitive and loving dedication to our family and the church. Thank you, Curt, for your sensitive and loving dedication to our family and the church.

> *Have you had an opportunity to thank someone for his or her loving and long service to you or someone in your family? If not, it's not too late. Grab that pen and paper and just say, "I'm grateful."*

November 16

Day 177: Lessons

It's been six months today since Curt left this earth and found paradise. I can't believe I've lived six months without him. Six months since we talked. Six months since we went to coffee. Six months since we smiled at each other while admiring our grandkids. Six months since we talked about our work. Six months since we worked in the yard together. Six months since we sat in our chairs and relaxed. Six months since we held hands.

Six months is a half of a year. I've been through a lot in six months. I've learned how to do things I thought I couldn't do, like take care of the cars, take the garbage out, and do the taxes. I've learned to do some things that are hard because it might be a good thing for somebody else. I've learned I am not at my best when I'm alone, but that I also need some alone time. And I've learned to lean on people who can help me.

I've learned that work is a great antidote and gives me purpose. I've learned that I don't have the answers to a lot of things. I've learned that I can't control most things. I've learned that Curt loved me even more than I realized. I've learned that life is about day-to-day moments. I've learned that my family is the closest thing I have to paradise. And I've learned positive people heal more quickly than negative.

I've learned there are people who can hurt me even when they aren't meaning to, but I've learned that hundreds of people will show up and do acts of kindness that can literally heal my heart. I've learned my faith hasn't wavered, although I have fewer of the "right answers" than ever before. I've learned that writing these posts has healed me—both from the cathartic act of writing, but mostly because of people's kind responses.

I've learned that second firsts can be meaningful. I've learned my life will go on. I've learned that, to a large extent, I can choose how I live, invest, and think. I know the road ahead has so many hard parts yet, but I also know I must do my best to honor God, who has given me a life to fully live out, despite this season of grief.

What have you learned these past six months? How will your next six months be different? What's your story?

Day 178: A Mean Layup

Sunday afternoon, I went to Johnny's first basketball game of the season. As always, I wanted to be sitting next to Curt. The first points of the game came from a picture-perfect layup by his grandson. And as the ball swished through the net, those first tears welled up in my eyes.

It's odd. I know that what Curt has in heaven is more amazing than anything we can comprehend or imagine, but my widow-self still feels bad that Curt isn't seeing what's happening here on earth. I don't know if he sees it or not. Norah is convinced he sees everything we do—especially the good and funny things. If he is seeing it, I bet he threw his elbows out as he clapped pals on the back, cupped his hands, and yelled, "Way to go, Johnny!" He may even do one of those whistles when he blew through his thumbs. If you knew him at all, you knew that whistle. Then he'd do a blow by blow of this all-important fifth-grade game with whomever would listen.

Johnny asked me which part of the game I liked best. I said, "The layup." He smiled. I smiled. And although I'm sure he would have rather heard it from Curt, he seemed darned please his grandma is proud of him. Thank goodness I have basketball games that can fill me up and distract me from lonely Sunday afternoons. I'm grateful for smelly gyms, uncomfortable seats, and a grandson who does a mean layup.

Have you ever played basketball? Do you like watching basketball? Do you go support some kid as they play their first imperfect games of the season, like my sister and brother-in-law did Sunday? If you do, consider it a ministry. I do.

November 18

Day 179: Healing

Yesterday was a big day. Up and back to St. Louis, then Omaha overnight as I am teaching the next two days. I'm tired and feeling those life weights that make me weary. I miss Curt.

Memories screamed from the walls of the hotel I stayed in last night, but I couldn't cry. I felt like I was crying inside, and it wouldn't come out in the form of tears. This morning, as we started out in this room of eighteen individuals who are purpose-driven and starving for a strengths-based approach to life, I heard my Gallup colleague say, "My first encounter with strengths was with Curt. It just changed my life." I listened as my peers described how Curt often used my strengths as examples, and how they could tell how much he loved me and our family. I could feel the students look at me with admiration, intrigue, and sympathy—and maybe even envy for living with this man.

I feel better today. I'm doing something that helps me heal as I teach with my dear friend Maika. People and work help me heal, and, as hard as it is, I keep moving forward.

What is pulling you forward today? Is it outward-focused? Is it relationship-centered? Is it helping you move from good to great?

Day 180: Student Teacher

Yesterday a woman in my class approached me at lunch and handed me a card. She explained that she had never met Curt, but had learned so much from him on podcasts and the "Theme Thursday" webcast. Of course, her kindness and mention of Curt's name brought tears to my eyes. And of course, in my role as a professional, I tried to hide that emotion.

But she had that look that kind of melts me. She, too, is a widow. She lost her husband at age fifty-two in a terrible accident. So, I asked her for advice, as I have everyone who has gone through what I am going through. She said, "Be kind to yourself." I've heard other people say that, so I asked her to tell me what she thought that meant. She spoke of how she believed you should extend grace to yourself. For instance, sometimes if you don't feel like doing something, you are best off not doing it. Or if you fall apart when you think you should be strong, don't feel guilty. After many wise words, she ended by saying, "With your strengths, you'll be able to move forward in time and create a new and wonderful future."

I coach individuals around their strengths all the time, but in a few minutes, this woman was like my personal coach in a rather reversed role. I loved it that my student was also my teacher.

Have you ever had a student be a teacher to you?
Have you ever had a teacher who was willing to be student too?
What makes a good teacher? One who loves above all.

November 20

Day 181: Good Tears

I've made a discovery. I may cry sometimes, but now it isn't always about my loss. Last night at Johnny's choir concert, the tears came when they sang their first song. In my mind, the tears were associated with grief. I've cried more in the last six months than I cried in my entire life. After I thought about it a bit, I realized I would probably have had those same tears even if Curt was sitting beside me.

Prior to May 16th, I cried good tears far more than bad. I told the grandkids early on, when they'd see me tear up as a reaction to good music or seeing something beautiful—or just being moved watching an unlikely person find success—that those tears were happy tears. Curt teared up easily too, and I loved that about him. They got used to seeing me dab away tears and thought it was normal. I wanted them to know good emotions can evoke tears, and it's a beautiful thing.

I had to remind myself of that last night. I had gotten used to thinking only of tears associated with death. I'm going to try to remember that it's okay to cry, and that sometimes it means I'm happy. Or moved. Or just full of good and powerful feelings.

What causes you to tear up? Isn't it amazing that God gave us the ability to produce tears? Do you ever laugh while crying? Or at least smile? I hope to do more of that and bring back the good tears once in a while.

Day 182: The Tree

Yesterday I got my Christmas tree. It's earlier than usual, but I got a call from dear friends letting me know now was the time to come find one at their store. Two years ago, our tree fell over not once, but twice, breaking many ornaments and making a huge mess. Last year, Curt and I decided to get a tree from our local nursery, Campbell's, and have them put it in a stand and deliver it. It worked slick. After it was delivered, Curt put the lights on, and I decorated with the help of the grandkids.

Shortly after Curt died, my friend Ann asked what she could do for me. She asked specifically about a Christmas tree, and I told her I'd go get another one from her nursery. She asked me to bring the tree stand and lights to her yesterday. She wanted to help me pick out a tree. She couldn't stand the thought of me doing it alone.

When I walked into the nursery, she said, "I've been waiting all day to see you. I've been thinking how hard this will be, but we are going to pick a tree out together that will be perfect for you." She had done her elf work and had already found one she thought would be beautiful. So, there we were, standing outside in the middle of those gorgeous trees, two relatively new but old-soul friends, choosing a tree. Not Curt and me, but a loving, caring, person who stood in the gap.

How do you help a widow? Well, Ann helped me yesterday in a way I can't even describe. She did what she does best, and she did it with authentic care. She didn't try to replace Curt, but she ended up being the next best thing. Seriously.

> *Do you get a real tree? Who helps you pick it out? Or do you find the box in the basement with the tree you love to unpack? Who helps you do that? I think everyone needs a tree, even if it's a little one. And everyone needs someone to help them with picking it out or putting it up. I think it's a spiritual experience to pick out a tree. At least it is for me.*

November 22

Day 183: The Marker

A brochure advertising grave markers lays on my desk and stares at me every day. I hate it. Purchasing a headstone is not at the top of my list of things I look forward to doing. I realize that for many people, the headstone marks a place where they can visit their loved one, or leave meaningful objects. Everybody has their own way of connecting with and honoring their loved ones, but that's probably not quite me. For one thing, headstones cost a small fortune. Plus, my family and I will probably only be in the cemetery on Memorial Day. On top of that, I think most of the markers are not very much what Curt or I would want.

So, I've been procrastinating yet again on a death duty. I find myself frustrated and unable to go and pick one out by myself. I often wonder how many people never had a headstone: Syrian refugees who died in the last few months, Jews in the holocaust, soldiers all over the world who died in a foreign country, homeless people. I'm sometimes a little cynical about the business of headstones, although I believe everyone is entitled to have a business of their choice. I promise I will get one—one Curt would approve of, and I will have it by Memorial Day. It will be a simple marker in a simple, country cemetery that marks the life of a famous man.

I don't think there's a marker big or significant enough to match my love for Curt, so I'm not going to try. Instead, I will try to honor him in living ways. Telling his stories. Honoring people's natural strengths. Displaying his pictures. Loving his mom and family. Creating a memorial garden in the area of the yard where he died. Cheering on our grandkids. Above all, living a life that is still meaningful and honors God.

How do you memorialize your loved ones? What do you do to intentionally honor their memories and share their stories?

Day 184: New Eyes

Past. Present. Future. Is there another way to think about time?

I've been working really hard at figuring out how to tune my mind and heart in a way that helps me heal while still not denying the grief. The moments when I think about the past are still unbelievably hard. A few times I could smile when remembering something about Curt or hearing someone recall things that are funny, but not often. It's when I take the past and link it to the future that I get crazy sad. I'm working hard at still thinking of the past, but not attaching it to "what could be." That's easier said than done as the two seem to seamlessly link. They can and need to be separated for me to heal.

I'm reading a book called *Second Firsts* by Christina Rasmussen. She had done a lot of research on grief, then suddenly lost her husband while in her thirties. She talks about "re-wiring the brain" for the second firsts. Neuroplasticity is the official term. There are things I don't really understand about it, but I think some of it has helped me.

She helps grieving people consider the future with new eyes. She talks about honoring the past without attaching it completely to the future. Sometimes when I read her advice, I just want to say, "This is a bunch of malarkey." I'd like to say she doesn't know what she's talking about—but she really does.

How do you work to not avoid pictures of the past, while creating pictures of the future that are new... and good? That's the operative word—*good*. The past is still painfully hard to remember without tears. In the present, I'm working on each day's opportunities for growth and gratitude. And the future... well, I'm looking at it knowing it won't be the same as my former future, but believing that God can make it good. That sounds way more positive than I feel. As I write this, it helps me to focus on how to live—which hasn't been an easy challenge for the past six months.

*What kind of person are you? Past? Present? Future?
Does one inform the other? Can you live in more than one
of those worlds? Have you had any second firsts?*

November 24

Day 185: His Voice

Yesterday I had to make a call to one of my colleagues at Gallup. I dialed what I thought was her office phone. It's a number I call often so I thought I knew it by memory. After the phone rang a few times, I heard a different voice on the answering machine. It was Curt. I had accidentally dialed his old office number.

"This is Curt Liesveld. Please leave a message, and I'll get back to you as soon as possible."

I gasped. I couldn't believe it was his voice on the other end of the line. I've had a lot of things take my breath away in the last six months, but nothing quite like hearing his voice on that recording. I wish I could have left him a message. I would have told him I miss him. That he was my hero. That I'm trying to be brave. That I want to honor him in how I live. That I wish he could be with me for Christmas. But I didn't say those things. I just hung up. Then I realized how sweet it was to hear his voice again.

I'm glad I have some recordings of Curt's voice. I'm sure there are some of the hundreds of sermons he preached, including those he did at my parents' funerals. Gallup has recordings of him talking many, many places as he presented his concepts around living a strengths-based life.

Misdialing that number caused pain as I heard his voice that made him sound so alive, but I realized how amazing it is that we have the technology now to capture people's voices. I may want to call that number again. Maybe next time I'll even leave the message I have in my head and heart.

> *Whose voice makes your heart melt? Do you listen to recorded messages of loved ones? Should you be recording your voice and your thoughts for the future? Go ahead. It may make someone's day to hear your voice.*

November 25

Day 186: The List

Moments of grief yesterday:

1. Trying to put lightbulbs in outside lights with a ladder that was three inches too short.

2. Putting up outside Christmas decorations by myself.

3. Putting up outside Christmas decorations and not being able to figure out the electrical cords and timers. UGH!

4. Being alone at the end of the day.

5. Eating dinner alone (again).

6. Thinking about Thanksgiving at the Liesveld's without Curt and his dad.

7. Listening to the person I coached talk about how amazing her teacher was—his name was Curt. She didn't know.

8. Feeling like I am a bother when I need help.

9. Being bored and alone at night.

10. Missing Curt telling me how much he loves me.

Moments of gratitude yesterday:

1. Eating breakfast with Senia and Julie, friends from another life who are now our friends in a new life.

2. Having a brother-in-law who happened to drive up just when I was putting up those Christmas decorations. Claude brought a hug and received lots of tears that released some grief.

3. Having a pastor who texts me to say he's thinking of me.

4. Being blessed with a son who is willing to come over later and put in those dang light bulbs.

5. Having a job where I get to coach people and listen to them rave about that guy named Curt.

6. Having a sister-in-law, Sandy, who sends me amazing cards with poetry that goes deep in my soul.

7. Having electricity for those dang cords that will eventually work. (Please tell me they will be on sometime before Christmas.)

8. Knowing my new neighbor who yells, "Hi, Rosanne!"

9. Deciding to ask the grandkids to go eat dinner with me, and their excitement at being asked.

10. Knowing Curt loved me more than life itself.

11. Knowing Curt would love it that we're having Thanksgiving with his family. No matter how hard it is, we will be together.

Did you notice I had one more moment of gratitude than of grief? The bottom line is that people make the difference for me. In all the gratitude, people are the main subject.

> *What has created grief for you today? What has created gratitude? I'd suggest trying to outnumber the grief with gratitude.*

Day 187: Glorious Unfolding

It's Thanksgiving Day. Or Is it?

Yesterday I wasn't in a Thanksgiving mood. I was tired, but bored. I was lonelier than I remember being for weeks. I was frustrated with things breaking and being out of reach. When I finally quit trying to be strong for a minute, the floodgates opened. In a fetal position on my couch, I cried and asked myself how I can do these upcoming holidays without Curt. How can I do it physically? How can I do it mentally? And mostly, how can I do it emotionally?

I don't know for sure how I'll do it, but I know I find motivation largely out of needing to be strong for other people—especially my family and Curt's mom. Today we will go to Mom Liesveld's house for Thanksgiving. We haven't all been together there for a long time. Two chairs will be empty—two chairs once filled by amazing men. I have a feeling we'll shed a tear or two. I feel so for Curt's mom. This is not easy for her. But I will go, knowing how proud Curt would be that we are all together.

Yesterday I listened to a song by Steven Curtis Chapman called "The Glorious Unfolding." He and his wife lost their five-year-old daughter in a tragic accident, and this song is a true statement of faith after that horrific experience:

Lay your head down tonight.

Take a rest from the fight.

Don't try to figure it out.

Just listen to what I'm whispering to your heart

'Cause I know this is not like anything you thought the story of your life was gonna be.

And it feels like the end has started closing in on you. But it's just not true.

There's so much of the story that's still yet to unfold.

And this is going to be a glorious unfolding. Just you wait and see and you will be amazed.
You've just got to believe the story is so far from over.

So hold on to every promise God has made to us

And watch this glorious unfolding.

I can do this when I know there is yet to be a glorious unfolding. Yes, I believe there will be a glorious unfolding.

Happy Thanksgiving.

Have you experienced a glorious unfolding in your life? Are there chapters in your story that you could not have predicted? What makes them glorious?

Day 188: Love Overcomes Pain

Thanksgiving Day started out pretty raw. John was facing reality about the holidays, and his tears matched mine as we drove down to Mom Liesveld's. Then walking in to that house, although I've been there several times since Curt died, was so hard. Curt's mom hugged me, and we didn't have to say anything. We just hugged and cried. The bathroom was the only place I could find to catch my breath and find some level of composure. Everyone's hugs seemed to have a healing touch, and even the food seemed to reinvigorate.

The most poignant and healing part of the day was when John gave the prayer before we ate. He said simply, "Lord, we say thanks, not for always getting what we want, but for the love that overcomes the pain of not always getting what we want." The audible sobs during that prayer touched me more than grieved me. Curt would have been so proud of John's prayer with its depth and simplicity. And he would be proud of his family pitching in, showing love, and being so sensitive to both his mom and me. This morning I feel a little stronger again. It may only last a few hours, but I will take what I can get.

Thanksgiving brought so much gratitude. Black Friday will also be my day of gratitude, as I try to remember to be grateful for the love that overcomes pain, and that takes the place of the pain I feel when I don't always get what I want.

> *What pain do you have from not getting what you want?*
> *Is it legitimate pain? What kind of love can you pursue to fill the*
> *void left by the pain? Are you in pursuit of love—real love?*

November 28

Day 189: Decorating

This is the day I put up Christmas decorations. I usually love this day. Curt would sit in his chair and watch football while occasionally being bothered by me to help lift something, reach something, or just do something it takes two people to do. When I was done, he'd say, in his understated way, "The house looks nice." He must have said that every Christmas after I decorated.

Today I'll try to make the house look festive and beautiful. Well, festive may be a stretch for me this year. I know Curt would be both surprised and disappointed if I didn't work at making things look special—special for my grandchildren. Special for my children. Special for co-workers. Special for friends. Special for the church staff. Special for neighbors. Special for all the people who have been special to me in such incarnational ways these past few months.

Here is the gratitude: Jane said she'd come help me. No one really wants to help another person put up their Christmas decorations. Doing your own house is enough. Last night I put up a few things, and it wasn't as hard as I thought because, guess what, I knew someone was coming to help me do the rest. I could have done it (well, most of it) by myself, but the emotional support changed everything for me. Thank you, Jane, for what will be a good day. I hope I'm able to pay you back some day. You deserve it and so much more.

> *Who decorates your house for the holidays? Have you ever helped someone put up their decorations? It may be one of the best gifts you could give someone this Christmas.*

Day 190: Ambiguity

I've talked a lot about my faith in the past few months. Sometimes it's been a weak faith, but I haven't lost it. I've noticed that some people want to analyze how and why Curt died. They ask questions all the way from "Did he have symptoms?" to "Do you think it took too long for the ambulance to get there?"

I'm not sure why, but I don't really think about the reasons that could explain his death. Maybe it's because being naïve helps me cope. Or maybe it's because I don't think I can outsmart God. Or probably because I *do* know it does no good for me to ponder those whys. It doesn't help. In fact, it makes it worse. At times, I'd like to think I could blame someone or something, but I refuse to do that. Bottom line: I refuse to hate.

I will let myself grieve, but I stop the line at anger if I possibly can. Years ago, I heard Nebraska's former football coach, Tom Osborne, speak. He said he never pushed his players to hate the opponent because hate is the precedent to fear, and fear loses games. I think that applies to my grief too. If I end up hating someone or something because they may have contributed to Curt's death, I will soon learn to live in fear—fear of whether I will do something that will cause more grief. Fear that I can't go on. Fear that I'm not loved anymore. Fear of my fear. Fear that I will lose in the game of life.

So, I am grateful I can live with ambiguity—or maybe that's called faith.

What's your capacity for ambiguity? Does it help you? Can you avoid hate? Can you avoid fear? Can you claim to have faith? Ambiguous faith?

Day 191: First Snow

I woke up this morning to the first snow of the season. I'm the crazy person who loves it when it snows. Our pond looks most beautiful after a snow. And guess who else liked snow? Yes, Curt.

He was like a little kid when it snowed. He'd ask if I needed anything from the grocery store because he wanted to drive in the snow. He always wanted to scoop off our driveway, even though we get that done through our neighborhood association. And he loved shoveling off the pond, getting it ready for ice fun. Some of the hardest pictures for me to look at are those of him in his coveralls and boots clearing off a place on the pond for skating.

Curt probably liked snow most because he could take pictures. He took awesome pictures of snow scenes. I have many framed. I always told him that when he died, we'd have his photographs to remember him. Since gardening is done every season, there will be nothing left of my hobby after I'm gone. Maybe that's why he loved taking pictures of my flowers—so there was some evidence of both our hobbies.

Today I see the snow and miss him and his childlike love of something as simple and natural and beautiful as snow. The second verse to my favorite hymn, "Great is Thy Faithfulness" goes like this:

> *Summer and winter, springtime and harvest,*
> *Sun, moon and stars in the courses above,*
> *Join with all nature in manifold witness*
> *To Thy great faithfulness, mercy and love.*

So today, I will claim that promise that there is a seasonal greatness to God's faithfulness, even when it doesn't feel like it.

Do you like snow? Do you like the idea of seasons and change? I do. At least I like the idea of seasonal change. Maybe someday I will come to appreciate this change in my life, just as I appreciate the first snow of this season.

Liesveld Pond in Winter

Entertaining is one of my joys. I find the joy of the Creator
so much in hospitality. Setting this table for Christmas is an
act of worship that Curt found compelled to photograph.

December 1

Day 192: Joyful Spirits

I try hard to anticipate things and plan for potentially difficult situations or events. I realize I shouldn't try to escape the grief, and I don't think I do. I do think there are ways to deal with some things in a more realistic way that makes it easier to cope emotionally. Still, there are some things I can't anticipate.

I did think about the Christmas tree and how Curt always did the lights. I asked for professional help on that, but I dreaded the actual dressing of the tree. Even though I usually decorated the tree while Curt watched sports, we always sat back after it was done, soaking in the glory of the season together. I thought about inviting the kids and grandkids to decorate the tree, but they so often get the brunt of my neediness, so I wanted to figure something else out. I invited my close group of girlfriends to help me.

The friends are part of the walkers. Almost thirty years ago, I started walking early in the morning with one of them, and after about a year, the rest joined. Soon, our walking days gave way to only talking days. We met two days a week at 6:30 in the morning. Occasionally one of us didn't show up because we overslept, or we were out of town, or we had cramps (yes, that was a long time ago), but our loyalty was amazing.

Over wine, pizza, and chocolate, we hung the decorations. The music played in the background, and I had tears, but they didn't control me. Hugs and words of "I get this," "I wish I could take away this hard time," "It's okay," and

"We are with you," soothed my occasional sighs and tears. When we were done, the tree looked awesome. Deb was even tall enough to put the star at the top. What could have been a total meltdown turned out to be a special night. I'm so grateful I asked my friends to help me and they agreed. I'm so grateful for friends who serve with joyful spirits.

Where is your joyful spirit this season? Can you lend your joy to someone? Do you need to ask someone for help to get back your joy? Don't be afraid to do that.

The Walkers decorating the tree

Day 193: The Blue Dress

Last night it was Norah's Christmas Program at her preschool. In past years, Curt and I usually bought her a dress together, often at a Macy's sale. In fact, one year when we couldn't decide between two, Curt grabbed both and took them to the counter to pay for them. That's how he was. I believe what he said was, "I can only buy her cute little dresses for so long." At that time, I thought it was because she would eventually not appreciate our taste in dresses. Now I know it was because he wouldn't be here forever.

This year, I went by myself and got Norah a dress—a light blue dress with a few sparkles and some fur. She looked very sweet. It was hard not thinking of how much Curt liked to take pictures of the kids during the holidays, so I took a picture, and it made her smile. Me too. Better yet, Meagan used Curt's camera and took several really good pictures.

The evening was a success, and Norah sang and danced with the great stage presence of a preschooler. I missed Curt wrinkling his nose and smiling broadly as he watched her antics. I'm thrilled that colleagues Melissa and JerLene rearranged our business trip so that I could stay home for Norah's program. I have great colleagues.

I hope you get to spoil your grandchildren. Curt thought that was a little of his role, and maybe it is yours too. My mom used to tell me, "You've got to make your kids behave, so I don't have to." She wanted to remain in her spoiler role as much as possible. I liked that, and we are happy our kids are raising our grandkids so well, so we get to spoil them. I think Curt would have bought that second dress again in a heartbeat—especially knowing he'd not be here a few years later.

> *I hope you get to spoil your grandchildren. What can you do that will leave a lasting impact on their young lives?*

Norah in her blue dress

December 3

Day 194: Chicago

Today I went to Chicago with some of my best friends. We've gone to the Windy City for a little Christmas getaway for several years. Chicago is a city Curt and I loved as well, so today, everywhere I went reminded me of time with him here. I keep wanting to text him or call him and tell him what I'm doing. Tell him what we did for lunch. Tell him what ideas I had for presents for the kids. Tell him that the lights on Michigan Avenue are spectacular. Tell him I miss him.

As always, memories sneak out of my heart and cause heavy sighs or moments of tearing up. How blessed I am to be with friends who don't care when I mention Curt multiple times in a day and understand that I still lack energy and that my laughter isn't as raucous as other years.

> *I hope you get an opportunity to visit a new city sometime during the holidays, and that you do it with your best friend or best friends. It's sweet even in times of grief.*

Best friends for dinner

December 4

Day 195: Passionate

What one word would best describe Curt? In many ways, I'd say passionate. I've been described that way by some people, and that is how I remember Curt. He didn't always express his passion out loud, but his passion went very, very deep in his soul and heart.

There were many things he was passionate about: Nebraska football (all Nebraska sports), pizza, photography, music, and books. Even more, I'd say he was passionate about:

- Not stereotyping people.

- Owning your strengths instead of relishing in false humility.

- Playing "name that tune" at parties. (Yes, Curt often was the life of the party!)

- Always saying yes to the grandkids.

- Giving generous tokens of love.

- Teaching the truths of the Gospel.

- Taking care of his mom and dad.

- Believing each of us have unique strengths, and they are all good ones.

- Believing things are more grey than black and white.

- Not being "tight" about things.

- Not saying negative things around people when it might be hurtful.

- Believing that moderation in all things is a good philosophy.

❀ Supporting your kids but being clear where the line is.

❀ Believing that nurturing your marriage trumped all.

❀ Being responsible and doing what you're supposed to do.

❀ Not living like you're afraid you will run out of something.

❀ Not talking politics in groups.

❀ Listening to people with all-powerful care.

❀ Making grandchildren feel like they are the most important things in the world.

❀ Walking your faith more than talking it.

❀ Being honest.

❀ Showing his wife he loved her.

Still waters ran deep, and I miss that quiet undercurrent of passion I felt from Curt in ways perhaps no one else ever knew. He shared his passion openly with me, and I loved that about him. One thing I do know: he would be passionate about wanting life to go on for the kids and me.

> *What are you passionate about? Could you make a list? What are you known for? How can you be passionate and still be loving?*

December 5

Day 196: Grief Traits

Being with some of my best friends the last couple of days has helped me process and talk through many aspects of my grief. As I reflect on how I've naturally grieved, I realize it's very much like the way I live.

I'm sure someone has studied whether personality traits remain consistent in times of trauma and grief. I have no idea what the research says, but I can tell you what makes sense to me at this point of my life. I feel I've grieved in a manner typical of my natural self.

Curt would sometimes call me tenacious. Since his death, I've been tenacious as I pursue good things that I can possibly find to live for. He also said I have social responsibility. I do often go to things, say things, or get involved because I think it's good for other people, not just myself. That characteristic clearly has shown up in the last few months.

I think Curt liked to watch me use my Futuristic strength to imagine what could be, and I've certainly talked about how hard that part is for me now. Yet I have forced myself to think and write about short-term future and longer-term future in a way that helps me get up every morning.

Curt would say I like to be around people. I still like to be around people, even when I'm feeling horrible. And he would say that beauty heals me and brings me closer to God—beauty in the form of nature, in the form of people, or humanly created beauty. He was right. Deep inside I still crave and appreciate beauty, even when it's very difficult to see.

I've never been much of a procrastinator, sometimes to Curt's disdain. I think that has helped me take difficult issues head-on many times. Before Curt's death I was his cheerleader. I still am.

This may seem like a jumbled bunch of words, but I take a bit of solace from the fact that who I was before has not really changed, in spite of horrible grief.

> *If you wonder how you'll grieve, just look at how you're living. Is there something you need to change in the way you live so that you'll be able to grieve better someday? Perhaps not, but at least marvel with me that the God-created DNA in us has amazing and unique staying power through good times and bad. In some odd way, that gives me comfort.*

December 6

Day 197: Swish

Everyone who has lost someone close knows that waves of grief are unpredictable and can come as a result of very odd things.

On Sunday mornings, Curt and I always went out for coffee before church. I often still do. This morning I took the paper with me just as he always did. As I carefully pulled out the front page, so as not to disturb the rest of the sections, it made a "swish" sound. That sound did it for me. And all I could think about was how Curt always went straight to the sports page, and sections would fly all over. I used to tell him he needed to read something more important first, and he would say, "This is important."

It's the little things—the little sounds, the little memories—that are relentless yet. The truth though? I didn't tear up when I thought about it this morning. Grief was only a ten-foot wave that didn't drown me.

> *Do you read the newspaper? Which section do you dig for first? Curt was a big sports page guy. Thanks to all you sportswriters who gave him a lot of joy over the years. And listen to the papers swish next time you pull out a section. It's a sweet sound.*

Day 198: Dominus Illuminatio Mea

Yesterday at church, our youth pastor, Troy, gave the message. The topic was light. Troy was a science teacher at one time in his career, so I always appreciate how he brings things to his message that reflect on science.

He talked about the fact that sometimes we cannot see or feel light even though it's shining. For instance, he said that the moon is just a rock running around the sun, and sometimes the sun's light hits it just right to show the reflection. It also reminded me of a song I used to teach my fifth graders out of Marlo Thomas's book *Free to Be… You and Me*. Those lyrics went like this:

> *I'd rather be the sun above that shines so bold and bright,*
> *than be the moon that only shines with someone else's light.*

The topic of light has been big for me since it was Curt's word for the year. I see the Christmas lights all around and think about how he would have appreciated them this year with his understanding and commitment to following the light. Curt wrote on Facebook about the Latin phrase "Dominus illuminatio mea"—translated, "God is my Light." He was very fond of those Latin words. I chose them for the inscription on the rock that will be placed in the memorial garden in my yard.

God is my light. I can't always see the light during this time of grief, but I know it's always there.

> **What do you think of when you see Christmas lights? Do you believe there is light even when you can't see or feel it? You should. It's a scientific fact. Even more, it's a spiritual truth.**

Day 199: Finding Joy

Another tough day. I was home again and feeling the quiet of the house, and I had a song relentlessly playing in my head. It was Mariah Carey's, "Miss You Most (At Christmas Time)." I remember hearing it after my mom died and crying almost every year when it plays. Curt would come and put his arm around me and comfort me.

Yesterday when I heard it, no one was there to put his arms around me and comfort me. It's a haunting melody with words that are spot on for a widow. It looped over and over and over again in my head. I tried listening to other music, and I tried distracting myself with other things, but it was tenacious. Music, pictures of Curt, and his handwriting are perhaps still the biggest triggers of grief.

The day was long until I went to help my friend Rita decorate her house. She's been busy with her business, her family, and travel, so I wanted to pay her back for helping me with my tree. The two of us and our friend, Deb, spent two hours decorating. I can even say it was fun. Afterward, we enjoyed Chinese food as we admired our handiwork.

Once again, doing something for someone else (I've been on the receiving end so much) and being with people cured my ills. Even though the house was still quiet and void of Curt when I got home, I had some joy in my heart.

Do you take control of your life to find some joy? Sometimes it's just too hard to do, but maybe you can try. Even on a day when song lyrics haunt you, and you want to give up, you can usually find a bit of joy. In the end, I had someone put an arm around me and give me comfort.

December 9

Day 200: Public Grief

I can't believe two hundred days have gone by, and that each day I've had something to express about my grief and gratitude. Just as I was questioning even this morning whether I should continue my posts, I saw Sheryl Sandberg talk about how being public about her grief on Facebook helped her heal. One month after the Facebook COO's husband died suddenly, she posted these words: "I know that many future moments will be consumed by the vast emptiness as well, but when I can, I want to choose life and meaning."

Her Facebook post was both strikingly candid and strikingly public. Few people of Sandberg's stature reveal their inner grief to the world. As it turns out, she almost didn't press "publish," but now says that sharing her feelings with strangers has helped her undo the isolation of grief and begin to heal.

"It's a pretty isolating thing to live through. No one quite knows what to say. Everyone looks at you like a deer in the headlights," Sandberg told Savannah Guthrie during an interview on *The Today Show*. After the post, however, she says, "People started talking to me more openly, even strangers."

"I think loss and trying to rebuild and resilience are such a huge part of the human condition," she continued. "By sharing on Facebook, I felt part of that global community."

Need I say more? I feel better knowing someone else finds solace in public grief. I don't share every intimate detail, but I've found it a holy and good thing to be able to share with friends, family, and even relative strangers.

I still don't know how long I'll continue to write these posts—and I promise it won't be forever—but for now, I echo Sandberg's words that the global community has been a blessing to me in helping me to rebuild and find resilience.

Are you willing to be public about some of the things in your life? How might public authenticity make you better?

Day 201: The Love Note

I often work on my computer on planes when I'm traveling for work. Yesterday on my way to Austin, I decided to purge some of my e-mail. I slide many of my messages into personal folders. After purging many messages, I came to a folder marked "Curt." I had a lot of practical, work-related messages in there, but down at the bottom was an e-mail he had sent me almost to the day in 2010. I share his words, not to promote me, but to shine a light once again on the beautiful and generous way he communicated his feelings:

> It is 12:30 a.m. Seattle time, and I just got into my room. I read on the flight from Lincoln to Denver and listened to Christmas music and tried to sleep from Denver to Seattle. I found myself thinking fondly of you. This weekend I was reminded what a wonderful person you are and how much you are loved by those whose lives you touch. You are leaving a legacy of love for many. I am blessed to be one of that number. Watching you reminded me of the best of your mom: gracious host (even to difficult guests), loving mother (You tenaciously seek the best for them, even when they don't), loving mother-in-law (I always felt very loved by your mom and I know Meagan feels the same. It is easy to see she loves being around you), loving grandmother (Johnny and Norah love you as much as you love them), and loving wife (I know you love me even when I am not always lovable). I will miss you this week. See you on Friday. Better get to bed. 5:30 a.m. will come early.
>
> Love,
>
> Curt

Maybe today is good day to send someone a love note. They may find it five years later and cherish it again.

December 11

Day 202: Highlight Reel

Sometimes I feel like a bad trick is being played on me. I have some chunks of time when I am fairly distracted from my grief and may even feel quite strong and happy. Yesterday I led a workshop that was about an hour in length. It felt good to do that, and immediately after I was done, I had this almost euphoric feeling of being strong and in control.

As I walked out of the room, I almost felt like my old self. But in a nanosecond, I remembered. I remembered that my life is not perfect and that I am now a widow. My high crashed into an even lower low.

I now have this occasional ability to think that everything is normal for a while, then realize it's not at all. It feels like the meanest trick in the world, but as I was thinking about it, I remembered what I often say to my students when I teach them about strengths. I ask them to spend more time studying their successes and what goes right, so that they can do more of what they're already good at. Maybe I should listen to my own advice. Maybe I should learn from the strong moments and lean into them so they can come more often. I don't know.

What does your highlight reel look like? Can you study yourself? And can you be more of what you're already good at being?

Day 203: Gift Wrapping

Curt always wrapped all our Christmas presents. I rank having to wrap gifts with cleaning a toilet. I am horrible at it, and the gifts look like they were wrapped by a first grader. As I was getting ready to host a gathering this weekend, I noticed how bare the bottom of the tree looked. So, I did what Curt did. I got out the wrapping paper, bows, tape, and scissors and used the desk in our bedroom to wrap gifts. When Curt wrapped gifts, he put a big piece of plywood on the bed, but I wasn't physically able to do that. Sometimes he wrapped gifts upstairs while watching a game.

I had to clear off my desk, which holds pictures of us on our many trips. Taking down those pictures one by one was the first hard part. (Well, maybe the second hard part since just the thought of wrapping gifts made me shudder.) Then I got that same feeling I get when I try to do a math problem. I feel stupid and confused, and the outcome is always the same—below average. Period. But I wrapped five gifts— one for each of the individuals in our family. I tried to be brave, but I wasn't. I was angry at having to do all the work this Christmas. Even more, I was sad and achy that I am so alone during this time of year. I wrapped because I have to. I gutted through another thing that I didn't want to do, and it only made me feel lonelier.

Then I remembered I could maybe take Anne and her friend Jenni up on their offer to help wrap gifts. They like doing it! All this to say, it was a tough day again. I'm looking for gratitude, so here it is: I have the money to buy gifts. I have friends and family whom I can watch open the gifts. I have volunteers who may even come help wrap some of the gifts, and I had a great husband who wrapped lots of gifts over lots of years. Gratitude isn't equal to grief today, but it will take up a little real estate in my heart if I let it.

Who does your wrapping? Do you like to wrap gifts? It's such a talent—maybe you can share that talent with others who might appreciate your help.

December 13

Day 204: Candle Light

Last night I hosted a Christmas dinner for our small group. When I said I wanted to host, they all questioned me, but I said I needed something to push me forward during this season, and they were the best group I could think of to host. So, I did.

I did the prep work and, as I always do before a party in my home, I started to light the candles. As I lit the last one in the living room, I remembered that I always lit one in our bedroom. I loved the feeling it gave us after the party was over, and we had cleaned everything up. I loved going to bed with Curt with that candle glowing. It was like a sweet sign of the best part of any party—being together in the end to feel the pure joy and affection we had for each other. I lit no bedroom candle last night, and I hit reality unusually hard with that memory.

The party was a huge success because the people were amazing. We finished the evening reflecting on Christmas and how our lives were different because of our faith. Then the guys in the group, who were Curt's true confidantes, told me they had arranged to pay for the light that will go in the memorial garden. That is no small gift.

It was this group that listened to some of Curt's last words about light. What a powerful and meaningful gesture of love. I am so, so grateful for these friends, for their amazing love. My candle in the bedroom did not burn last night, but the one in my heart did.

Do you like candles? Where do you like to place them in your home? Perhaps next time you light a candle, say thank you—for the light.

*Winter candle, one of
Curt's gifts to Rosanne*

December 14

Day 205: Extras

Yesterday John, Meagan, and I talked about this Christmas Eve. I think we were all dreading talking about yet another hard first. We've always had rather quiet Christmas Eves—church, a traditional dinner often prepared by Curt himself, watching choirs and movies on TV, and just having a sweet time together. We're unsure what to do this year.

The question I face repeatedly is "Shall we do what we've always done, or shall we do something different?" That's the way a person in grief looks at most occasions that first year. Part of me wants to be around some other people that night, but I honestly hate to inflict my potential sadness on others. I had mentioned to Jane that she and her family are welcome to come over on Christmas Eve. Today, I got a text from her saying, "Yes, we will come." I was so relieved. I'm not sure who else will join us. That may not seem like a big deal, but it's such a comforting thought to know we'll have some extra family with us as we face this first Christmas Eve.

> *What do you do on Christmas Eve? Do you have traditions? Do you ever take in someone who doesn't have a place to go on that special night? Are you like the innkeeper? Do you find room for some special people?*

December 15

Day 206: Futuristic

There's such a fine line for me between inviting in memories of the past and blocking them out. I find myself crossing that line several times each day. I don't usually intentionally go down memory lane, but things just happen. I think it's probably normal and necessary and impossible to avoid. I am trying more and more to move into the future on the heels of the past. I'm not even sure how to do that, but I'm trying to fine-tune a strategy.

Today, I will be on "Theme Thursday"—the strengths webcast Curt initiated and hosted for twenty-four of the thirty-four strengths. Many of you have watched them. (Just search "Theme Thursday" on YouTube.) I can't get myself to watch them much yet, but I know sometime in the future, they will be incredibly powerful for me. Today, one of Curt's best friends at work will host the program and interview me on my number-one strength, Futuristic.

I have no idea what I'm going to say, and that's the honest truth. I've often said how having Futuristic as a strength is about as tough as it gets now. I don't think everyone wants to hear a grieving person's point of view on the future, so this could be interesting.

I hope Curt's love of one of my Signature Themes will shine through me today. I will invoke his presence as well as the Giver of all Strengths.

> *What takes you into the future? Do you have pictures in your head of what can be?*

December 16

Day 207: The Voice

Last night when I got home, John and the grandkids were at my house. They were watching a popular show called *The Voice*. They follow the show as a family; they feel it's great entertainment and one of the few shows kids and adults can enjoy together. John badly wanted me to hear one of the finalists, Jordan Smith. Jordan is an average looking kid from Kentucky who has this amazing tenor voice. John had me listen to Jordan perform three of his favorites: "Great is Thy Faithfulness," "Mary, Did You Know?" and "Climb Every Mountain."

As we listened together, sitting there with the Christmas lights on, with tears running down our faces, I said, "My gosh, his voice sounds exactly like the kind of voice Curt loved. It makes me think, in heaven, Dad is listening to music like this." This is music that is big—music that stretches the voice. Music that moves you to more emotion than you ever knew was possible. Music that gives you goose bumps on both legs.

Then a weird thing happened. I wished I was with Curt in heaven. I usually wish he was here on earth with me, but for the first time, I think I had a glimpse of heaven and was glad he was there—except that I wanted to be with him. It was a little sad, but mostly a glorious and compelling feeling.

Later in the evening, Jane texted that she, too, was listening to Jordan on *The Voice*. Her text read, "That guy is an amazing singer. I'm sure Curt is not only listening to great singers; he is now one of them. I love that thought." I think she's right. Curt loved to sing. He, too, had quite a stunning tenor voice, and I bet he got to be in first chair of the choir. Someone told me once they thought I would get to direct one of the choirs in heaven.

Today, I have a new image of the future. It is Curt and me in heaven, singing, with only the best singers (like Jordan Smith), and feeling the power of eternity with each other in all its glory. Maybe I will even get to direct a song or two.

> *Do you belong to a choir? Who is your favorite singer?*
> *What kind of music do you expect in heaven?*

December 17

Day 208: In His Light

Previously I've written about creating a type of memorial garden in the area of my yard where Curt left for heaven. It has taken many months of planning and thought, but yesterday the landscapers came to do the first stage of the garden. They cleaned the area of brush and placed a beautiful arbor made of birch poles. The part I was most anticipating was the placement of the stone that will mark the spot and memorialize Curt.

I had looked at dozens of verses on light and finally found one that fit—Psalm 36:9. The personal translation I came to love is, "In His light, we saw light." I know *His* is a reference to God, but I like to think it also refers to Curt—or at least Curt as God shone through him. "Dominus illuminatio mea," the Latin phrase Curt wrote about on Facebook, will also be inscribed on the stone. Near the stone will be the light—a light symbolic of so many things. A light that will be seen from my house, my yard, and my heart. There will also be dozens of tulips and daffodils along with some new plantings that have special meaning to me.

I do want you to share this journey with me. The final product won't be done until next May, but this start gave me so much joy. When I first saw the stone, the tears welled in my eyes, but soon, I found it so beautiful and fitting. Stayed tuned. I may have more pictures and thoughts on this sacred space in my yard.

In the meantime, do you have a special place where you remember someone who has left this earth? Do you go there? It's not too late. Maybe you can still create a space and feel the same joy I did yesterday.

The stone and the light

Day 209: The Fight for Gratitude

I woke up yesterday and thought I felt Curt touching me—grief. I had a great year-end review with my go-to at work, and I could feel Curt's healing touch since we both loved Benjamin so much—gratitude. I walked by the men's clothing section in a store and, for a second, thought, "I should get that sweater for Curt's Christmas present."—grief. I saw someone wearing one of Curt's shirts that I had given him—gratitude. I went out to look at the memorial garden and missed being able to tell Curt about the project—grief. I went out to the memorial garden and saw the new sitting boulders under the arbor—gratitude.

I went to Johnny's band concert without Curt—grief. I saw Curt's face all over Johnny's when he played his trumpet—gratitude. I remembered how Curt loved watching the Husker Volleyball team win championships—grief. I got to watch the Husker Volleyball game in the national semi-finals with the kids—gratitude. I had to come home to an empty house again—grief. I came home to a counter full of wrapped gifts compliments of a gift-wrapping saint named Jenni—gratitude. I walked outside with John on a chilly night to see the memorial light and felt the cold tears on my face—grief. I walked outside with John on a cold night to see the memorial light—gratitude.

And so each day goes; the grief and the gratitude fighting for the bigger spot in my heart. The tug of war between these emotions exhausts me most days. If you see me in the grief mode, you'll think I'm a wreck. But if you see me in gratitude mode, you'll think I'm doing well. Neither is 100 percent true. I am what I am most days, leaning toward finding more gratitude than grief as the days turn into weeks and the weeks into months.

> *How do you find gratitude in each day? Do you pray about it? Do you write about it? Do you talk about it? Can you try to at least think about it? Let it win in your life today amidst any negativity and grief you may feel.*

Day 210: Christmas Heaven

I'll never be able to figure out why some days are just harder than others. Sometimes it's about being physically tired. Sometimes it's about being overwhelmed with the work I need to do now as a single person. But always, it starts with a memory, then those other factors kick that memory into uncontrollable despondency.

Yesterday was one of those days. I had a normal day—coaching calls to do, errands to run, food to make, etc. Last night was one of the holiday parties I've always looked forward to the most. My four wonderful "old" friends had their annual Christmas dinner. I'm sure the anticipation of that triggered my hard day. Some of it was practical. I wanted Curt to help get the groceries I needed, but he wasn't there to pitch in. I wanted to walk out after getting dressed up for the night and see him smile and raise his eyebrows at me as if to say, "I like what I see." I miss that look on his face. I hated getting in the car by myself and driving to the party.

I sighed a lot yesterday. I had a headache. I needed to cry but wouldn't let myself go far enough down the road because I was afraid it would be a night of deep weeping. I forced myself not to think of other years. It was hard—so hard that I wanted to give up and just stay home with a remote in one hand and a glass of wine in the other. But I went with my pecan pie and hurting body.

Once there, the group must have felt my heavy heart because they acknowledged Curt's absence out loud. Out loud is the key—talking about him naturally and asking how I'm doing. I need that to clear the air some times. We stood around the kitchen table and reflected naturally on the missing person. They talked about how they missed him too. Missed his competitive softball days. Missed his Christmas Eve services—always simple and meaningful. Missed his intellect. Missed him as their pastor. Missed him as a friend.

Then we imagined Curt in Christmas heaven. What a picture. As much as I wish he was on Christmas earth, I know he has more ecstasy and joy than ever before.

December 20

Day 211: Family Christmas

Last night I had Curt's family over for an early Christmas, and the night was wrapped in so much love. The food, the hugs, the Husker Volleyball National Championship (Curt's mom is a huge fan), and the gifts for little ones were all so joyous.

Only twice did tears flow. Several of his family members walked out on the mild night to see the space in the yard dedicated to Curt. The stunning light and memorial stone took people's breath away, and that made me feel so good. The two whose tears flowed most were Johnny and John. I've always said it's the little, unexpected things that cause grief. They had gone out to the garage to set up the ping-pong table, and grief in the form of ping-pong memories flooded their hearts and tear ducts.

We have so many good memories of Curt and his crazy love of the game. Of Curt playing and rather enjoying the fact that he was the reigning champion. Of Curt and John and Johnny and any other willing partner slamming the ball, running around like crazy and always ending with, "Good game!"

So, there was some grief amid an almost perfect family gathering—but the grief had sisters and nieces and grandmas and brothers-in-law to hold it in its arms and cradle it until it felt a little better. Thank God for families. All families. Every size, shape, personality, and age can make up a great family because it's the place where laughing and crying can be first cousins.

Who makes up your family? Do you tell them you love them?
Can you cry a little with them too?

Day 212: Music

I've said this before, but music is one of the things that triggers deep emotions for me. Last night was another Boys' Choir Concert. With tears running down our faces, we listened to Johnny sing beautiful Christmas songs. It probably helped that he had a solo that he sang perfectly. (There's no bias to that, of course.)

Curt loved music. Sometimes when I couldn't find him, he'd be sequestered in his office, listening to music on his computer. He rarely listened to a whole song, and that always drove me crazy. I think he couldn't wait to get to the next song and see if it was even better than the previous one. He liked close harmonies, more often male voices, usually with a pretty wide range that favored the top.

Music was always an emotion-producer for both of us. I was a vocal music major in my undergraduate years. I went on to teach vocal music at almost every level of K-12 schools in three different states. I played the piano and directed choirs for years. Curt was in the choir I directed at the last church we served, and we loved that group of people. I sometimes think Curt loved me as the choir director more than any other role I played. Music was a big part of our lives.

I've noticed this year how many things at Christmas are romanticized rather than spiritualized, including advertisements, movies, and music. I've tried to separate the romantic songs from the truly spiritual songs and focus on the real meaning of Christmas.

I'd suggest you try sorting out the idyllic and romantic holiday messages from the spiritual message. It may lift you up to new heights and to new depths of meaning—especially if you are in some grief—and who of us isn't in some form of grief?

December 22

Day 213: What Awaits

Each day during this Christmas season, I go to the mailbox and find beautiful cards with such kind and heartfelt messages. I read them all and cherish them all. I've received so many blog posts, poems, sayings, and stories via Facebook, e-mail, the mailbox, and even in person. They all speak to me—some making me even more sad, others giving me hope, and some evoking deeper thinking on my part. Yesterday, my dear friend, Jo Ann, sent me something particularly powerful. Jo Ann is a Franciscan Catholic Sister, and I love her sister friends, who provide her with amazing writing. This was written by one of those friends:

> "The difficult thing about the trip to Bethlehem, the scripture is clear, was the question of having to go at all. Nothing about the trip was right. It was a long way from Nazareth. The baby was almost due. It wasn't their choice to go. They had no idea where they would stay when they got there. But that's exactly what important change is all about: not wanting it, not being able to control it, not resisting the situation to the point that we refuse to find there what awaits us for the rest of our lives."

Isn't that wonderful? I've never heard anything during this season that was so meaningful—and I've heard a lot.

The challenge to me, and perhaps to all of us, is this: how can we avoid resisting things that we don't want and can't control? Do we resist to the point that we refuse to find what awaits us for the rest of our lives? With my spiritual grounding and Futuristic thinking, that thought gives me hope and strength like none other.

What change are you resisting? What might await you for the rest of your life if you lean into the change with faith and courage?

Day 214: Sick and Tired

It's rainy and dreary today. I couldn't sleep last night, so I'm tired, and I think I have a cold. I've tried so hard to be proactive and face these holidays with strength and joy, but today I'm just done with trying. Work is slow, so I'm home alone and have only mundane things to do like get gas in the car and clean out the refrigerator. I mostly want to curl up in a blanket and sleep today. I may do that.

Gratitude is hard to find. I want my life to be back to normal and that just isn't going to be. How do I find joy? How do I find gratitude? Are we really expected to give thanks in all things? Everyone tells me to be grateful I have such good friends and family, and I am. So today, I'm going to start by thinking about how people have gone way beyond the call of duty to help me, empathize with me, and include me. During this season, they have been incarnate—God in flesh.

Grief is winning so far this morning. I pray that gratitude will squash it by the end of the day. Will you pray for that to happen for me? Pray for me to physically find healing, and emotionally to have enough to at least be an incarnational human being for someone else in the next few days.

> *Right now, can you write down a list of people you are grateful for? Even better, can you let at least one of those people know they made your list?*

December 24

Day 215: A Miracle

Well, this is the day I've probably dreaded the most since May 16th, but something happened. I woke up to a white Christmas Eve day and felt peaceful. What a difference twenty-four hours made.

Perhaps it was the snow with its peace and beauty that made a difference. Maybe it was a son and a sister who both asked me to go out for breakfast, which made it easier to get out of the house and start the day. Maybe it was knowing John and his family will spend much of the day at my house, cooking, and setting a table (thanks, Norah). Maybe it was a friend named Linda who just called and asked if she and her husband could take me out for a glass of wine this afternoon.

Here is what I know: I started this post with gratitude. Who would have thought that would be possible on this very special day without Curt? I'm not without grief. I remember years of Curt as pastor where he was busy all day getting ready for another Christmas Eve service. I remember trips from Mitchell to Lincoln, driving until 2:00 a.m. to get home for Christmas, a sense of anticipation and love with every snowy mile we drove. I remember those candlelight services that only Curt could do with such depth, simplicity, and meaning. I remember Christmas Eves in the past years when he didn't have to preach, but spent time in the kitchen making the traditional meatloaf (that may not be your idea of Christmas dinner), crème brulee, and other signature Liesveld dishes. I will miss sitting beside him tonight at church when we sing "Silent Night." I'm sure I will shed tears along with the rest of my family.

But today, for right now, I feel more gratitude than grief, and that's my Christmas miracle.

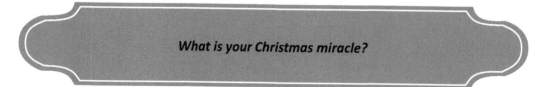

What is your Christmas miracle?

Day 216: I Miss You

Merry Christmas, Curt. I want so badly to talk with you tonight. Many people tell me to go ahead and do that. I managed to get through Christmas Day without you. My eyes sting from the many tears.

I woke up to Liesveld Pond in all its glory. You know how it looks when the snow and fog mix in the air to form an amazingly beautiful scene only God could create. The kids were extra thoughtful today. I think they knew I would not have presents from you this year, so they were extra generous. Johnny had a tough time today when we opened gifts. He misses you so much. I told him that he only had ten years with you, but that those ten years were amazing. I told him you adored him and his sister. I told him I don't know what I'd do without him because he reminds me so much of his Poppo. Then I told him the best thing he can do to feel better and to honor you is just try to be the kind of person Poppo knew him to be.

Norah gave me earrings that looked like the diamond ring you gave me a couple years ago. She lovingly patted Johnny and me on the back when we cried. Meagan made me note cards of the four seasons with your photographs on them. That's when I cried the most. You know, your photography still amazes me, and I think none compares to yours.

Tonight our house is still beautiful from Christmas decorations, but so very quiet. I wish we could talk about our awesome season. About Norah, and how she can read the Christmas story as a five-year-old like she was eight years old. How Johnny loved getting his Royals shirt.

I'd tell you to walk over to the window and look outside at the full moon on the pond and the lights reflecting in the snow. I'd say, "Isn't it beautiful?" And you'd probably say, like you always said to me, "But not as beautiful as you."

Curt, I looked out at your memorial light and I felt you close. Not close enough, but close. It shone through the white snow like a beacon. I think you are encouraging me to keep going and look for more gratitude. Thanks for so many Christmases. I miss you tonight, but I'm glad you are in a place where Christmas day never ends, where the snow is always glistening, and the lights are as bright as the light you've left in my heart.

> *What's your best Christmas memory? Who made that memory special? How can you have more glorious Christmas Days?*

Winter on Liesveld Pond

Day 217: Undecorating

The day after Christmas. Thank goodness my friends Rita and Deb asked me to go to coffee and then do a little post-Christmas shopping. It made it easier to get out of bed this morning. I got home and thought I'd take the ornaments off the tree. I usually don't do it this early, but I will be gone for a couple days, and then work starts back full force on Tuesday.

This is one of those jobs Curt normally did. While I got Christmas decorations packed back up, he would dismantle the tree and, with my help, put it out for recycling. The tree suddenly looked huge. I honestly wondered how I'd get the lights undone and reach those highest ornaments. Then John and Johnny came over. John is determined to get all of Curt's pictures on the computer, and it's a huge job. While he worked on that, Johnny helped me take some ornaments off; then we all ended up undoing the lights and taking the tree out of the house. It was a huge help to me.

I'm constantly amazed at how much help I've been given and how much that means to me. Today, I'm so grateful for the tree and for the son and grandson who helped me do what Curt has done every year. As I think of all the things people did for me this season—thank you from the bottom of my heart. You are all angels in my mind, and Curt is, no doubt, smiling down on your help and thinking you are using your strengths for good. He's like that, you know.

What is the day after Christmas like for you? Have you ever helped someone undecorate their Christmas tree? How do you use your unique strengths for good?

December 27

Day 218: The Right Way

Lately I find myself wondering if I'm doing grief in the right way. I sometimes wonder if I'm trying to be too strong or just the opposite—if I'm giving in too much to my feelings. Or if I try to prepare myself too much for the future, or the opposite again—do I need to remember more? Should I be more able to conquer grief? Or should I walk through it with the belief that I will not heal if I don't tromp through the messiness?

Second guessing myself is not something I've normally done. I find myself doing that now, especially when someone says something (not on purpose) that makes me lose confidence. A simple remark can make me feel guilty, or scared, or inadequate. It's rarely that person's fault. It's just that I'm too sensitive now. So many questions. So few answers. Grief forced the questions. Sometimes gratitude forced an ambiguous acceptance.

I need to talk about these things often and I am grateful when dear friends ask me the right questions and help me process.

> *What good questions can you ask that help people process?*
> *Can you perfect some questions? Or maybe just ask your questions*
> *with care and acceptance, and they will be*
> *perfect—perfectly needed. Perfectly appreciated.*

Day 219: The Scratch

The morphing of grief is an amazingly complex thing. I feel like I have moved past the shock that Curt isn't here anymore, and now am more aware that this is permanent.

But what is permanent? Something that lasts forever? Yesterday, when I was getting my big Christmas tree out of the house, I scratched the wood floor. Not a small scratch either—a long one and deep. There must have been something I wasn't aware of under that plastic and tree bowl. I looked at that scratch and wanted to cry. Of course, it is in the most prominent place in the house—right in front of the patio door. I went to get my trusty Old English Wood Stain that I've used for many years on wood scratches. I put it on and stepped back. The raw wood no longer showed, so it wasn't as glaring, but the scratch was still there. The sharp groove isn't gone and never will be. I've noticed with other scratches that, after a while, they almost blend into the floor—not 100 percent, but they get more worn, or dirty (It's interesting that dirt makes them look better), or I just get used to them being there.

That's so much like grief. The scratch, the wound, the hurt will always be there. But with intentional attention (like what I did initially with my Old English stain), the raw wood and the raw wound can be a bit disguised. And over time, it will be less prominent. The natural things in life will make it blend in a bit more and seem almost normal.

I'm not so grateful for a scratch on my wood floor, but I am grateful for how that scratch can teach me a lesson since I look at it almost every day.

What lesson have you learned lately? Do you have reminders in your home that teach life lessons? Has time healed any of your scars?

Day 220: Cleaning the Floors

Yesterday I went to clean the floors and had a memory of Curt doing them on almost the same day last year. Once or twice a year, he did the big job of cleaning the floors and then using a polisher to make them nice and shiny.

I remember so well him cleaning the floors last year. I was in the office doing something and, suddenly, I heard the polisher shut down and Curt sobbing. I ran to see what was wrong. This emotional breakdown seemed to come so out of the blue. He stood in the middle of the half-polished floor, his head in his hands, weeping. When I asked what was wrong, he said simply, "I feel so bad for my dad and mom."

Curt's dad had dementia after a fall out of a tree at age eighty, and his Mom had the big job of being his caretaker for the past eleven years. I can remember so many nights in the last year when Curt couldn't sleep as he worried about his parents. Curt's heart was breaking for them. For his dad, who had been perhaps one of the quickest, friendliest, most spiritually grounded and physically fit people you would ever know, but was now withering away both physically and mentally. And for his Mom, whose last eleven years had not been what she expected. She served as primary caretaker in situations that were not always easy, but she did her caretaking with diligence, fulfilling the "in sickness and health" part of the vows.

As I cleaned my floor this year, I thought about the huge depth of sadness Curt carried for his parents in their aging years. His dad was in hospice when Curt died, and I believe for the first time in several years, Curt had some peace about his Dad. And that gives me peace.

I wish Curt could have spoken at his Dad's funeral. I'm sure he had written the sermon in his head many times, but John was able to fill in and do the service with some amazing strength, considering he had lost his dad just a few days before. John's message title, reflecting his Grandpa's life, was "Relentless Positivity."

That's what cleaning your floor does—brings back memories. Some hard, some good. But all of them worth pondering.

> **What mundane tasks do you have in your life?**
> **Do they offer think time? What's worth pondering?**

Day 221: Down to Our Toes

Work is always a little slow between Christmas and the New Year, so it was a perfect time to meet a good friend for coffee.

Helen is one of those women who can make a routine coffee meeting seem like a blessed event. Her home was still beautifully decorated from the holidays, setting the perfect stage for her almond coffee cake and rich coffee. But the highlight of our time together was her willingness to share, listen, and encourage. She is one of those people who can truly speak the truth in love. She and her husband, Dave, spent many, many hours with Curt and me. We went to concerts, out for dinner, and spent time with them as pastor and amazing parishioners. Dave rode by on his bike just minutes before Curt died and was the second-to-last person to talk to him.

One of the things Helen said today was, "When Curt prayed, we all felt it down to our toes." Helen told me how much they miss Curt. After his funeral, Dave put Curt's memorial picture right by their phone on the desk. Neither of them wants to take it down.

For some reason, that small gesture made my morning. Helen knows how to encourage. She helped me see my growth and healing in this godawful process. She understood the value I have for being thankful in all things (well, most of the time). And she just knows how to be loving. I wish the four of us could be going to a concert tonight. I miss those dates, but Helen gave me so much to think about and so much genuine love.

> *Do you have a Helen in your life? Do you know someone whose prayers go to your toes? Whose picture do you keep in a prominent place because they are important to you? Hodge podge pondering today; are you up for it?*

Curt

December 31

Day 222: What I Can Do

It's December 31st. It's the day I've always been energized for, as I write goals for the next year. I looked back to see how long I've been writing goals, and I can find them dating back to 1986.

I don't always accomplish those goals, but most of the time, I've made a good dent in them. This year was the biggest flop of all. So much for that trip to Switzerland.

So much for retirement plans. So much for writing a book together. Today I will take out my computer and hammer out some goals. Physical, spiritual, work, family, home, and perhaps the most important—a category called giving back.

My grief wants to have goals like "don't cry all day" or "don't think about my loss the first thing when I wake up." But instead, I will try at my new normal goals. My gratitude will beckon me to focus on what I can do and what my new life will look like in the new year. Focus on what I have, not what I've lost. Focus on what I can do, not what I can't. Focus on new joy instead of depending on past joy to replicate itself. This year, I will have a new category. It will be called Curt. It will be about putting some finishing touches on how to honor him.

Feel free to ask me about my goals when we are together. I may need some accountability. I may need some encouragement. I may need someone to care. I've used goals in the past to get me where I want and need to be. Maybe this year I will need them more than ever.

> *How about you? What's your hope for the new year? What's your goal for the new year? What's your dream for the new year? Perhaps you can write it down and create a plan where you can turn dreams into reality.*

January 1

Day 223: A New Year

New Year's Day. I've never made New Year's resolutions, but today, I do resolve to do a couple things regarding my grief and gratitude posts. I resolve that they will be shorter. I resolve that I will do these only until it gets close to the anniversary of Curt's death.

Some of you are probably saying, "It's about time!" But selfishly and truthfully, these have come very naturally to me and have helped me so much to heal. I know these posts are not what everyone would want to do. I would not have thought I could grieve rather publicly until I found out how it helped me to process with words, how it helped me to know the power of my circle of support, and how much it helped to know that others occasionally benefit from the words.

Everything and everyone says you should grieve the way you need to. I'd say I grieve the way I have lived and loved. Anyway, tomorrow and for the next amount of time, I resolve to try to be as helpful and grateful to all of you as you've been to me the past seven and a half months.

Today is a new year. I'm done with last year, and glad to be done with it in most ways. I'm certainly glad I didn't know a year ago what was in store. Thankfully, it didn't change the way I lived or the way Curt lived his life.

What does the new year hold for you?
How will you make a difference not just for yourself,
but for others? Here's to a new year—to a new beginning—and to
the courage to live fully, no matter what you face.

The bench behind our home in winter

January 2

Day 224: Saturday Grief

The first few months after Curt died, Sundays were the hardest, and they still are hard. But now, Saturdays have become my new Sundays.

Since both of us traveled a lot for work and had busy weekday lives, we always cherished our Saturdays. Not to mention, for twenty-three years while Curt was a pastor, we never had a real weekend. I remember when Curt was first done with his jobs as a pastor, it was like we were on vacation all the time because we had weekends to anticipate.

Now Saturdays feel different. In many ways, it's the hardest day to wake up to. For me, Sunday was a complete day of rest, and Saturday was the day I loved getting things done. I loved that I always had a coffee/breakfast partner. And I loved getting work done with Curt as my partner. Then at night, we usually had plans or made our own.

So today, I hated getting up and facing the day alone—especially an open and alone Saturday night. As time has progressed, I've learned to embrace being alone at times. I will never choose that because I'm much more a person who needs social stimulation, but there are some days I even crave it—at least for a while. Not today though.

> *Do you get alone time? Do you need alone time? How do you spend your alone time when you get it? Are you productive, getting things done? Or do you cherish time to read and relax? What do Saturdays mean to you? Work day or play day? Or both? If you are alone on a Saturday night, do you like that? Or loathe it? And perhaps, most importantly, how can you make your Saturday a day you love?*

January 3

Day 225: Lavish Devotion

Each year after the holidays, I attack each room in the house to declutter and deep clean. I considered not doing it this year as I have plenty of other painful things to experience. But I'm fairly focused in some ways, and I knew completing this annual task would give me a little sense of control.

I had always started in Curt's office. I didn't usually wade through much of his stuff, but yesterday I did. Although I'd earlier dealt with parts of the office that had items I needed after Curt's death, there were spots I hadn't touched, like a big bin of his handwritten sermons. Twenty-three years of forty-eight weeks of sermons. He even kept the ones he did on his seminary summer assignment, and now I'm glad he did.

Curt pretty much never used an old sermon. What I found in that bin full of handwritten sermons was a goldmine of his thoughts. One by one, I went through most of them, finding treasures like one on grief, a few explaining his resignations, and one on the afterlife.

Then I found my favorite one—Curt's message on lavish devotion. It's based on the scripture where Mary pours expensive perfume on Jesus's feet and was met by angry comments from religious leaders of the day. It's the sermon I hear people talk about often. Some say it changed their lives.

So, I had a day of hard work and hard emotions, but I found my Curt's heart and mind, and that made for a better Saturday than I expected.

> *Do any sermons you've heard carry real meaning in your life? Has a sermon ever provoked you to act or to change something in your life?*

January 4

Day 226: Activator

I've read more things on grief and recovery than I ever thought I could. Some of it is good. Some makes me feel terrible. A line that struck me from my reading today was this: "No matter what life hands you, take an active part in your own recovery and healing."

That strikes a chord with me. How often is it easy not to take initiative in our own healing? Healing from failure? Healing from health issues? Healing from losing control? Healing from loss? I think the operative word is *active*. Perhaps I'm drawn to that thought because I have the strength of Activator. Curt called it the "hate to wait" theme. I try hard to think ahead (Futuristic), and take some proactive actions (Activator).

Who would have thought a year ago I would be applying strengths theory to grief? It makes me want to help others in grief understand more about their strengths. I honestly believe the differences in how we grieve reflect how we use our strengths or fail to use our strengths. I sometimes still feel paralyzed—paralyzed when I think of people judging me. Paralyzed when I'm exhausted. Paralyzed because I need help.

I want to commit to continue to take an active part in my recovery and healing. I'm determined to heal but I will need people standing by with the salve and Band-Aids.

> *What do you need to take an active part in doing? What holds you back from being active in your own healing process? Who can bring you Band-Aids and salve along the way?*

Day 227: Longevity

When we went to our financial planners, they talked about how much money we would need for the future and projected us both living to age ninety-two. I told them that was crazy because with my genes I'd never live that long. Dad was in his early seventies when he died, and Mom was eighty. Curt's mom and dad, however, both reached ninety-two. So much for statistics. This was not the area where I wanted to buck the proverbial system.

We try hard to project life expectancy, just like we try to scientifically *know* so much with certainty. Curt's life didn't follow the projected timeline. He didn't smoke, he was physically active, and he only drank alcohol occasionally. He passed his last physical with flying colors. Yet he died thirty years younger than what we had saved and planned for.

What's the lesson? I have even less faith in those trends and projections than ever, or even in what healthcare can provide us for warranties. Having said that, data can tell us something—just not everything. If we think we can know it all, it's just simply not true.

> *How long do you expect to live? What data do you put your trust in? How would you feel if the data didn't project accurately? Most importantly, how are you living today? Do you live like tomorrow may never come, or like you will live until ninety-two?*

January 6

Day 228: Joyful Defiance

I wonder sometimes how people find the determination to seek joy and hope. For me, it's a mental exercise largely driven by the discipline of gratitude. I think the determination also comes from living life in an authentic way—the way I am most naturally productive and happy. But it's also a spiritual discipline.

When I read Curt's sermons on grief, he references the grief of many of the people written about in the Bible: Job, David, Paul, and Judas in his deep remorse. I most appreciate Curt's observations about the Apostle Paul. Paul knew persecution, but his letters are full of determination and focus on gratitude. My new challenge is to add joy to gratitude. Joy sounds a little too fun for a widow, but I honestly think I should be internationalizing the discipline of joy. I do know I'm most vulnerable when I am most self-absorbed. In the words of the great Bono, "Joy is the ultimate act of defiance." I love that. We live in a culture where fun seems to be more important than joy.

Today I will look for joy. My defiant, headstrong, tenacious self will look for joy.

> **Do you look for things to bring you joy, or do you claim joy first and then that joy brings you good things? Either way, defiantly choose joy if possible.**

Day 229: Weather

I'm spending a few days in Arizona with some precious friends. I tried to anticipate the hard first week after the holidays by planning this get away. The trip has started with several bumps along the way—nothing major, just the usual trying things like forgetting all my makeup and needing to rearrange my schedule.

One of those other bumps is the weather. Although I'm not in the twenty-five degree temps they are having at home, the weather here is a little... meh. Partly cloudy with highs only in the fifties, and even worse—a fair amount of rain! In the desert? Who but me could get so lucky this year?

Despite these bumps, I'm having a time of joy. People make life, not weather. Curt used to say, "The mountains and ocean won't show up at your funeral, but people will. Invest in them, and one day you'll be glad you did." As usual, he was right. People showed up at his funeral, and I was so thrilled to see the hundreds of people who cared for him.

The people I've been with on this trip give my soul and heart joy. They amaze me with their graciousness and generosity. They make conversations the sunshine on a dreary day. For me, joy originates from relationships.

Today, it feels good to say I have joy for a while. And hey, if the sun shines tomorrow, I could have a really good day.

> *What's your reaction to Curt's remark that mountains and oceans won't show up at your funeral, but people will? Where do you make your greatest investments of time and money? Can vacations and relationships make a marriage stronger?*

January 8

Day 230: Baby Steps

I read a blog written by a widow the other day, and she opened by saying, "In the end when I die, I want to be known more for my living than my grieving." That took my breath away. The thought of leaving a legacy of grieving seemed so wrong to me. Yet, I have no idea how you get to that place where I am living more than grieving.

Oh, yes I do. Baby steps. Intentional baby steps. Crawl. Toddle. Walk. Run? Well, maybe never run for me, but walking seems okay. I walked 1.3 miles today—not much, but walking feels good. I'm hoping to take a lot of baby steps, and though they may seem miniscule for most people, they are forward movement—forward, not backwards.

> *What baby steps have you taken in your life that eventually lead to a stride? Don't be afraid to share those with others. They may be a magnificent encouragement.*

Day 231: Affection

I often hear husbands call their wives endearing names such as honey, dear, or sweet heart. I always envied that. Curt was not very demonstrative with his affection, especially in public (maybe it was his stoic Dutch blood). Looking back on it, I was kind of okay with that. Holding hands was our go-to whether in church or the car or in a restaurant. His other favorite—much like other husbands, I'm sure—was to pinch my behind. I've noticed football players often slap each other on the butt. Must be a guy thing.

My name to him was always just Rosanne—not Rosey (which I prefer) or Rose (which his family calls me and I also like). But Curt was a true romantic, and his written and spoken words were passionate and authentic. So many of his colleagues and parishioners knew him for his powerful command of language, and that is what I knew too. Even though I sometimes wanted to be called honey, that was not his style. In private moments, he was never shy about expressing his love for me and his appreciation for me as his wife. I hear from his strengths students all over the world how much he talked about me. His words were often simple yet profound when he talked about our relationship.

He wrote the best cards, notes, and even letters to me. I have many, many notes with words that I will never get tired of reading. We even told each other what kind of affection we appreciated most. He liked it when I rubbed my fingers through his hair, bought him small gifts, and supported him in his work, so I did that.

What form of affection is meaningful to you? What is your love language? Have you ever told your significant other or family what it is? My guess is that the most important thing about expressing affection is like the Nike ad: "Just do it."

January 10

Day 232: Tears in Church

Today I went to a traditional Presbyterian church in Fountain Hills, Arizona. I once again became friends with the Doxology, The Lord's Prayer, and hymns. As my friend Linda and I sat side by side in church and sang "How Great Thou Art," the tears flowed. I thought maybe her tears were for her loss of her husband Tom several years ago, but no. She told me that she could hear Curt belting out that song.

So, we cried in church and searched for Kleenex in our messy purses. Again, out of the blue, I felt Curt come to life, and I felt God's deep presence. I also found the joy of Linda's love and deep friendship. We left church and we laughed—laughed about our tears.

Some days, tears and laughter are as close as best friends. How great Thou art. Yup. How great Thou art.

> *Do you attend church? What do you experience there? How would you describe your church to someone? Is it a place of solace? Discovery? Power?*

January 11

Day 233: Vacation

I'm on the way home after a week away. This was the first real vacation of any length I've had since Curt died, and I wondered how it would go. One of my new realities is not only missing the fun of our past vacations, but worrying that I may never again have that reprieve, that Sabbath, that time to revive. But I did, and I'm so grateful.

I've traveled alone often for work for almost thirty years, but going away for a week of vacation by myself was a first. Yesterday, I got to spend most of the day with my good friend Donna and Marlene and her hubby.

I remembered I'd forgotten to put water in an outdoor bubbler (one of the things Curt would have done), so I called my neighbor Becky to ask if she could run over and add a little water so it wouldn't burn out. A bit later her husband Gale called and said he thought the faucet was frozen, and on top of that, he thought he smelled gas outside my house. Now that made me stop in my tracks. He called the gas company and sure enough, there was a small leak by the gas meter. Everything was checked inside and out, and the meter was replaced—all on a fifteen-degree Sunday. How fun was that for Becky and Gale? That's the kind of neighbors I have—go-the-second-mile neighbors.

I thought my vacation might end on a sour note, but it ended on a very high note thanks to good neighbors.

Who is like a good neighbor to you? Who is in your phone contacts under "emergency"? Whom would call you when they need help?

January 12

Day 234: The Retreat

For years, I've kept a binder by my desk and every few days I chronicle something. It's often just dumb stuff like the weather, or that I changed filters in the furnace, or cleaned out a closet. Occasionally I write more interesting things like where I went, who I was with for dinner, or where we went on vacations. I always look back to the year before just to see what I was doing—to see if something jogs a memory of what I should be doing or thinking about in the future.

Yesterday I glanced at last January. Lots of entries are about either Curt or me traveling for work, but one entry caught my eye. It said that we had just gotten home from Beaver Creek, Colorado, after our winter retreat. We loved going to winter places because of the unbelievable beauty. Curt loved photographing snow in the mountains. We sometimes would ski, but we would always reflect, and plan, and just enjoy our time together.

Last year, we took one afternoon and sat by the fireplace in the lodge and planned the next five years. We had three different scenarios we were going to consider and land on one by the end of this year. Yeah, none of them worked out like we'd hoped. There was an option number four that wasn't in our plans. Who plans on death? Some people might if they have a serious illness, or if they've lived to a very old age, but most of us plan on life. We had some very romantic, loving, honeymoon-like days and nights in Beaver Creek. It centered us as a couple, and we basked in the winter beauty.

I recommend that everybody plan and dream. It fueled us for so many years. Now I need to continue to plan and dream in a new way. Option number four, I didn't plan on you, but I know Curt would want me to dream once again.

What are your options for the next five years? I'd still say, "Go for it." Just know you may not always get what you plan on, but love, strength, and faith can carry you through to new options.

Curt relaxes in Beaver Creek, Colorado

Day 235: Melancholy

I've had several days of feeling strong, but last night brought out the weak me. I had a quick turnaround getting off the plane from vacation, heading to work, then boarding a plane to San Antonio. It was on that last leg of that trip that I felt weak, alone, and even scared. Something about the darkness in the plane and tiny lights of cities below seemed to have an impact on me. I felt so small, and insignificant, and helpless as I looked out the window. Seat 19F seemed to scream at me, "You are alone. You don't have anyone to text or call when you land. You are always going to be alone now."

Even before Curt died, I sometimes feel melancholy in planes during the evening hours, but this one was worse. Maybe it was the hour delay. Maybe I was tired. Maybe I was worried about rolling out new curriculum to a new client.

But I pushed through and when I landed, my good friend Jenny was there to greet me and share a late dinner. Before bed, I sent a too-late text to John and Meagan just saying, "I miss texting or talking to your dad tonight. No need to respond." I went to sleep and this morning, John's text was there. "I went to the Husker BB game. They won by 30." Gotta love that. It sounded like what Curt would have texted me.

Today the sun is shining in San Antonio, it will be seventy degrees, and I have one hundred people to teach. So, I'm feeling better. Sometimes, you must wait. "Wait" was my word last year. You think I've learned something?

> *Do you wait well? When have you waited for something and had the wait be well worth it? What do you need to wait for now?*

January 14

Day 236: Try

Each day, I'm more aware of my life taking a new form. I no longer forget as often that I am a widow. I no longer walk into the house at the end of a trip and expect Curt to be there. I don't expect that maybe Curt will fill the car up with gas if I procrastinate long enough. Even if I'm more aware of my new normal, it still isn't easy.

I was praying today and I had a moment when I wanted to say to God, "What were you thinking? Why did you choose to do this to me? What did I do to deserve this grief?" I didn't say that in my prayer, but I'm pretty sure God heard me think it. I feel like I'm at the stage when I more often forget about my grief, and then abruptly remember it, like a slap in the face. That slap often happens right after I'm feeling good, or strong, or valuable in some way.

Today, I finished teaching a large group of people and felt good about how it went. Then I remembered I can't tell Curt about my day. Gosh, I miss that. Sometimes, I just want to say, "Hey, I'll be home in two hours. Let's go out for dinner." Or I just want to know the black chair next to mine will be filled with my lifelong partner.

I'm glad I'm moving through the grief process and have made some progress. What a weird concept—progress with grief. But I also know I have a long way to go. I have tried to lean into my strengths in grief. I've tried to do hard things. I've tried to be honest. I've tried to initiate when I wish someone would initiate to me. I have tried to fill the void for my kids and grandkids, and I've tried hard to believe there is a divine plan to life.

What hard thing have you tried to do lately? Is there something you need to change in your life to help yourself live fully? What are you doing now that can prepare you for a better future?

Day 237: Self-Pity

I sometimes feel sorry for myself—actually I often feel sorry for myself, and I hate that. Sometimes it's about the things I need to take care of as a single person. There are many, many single women in this world who figure out how to do things on their own. I know that. Last year, I often tried not to ask Curt to do things, just to see if I could do them myself. I think now how odd that was.

Today, when my outdoor lights wouldn't work, I know plenty of single women could be figuring that out without a man. When the gas fireplace in my bedroom won't light, I bet there's an easy answer. When I have to figure out my taxes, I know all single people do that. When I can't reach things that are up too high, I know lots of single, short people always deal with that.

Here's to those of you who live alone and figure it out—and do it without whining. I admire that you don't feel sorry for yourself like I've tended to do lately. I'm trying to quit whining to myself. Really, I am.

> *What should you learn to do for yourself? If you suddenly become single, what will you wish you knew how to do? Maybe it's time to learn some of those things.*

January 16

Day 238: Time

Eight months today. Some days I think time has gone so slow, and in other odd ways, it has gone fast. Slow in that the days seem long as I live in this new awareness. Fast in that it seems like just yesterday was the Saturday Curt left us so abruptly.

Time has a way of changing things. I remember when the kids were babies, and they would cry and fuss and not sleep all night. I thought that stage would never end. Now they are all grown up, wondering when they will get their own sleep. That went fast. The concept of time is so complex—it must have taken God a long time to come up with it. There's a saying that time heals all wounds. I don't know if I believe that or not. What should be added to that adage is, "but the scar remains."

This I know: eternity is endless and timeless—no day or no night. I bet Curt isn't wearing a watch in heaven or looking at a phone. That, itself, is a pretty amazing thought to me.

How do you look at time? Does it go quickly for you, or is every day as drawn out and endless? How much do you value your time, or the time of others? Do you fill each minute with activity and productivity, or do you let the moments create your day?

Day 239: Meagan

Today is Meagan's birthday. She has been the perfect addition to our family, and every day I'm so grateful our son saw her value and goodness and pursued her. I tried to coach John on how important it was for him to embrace her family as his own because I think that is key to a great relationship with in-laws. Meagan isn't my daughter, but I wanted to treat her like she was.

Curt was a good judge of character and he always saw and loved Meagan's character. She is sensitive, hard-working, inviting, smart, and just plain beautiful inside and out. She is an amazing wife and mother and a generous contributor to our society. She is a person of strong faith and lends her leadership that way as well. She should win a prize for how well she fell in love with her husband's family. Many of us could take a lesson from her. Curt thought so much of Meagan, and he loved that she and I are close. I think that gave him a lot of joy.

Meagan is a photographer, and I watch her talent and see how much it resembles Curt's. I gave her Curt's camera, and I kept her camera at our house. That was the best act of love I could think of for her. Curt loved his camera and would have wanted Meagan to use it to its fullest, capturing human emotion, family times, and the beauty of God's nature.

So today, I want Meagan to know how much Curt loved her, and that I love her. I think she knows, but birthdays are a great time to pull out all the stops and celebrate and appreciate a life well-lived.

> *How do you treat your in-laws? How would you like your in-laws to treat you? As much as you want to be loved and appreciated by your in-laws, that's how much they want to be loved and appreciated by you.*

Norah and Meagan

January 18

Day 240: Teacher

Curt taught with many amazingly talented colleagues at Gallup. He honestly appreciated every one of them. My guess is the feeling was reciprocal. Today when I got to work, I found a card from the inter-office mail. It was from a colleague whom Curt taught with often. I met her and got to know her over a couple dinners when I was lucky enough to be in the same city as Curt.

Mara is an amazing teacher and is especially good with client culture. Curt always said she understood companies and could advise so powerfully. The card she sent said this: "A good education can change anyone, but a good teacher can change everything." Inside the card, she wrote her own version of that message. "When I saw this card, I immediately knew I had to send it to you. In the two-and-half years I got to work with Curt, he changed my life. His words continue to guide me in my career, even since his passing. And since he often spoke of how much you had impacted his life, I suppose I owe you a debt of gratitude as well."

Wow. She owes me gratitude? What an unusually kind thought to hear on a Monday morning. I continue to be amazed at how Curt's legacy is evidenced, and I continue to be so grateful that I get to hear secondhand how our relationship influenced him, and then influenced others. I feel oddly serene today about his death. Not happy, just a little serene.

> *What teacher changed your life? Have you told him or her? And what will your legacy be? It's not too late to create that kind of impact.*

January 19

Day 241: Complex Faith

I still struggle with the idea that God blesses some people with good things and for others, there is not only a lack of blessing, but grievous life change. Just the other day I heard someone say, "God answered our prayers." Of course, it all worked out great for them.

Even before Curt died, I struggled with the idea that you can see how God's hand was involved only when things all work out the way we want. And now, well, it is even harder to understand that kind of theology. I don't think I'll ever understand why Curt's life was cut short. It will never feel like God heard my prayers as Curt lie there in our yard. It will never feel like I was blessed. So, what's the difference between my (or my son's or my friends' or my neighbors') prayers and someone else's? I know—you're probably tired of me going over this again, but I had such a hard time yesterday after hearing someone talk so victoriously about how God heard their prayers and made all things turn out to their liking.

So how does that change me? I still pray for God's intervention. You would think I'd given up on that idea. I don't know that I can explain it. I just know I don't love it when people tout that their God heard their prayers or blessed them. Theologians are some of the smartest people I know, yet they haven't answered this one in a way that makes a lot of sense to me. Faith is complex and ambiguous and yet needs to be simple and sincere. The other day I read this in the book *Jesus Calling*:

> "When you thank Me for the many pleasures I provide, you affirm that I am God, from whom all blessings flow. When adversity strikes and you thank Me anyway, your trust in My sovereignty is a showpiece in invisible realms. Fill up the spare moments of your life with praise and thanksgiving. This joyous discipline will help you live in the intimacy of My Presence."

Have you ever been grateful for adversity? Can you be thankful for something that wasn't a part of your perfect plan? How can you fill the spare moments of life with praise and thanksgiving?

January 20

Day 242: The Top of Someone's List

Grief feels like not getting texts when you are on the road. Or phone calls. I'm traveling again for work and I'm noticing how quiet my phone is compared to my colleagues'. I miss being contacted. I miss someone checking in with me. I miss someone asking if I got somewhere safely when roads are bad. I'm almost a little jealous when I hear someone else's phone buzz, or beep, or ring. Mine sits there like it's broken most of the time—its glaring lack of sound reminding me I'm no longer at the top of someone's list.

I liked being on the top of Curt's list. He always checked in. He always sympathized when my flights were late. He always warned me to be careful. He always asked when I'd be getting home.

Grief has so many faces and challenges. Gratitude has a lot of faces too. I'm grateful I made it to my destination just fine after some less-than-stellar driving conditions. I'm grateful I have a colleague who makes traveling for work feel a bit like traveling for pleasure. And I'm grateful I am strong enough to push through lonely phone days.

> *Do you realize how your phone connects you to people? Do you use it to make relationships stronger? I think it really can do that if you let it. Pick it up today and text or call somebody you love. Just let them know you are wondering how they are.*

January 21

Day 243: Shock

I'm not an early morning person, but for some reason I woke up early and couldn't quit thinking about the first few hours immediately after Curt died. I don't remember large chunks of that timeframe, but my mind wouldn't let me give up on trying to retrace it.

I haven't done that very much until this morning. I tried as hard as I could to quit seeing the images, questioning things I can't remember, and experiencing some of those feelings again. It wasn't fun. I had this relentless reel going in my brain for about two hours as I lie in bed.

Shock does weird things to you and to your reactions and your memories. I remember feeling oddly calm when the doctor confirmed what I knew already—

that I had lost the love of my life. I remember hearing my son assure me that I'd never be alone because they would always be there for me. I remember the dreaded long interview so we could donate Curt's organs. I remember the weeping in the room.

And I remember how full that room at the hospital was. All these people who normally would have been at some joyous party in our house, gathered in that sterile, unfriendly hospital waiting room. I've often wondered what it would be like to get news like that by yourself. I know how this cloud of witnesses in the room seemed to shout of Curt's impact in their lives. I remember how Curt had said just a week before with our small group that he hoped in heaven we wouldn't have small plastic glasses for communion, but would have the bottle of wine on the table—that we would drink of God's goodness without fear of running out.

This morning, I'm tired. I'm a bit spent. But I look back with an odd sense of peace on that Saturday afternoon when we all gathered unexpectedly to cry, hug, and question why. It was so, so hard, and it was so, so powerful. Although I still feel much more grief than gratitude thinking back on that afternoon, I hope that someday the gratitude will edge out the grief, even ever so slightly.

What are some images that often take up unwelcome residence in your mind? How do you deal with them? What beautiful pictures can you lean on in difficult times?

Day 244: Good Night

I slept well last night, which sure makes a difference in my emotional constitution today. After seeing the huge correlation between emotions and physical rest, I wonder if most people wouldn't be happier and more stable if they had better rest. I'm no expert on health, but I do think maybe our society has underestimated the power of sleep and rest in general. So many widows have told me to be sure and get my rest when I can. They said sleep would make all the difference in the healing process. As I think about it, why else would we want to sleep all the time when we are sick? It is, at least in part, the way the body heals. I get that now.

I'm grateful I can sleep okay most nights. I'm glad I slept better last night because today I feel more prepared to be grateful and positive. It sure feels like our physical and emotional states are more closely connected than I ever knew.

> *I hope you get enough sleep and enough rest. If you don't, maybe that explains some emotional downs. Do what it takes to get your rest and a good night's sleep. You might be a happier person. And you may make the people around you happier too.*

January 23

Day 245: Touch

I have always been intrigued with the five senses that God designed. Many years ago, Curt gave me a book called *A History of the Senses*. It's was one of the top five books that's had an impact on me. I loved reading about each of the senses and their power—sight, smell, hearing, taste, and touch. Lately, I've thought about those five senses relative to missing Curt.

I'm blessed to have so many pictures of both him and of the things he photographed. I see and hear him both in videos. As I watch, I feel his presence so closely. Because Curt was videotaped so much in his work at Gallup, it is a beautiful and intimate way to remember how he looked and sounded. Just type in the YouTube search engine his name and "Theme Thursday," and you can see that too. I'm sure many wedding videos include him as well—standing so handsomely in his robe or suit marrying many special couples. I still can detect Curt's scent in both his office and his closet. I often breathe in deeply as I walk into those spaces, stirring memories of him.

It's the sense of touch that I cannot really get back in any form—and it's what I miss so much. When I come home, I want to go touch him—on the hand, on the head. on his knee. I would do anything to touch him again, and to have him touch me. So, I try to touch him through physically touching other people. I love hugging my male friends (How weird does that sound?) because it feels a little more like Curt. Mostly I love to hug my son and grandson and imagine I'm hugging Curt too. Touch is healing. Touch is love. Touch is powerful. I know I will never have the joy of touching Curt again on this earth. Still, I'm grateful for the power of the senses.

> *What sense do you most appreciate? Do you use them all?*
> *How can you expand your life by loving and embracing each of the five*
> *senses? Who can you touch that may need it today? Please don't deny*
> *someone of the power of the senses—especially touch.*

Day 246: Good Questions

Last night I was with some dear friends for dinner. Before we went out, four of us women sat around a table together and talked. It was a significant time for me. One of the women dared to ask me how I was really doing, and what had been healing. Then they talked about Curt and me and my new reality. What they did was ask good questions and listen.

It had been weeks since I'd had a safe place to talk about things. It had been weeks since I'd released some feelings. It had been weeks since I'd heard others talk about Curt naturally and often. It is hard for someone like me not to get to talk about things. And by talk, I mean talk so that I felt better. Talk about more than the weather, football, recipes, vacations. I mean talk so that I felt like I got something from inside that was begging to be released out. It's not always easy to do that. Many times, it's about being in the right place, but most times, it's about the people in the room. And it's about being willing to reveal, to be honest, and to cry when necessary.

So, I thank each one of you who have asked me good questions. Who have asked me what helps me so I know how to focus on doing more of that. Who have asked what I need, then offered encouragement. Ah, encouragement. In the end, I could walk away stronger because someone cared and encouraged.

What's your best way to show care? What's your best way to show encouragement? What great questions have you compiled so that you can pull them out easily? How have you asked someone to reflect on what helps them? Focusing on what is working instead of what is broken is a tried and true Gallup philosophy. It works well with grief too. Try these questions out if you don't have others: What best explains your success? What best explains when you feel good? What has helped you most? And then just listen and encourage.

January 25

Day 247: The Socks

Yesterday I went to Johnny's basketball games. His team won both games by two points on buzzer beaters. Johnny's three pointers in the first game were pretty impressive for an eleven-year-old (no bias there), but most impressive to me were the socks he was wearing. He told me they were Poppo's socks.

Now if you know eleven-year-old boys, they are just beginning to want to look cool. I've noticed that Johnny's coiffed hair is becoming more important to him, and he likes his sports attire to match nicely. But yesterday, he had on black socks with a very blue outfit. He told me later he liked to wear Poppo's socks for the games.

Little things can make my day. It wasn't easy yesterday. I could picture the exact expression that would have been on Curt's face after those three pointers, or imagine what he'd say to Johnny at the end of the game—and then I'd see Johnny's well-known smile. When I listened to Johnny talk to his other grandpa on the phone, I wished he could call up to heaven and review the games with Curt too.

Black socks were cool yesterday. Curt would be honored. I like how we all honor him in our own ways. My mind races with ways to honor him, and I love working on those things, but yesterday, a pair of black socks paid tribute to Poppo.

> *How would you like to be honored someday? Would it be someone wearing a special piece of your jewelry? Maybe someone reading a dog-eared copy of your favorite book? Your things, though seemingly just "things," may someday hold a lot of meaning for someone.*

Day 248: The Vow

Have any of you read *A Grief Observed* by C.S. Lewis? I came across a line in his writing that said, "Bereavement is not the truncation of married love but one of its regular phases." He writes, "What we want is to live our marriage well and faithfully through that phase too." In some ways, bereavement is not learning to completely separate from a spouse. Although Curt is not here in the flesh to care for, comfort, or physically touch, I can still live out the vows we made—to love him, to honor him, and to keep him. Maybe that "til death do us part" should be rewritten.

I find honoring him to be such a source of satisfaction and healing. He is darn easy to honor. I'm proposing a new take on the vows many of us took. "In good times and bad, in sickness and health, to love and to honor you all the days of my life." I like that. I will honor Curt all the days of my life, no matter how long I live or whatever my circumstances. That's my vow today.

What's your vow? Does it have an expiration date? How might you update it so it gives you a vision for how to live it out in the future?

Day 249: 6:00 p.m.

Last night I had an early dinner with a great friend and former colleague. Judy's husband died about three weeks ago from a terminal illness that had been diagnosed for more than a year. She and her family watched his physical body fail and knew it wouldn't be long before he would leave for his heavenly home.

Judy amazed and inspired me with her demeanor and outlook. The last hours of her husband's life on earth were filled with his precious family around his bedside talking, and loving on him, and facing reality together. That scene still gives her such secondary joy. She had a year to figure out how to take care of things around the house, where he had been the expert. She could ask him where things were and how to do things. She seemed to be thinking so clearly and realistically and hopefully. I was such a mess three weeks after Curt died.

There's something to be said for being prepared for death. There is even something to be said for being grateful someone isn't suffering anymore. I didn't have those things, but I watch Judy and want to learn from her. I left our dinner inspired by her and a bit disappointed in myself by comparison. What does any grieving and discouraged grandma do?

I stopped in at my grandkids' house. I didn't even ask if it was okay, like I usually try to do. I played dollhouse, and I listened to Johnny recite his spelling words. As I was playing with Norah, she said, in a hushed voice, "Can you ask my mom and dad if you can come over every night around 6:00?" Oh, my, I got a little of my mojo back. I felt needed. I felt loved. I felt a little happy.

Grief and gratitude. Last night was full of it. Grief that I had no time to prepare for Curt's departure. Grief that the shock is still taking its toll on me. Gratitude that my friend has such sweet memories of her husband's last days. Gratitude that she knows how to find the joy out of life and surrounds herself with friends and family. And gratitude that someone wants me to be in her life every day at 6:00 p.m. Little things can create gratitude if I let them.

January 28

Day 250: Angel in a Plaid Shirt

I finally went to pick out a headstone for the cemetery where Curt's ashes were buried. It's not something I ever imagined I would do. Yesterday was a gloomy, cloudy day. As I made my way to the little old house outside the mortuary, I felt alone and sad and in disbelief, even after eight months. I wove my way through the headstones scattered for display in the yard. I went in the house hoping to get this done as soon as possible. The house had a sickly sweet smell and had so many urns and samples of product that it even felt a bit like a cemetery—a weird cemetery.

I had decided last summer that I wanted to invest my money and energy in the memorial garden in our yard more than a headstone. Still, I needed to do my duty and find something to mark Curt's spot at the cemetery. I told the well-meaning but awkward woman that I wanted something simple and not expensive. Somehow that conversation took about forty-five minutes longer than I'd expected, and in the end, I was disappointed and discouraged. I hated it all and couldn't believe the expense involved. I thanked her politely and got in my car.

I drove to another monument place. I found a man there who understood in just a few minutes what I wanted for Curt's marker. He knew what simple meant. He knew what inexpensive meant. As I shook his hand as I was leaving, I said, "Tell me again your name." "I'm Curt," he said. He felt a little like an angel right then assuring me I had made the right decision.

I drove home, still a widow, but grateful I could survive another hard, hard day. I want to be done with these hard days when I feel so alone, but that angel, who looked like an ordinary man with a plaid shirt and a name that pierced my heart, helped me get through a day I won't soon forget.

> **Do you believe in angels? A friend of mine once asked,**
> **"Why are we so eager to believe in demons, but not in angels"?**
> **Well, maybe we should watch for angels, even angels unaware.**

January 29

Day 251: Initiate

Yesterday I was in a certification session at work. The certification process is designed to take a group of us to the next level as personal coaches. I see myself primarily as a teacher, but I love my other roles as coach and mentor. Coaching fits me, perhaps better than any other role I've had in my life at work.

I'm so grateful for my work. I sometimes worry about when I won't have my work. It's such a profound piece of my existence. The hard part of the day was when I walked out of my office and drove home. I was so full of thoughts, ideas, and feelings, and had nowhere to go with them. During much of this season of grief, I've learned to lean into my strength of Activator. Instead of feeling sorry for myself, I try to do something about it. It isn't always easy, but I try to take action.

So, I did. I decided to call my friend Maika. I knew she would get what I was talking about. When I picked up my phone, lo and behold, there was a text from her saying she'd been thinking of Curt and me. Talk about providence. I texted back and said, "Call me when you are free." And she did. We talked, and it was good. No, it was really good.

It takes all the strength I have to initiate some days, but I try to do that instead of feeling sorry for myself. Well, I do feel sorry for myself, but not as much when I try to lean into the responsibility I have not to be a martyr.

> *What can you initiate? With whom should you initiate? Who can help you initiate with hard things in your life? My experience is that you will be better if you use what strength you have to thoughtfully initiate instead of allowing yourself to wallow in pity.*

January 30

Day 252: *That's Just Delish*

This morning I had coffee with my son. Just the two of us. He used to have one-on-ones with his dad often, but not so much with me after he was married. I don't know if we've had coffee together by ourselves in more than ten years. At the beginning of his marriage, I was always careful not to promote our relationship, but to encourage John to invest in his relationship with Meagan.

This morning was a sweet time. We talked about lots of things, and I grew fond of listening to John and looking at him as he communicated so many smart and important things. I felt a bit like I was talking to Curt. I wanted to be more like his dad for John, but I know I really wasn't. He probably wasn't trying to be like his dad, but he was. I had a moment of sweetness that I've missed since May 16th, and perhaps for about ten years.

Gratitude comes in the shape of a son. I love that I can drive two minutes and meet John for coffee. What goodness, or in my new friend's words, "That's just delish."

(And she's not referring to food.) For once, my heart is filled with a bit more gratitude than grief. I'll take that for today.

Is it time to take your son or daughter out for coffee? Make a date for just the two of you. What might happen if you took time to do that?

John and Johnny

Day 253: Sister

I've learned so much from Curt's family. I only wish I had started earlier to know them, admire them, and love them like my own family. Today I am visiting Curt's sister Sandy, and it feels so good to be with her and her husband Rich. I feel like I have a safe place when I am with them, and they remind me of Curt's goodness. They don't tire of talking about Curt. That alone is so satisfying to me.

I stood next to Sandy in church this morning and when she sang, I had such strong memories of standing next to Curt in church. These siblings shared the talent of beautiful singing voices. I stood alone in church for most of our married life since Curt was in the pulpit, but I got to stand and sing next to Curt for the past fifteen years. It was a huge joy. Curt always put his heart into singing at church. I would often sneak a look at his face from the side when he sang because I loved the look of passion. Worship wasn't a passive experience for Curt.

I think Curt would love that I am spending his birthday week with his sister. I very consciously planned this trip the week of February 4th so that I could have some renewal and emotional support. I'm grateful for Curt's family.

> *What family do you have that does not share your DNA?*
> *What makes them close? Have you ever told someone they were like*
> *family to you? I bet they'd love to hear that.*

While in Paris, we walked by a shop that featured only roses. I love the French language, so Curt's picture of the dozens of roses is one of my favorites and seems to fit a month so associated with love.

{ February 1 }

Day 254: A Sanctuary

Curt's dad died the day before Curt's funeral. Just after Curt's graveside service, we learned Owen had died. Curt's family went from the cemetery straight to the hospital where Owen was on hospice and lived out his final hours.

I was so surprised when, a short time later, I saw them walking up the sidewalk to my house arm in arm. I quickly went out and said, "Oh, you didn't have to come here. I'm sure you want to just be together to mourn Dad." Curt's sister Sandy, with all her depth and sincerity and love, said, "No, this is where we want to be. Your house has always been our sanctuary."

I will never forget those words. We loved entertaining Curt's family. Our house was big enough to hold everyone, and we felt blessed to be the center of good times. Talking with Sandy today about so many poignant memories gave me pause, gratitude, and peace that our home was a sanctuary during some of our worst and most sorrowful days. I think Curt would have liked that.

Where is your family's sanctuary? Is it a summer home? Or an old farmstead? I think having a sanctuary is a blessed thing.

The extended Liesveld family

February 2

Day 255: What Can Be

I've thought a lot about verbs and tenses. I've figured out it's hard but good for me to think about the past—what we had. I've found it's healing and necessary for me to think about the future—what can be. What I need to avoid is thinking about the conditional—what could have been.

It's unproductive to let myself go down the road of, "If Curt were still alive, we could…" Or this is what he would have said, or done, or felt. It's getting easier to remember what was, rather than projecting that into the future. I have moments of peace and joy when I'm able to intentionally frame the past and the future with positivity and hope. Small moments to be sure, but I intentionally choose the future tense—wondering about what my life will and can be like. Wondering how I can keep Curt alive for myself and others. Wondering about my second firsts.

I know the futility of focusing on what could have been. I am not going there if I can help it. Enough talk of tenses. Grammar isn't very exciting, but intentionality about life is.

> *Do you think about what can be each day? Do you value parts of the past that give you joy? Can you work to avoid regretting what could have been? I'm trying. Maybe you can try with me.*

February 3

Day 256: Choosing Love

I write tonight with tears in my eyes. I can't begin to say all the reasons for those tears. As always, grief and gratitude. I've spent precious hours with Curt's sister, Sandy, and have had the privilege of talking openly as she listened, processed, and loved me through it all.

Curt used to say I needed to talk to process things and he needed to think to process things. Well, he was right. I've missed processing things with him. This has been a good week of laughter and tears. Tonight, I got to spend time not only with Sandy, but with my childhood friend Ellen—two women who are so wise and ready to be balm for my emotions. They knew the relationship Curt and I had and could honor it with me. They also knew how to let me be me and honor me. They were God living in human form for me tonight. I'm so blessed to have had these days.

I'm sure I will need a full emotional tank as tomorrow is Curt's birthday. It will be another grueling first. Tonight, I'm full of sadness and full of gratitude. I'm choosing to know the power of love tonight—both the love that was mine with Curt, and the love I now feel more deeply than ever with other precious humans. These Christ-like people are so beautiful in my eyes.

> *Do you ever think of your life as having God-like characteristics? Which of these can you live out today? Patience? Grace? Encouragement? Wisdom? Love?*

February 4

Day 257: Happy Birthday

Happy birthday, Curt. I'm going to spend this day not thinking about what would have been your sixty-fifth birthday, but instead, what will be your first birthday in heaven.

Last year, I was sitting in a class you were teaching along with our good friend Heather and getting certified as a strengths coach. Heather wrote me this morning, "I have such fond memories of teaching with Curt last February. It was magical having you in that room and seeing you admire his teaching and him sharing so openly with the rest of the room how much he admired your strengths." I believe we celebrated well in a hotel room that night.

We had some great celebrations of you over the years. Remember when you turned forty, and I had a dinner party at Misty's with close friends? Then I surprised you with an overnight in a bed and breakfast. I remember sitting by the fireplace in that room and talking about how much I loved you. On your fiftieth birthday, I pulled off quite the surprise when we had a huge room full of your fans at the Apothecary. We went around the room and each person told how you had influenced them and how they loved you. We stayed there that night, and you told me how special that night was for you.

We celebrated many birthdays with you and your dad and sister since you all had February birthdays. How precious those celebrations with your family were! Then there was your sixtieth birthday when we were in Beaver Creek doing our annual winter retreat. I told you when we got there that every time we ate a meal or had a drink I was going to tell you something I loved about you. You didn't even argue with me when I wanted to do that.

I will never regret all those celebrations I created for you. I know you knew how much I loved you and wanted you to be celebrated. No regrets. So, enjoy this first birthday in heaven. Sing some good gospel music with your beautiful tenor voice. Watch a Husker game (where they win). Eat some pizza and have a Goodrich malt. Talk to someone about their strengths. Take a bike ride. Photograph those streets of gold. Catch a couple of bass. Hug your dad. And then, tonight, look down on Anne, John, Meagan, Johnny, Norah, and me because we are going to celebrate you again. John is getting steaks, and Anne is making a cake. And if you listen closely, you will hear us talk about what we loved about you, and that our love for you will always outlast death.

Don't be afraid to let people know how you like to celebrate your birthday. It's a big deal. You were uniquely designed and born for something good!

February 5

Day 258: Benediction

I've been reading a devotional book called *Jesus Calling*. So many of my friends have read it and speak of its power in their lives. Yesterday, on February 4th, Curt's birthday, the reading was about peace. It started with, "Bring Me your weakness, and receive My peace. Accept yourself and your circumstances just as they are, remembering that

I am sovereign over everything… Let thankfulness and trust be your guide through this day." I loved that, but I loved even more the verse that accompanied yesterday's reflection. "The Lord bless you and keep you, the Lord make His face shine upon you and be gracious unto you. The Lord turn His face toward you and give you peace through Jesus Christ our Lord. Amen." Numbers 6:24-26

When I read that verse, I could hear Curt's voice so beautifully reciting that benediction. The cadence. The inflection. The volume. The confidence. He must have said that benediction hundreds, if not thousands, of times. I loved his benedictions—bene (well) dictions (to speak). An invocation for divine help, blessing, and guidance. I can still see Curt's arms and hands reach out and over his congregation to give them a blessing as they left worship. And his eyes wide open. This was no prayer. He was speaking that benediction over and for his congregation.

The words from *Jesus Calling* seemed so ordained for me this February 4th. Benediction. Good words.

> **Curt was good with words and he liked good words.**
> **How about you? What is your favorite benediction?**
> **How do you use words for good? Whom can you bless today?**

February 6

Day 259: Connections

Last night a friend came over and brought me dinner. Christine and I came to know each other when her son and my husband were co-hosts on the radio.

The food was delicious, but talking with her was the best part of the evening. She is an honest, determined, and kind woman. She reminded me that everyone has a story.

She helped me see how connected things are in our world. She spoke confidently and humbly of her spiritual life. She has gone through a lot, especially in the last year as she watched her son go through treatments for cancer.

Christine reminded me that we need to own our actions. That we can't blame God for hard things. That we can be peaceful during difficulties. I love good human models. They help me move forward with focused determination. She would say she has changed—that she is now a person of deep faith and truly at peace. For some reason, I felt compelled to pray for her some time ago when I hardly knew her, and I did. Talk about connections.

Thanks, Chris, for amazing homemade food, but also for teaching me how to face grief. You are brave and victorious. Your story is worth sharing with more people. You made a difference.

> *Are you sometimes nudged to pray for someone you hardly know? Do it. For me, these are my most powerful and heartfelt prayers. You never know how God might connect you with that other person in time.*

February 7

Day 260: Déjà Vu

Yesterday I went to a Husker basketball game with John and family. I have fond memories of going to games with Curt. We had great seats, and I particularly enjoyed watching Norah meticulously keep stats on each player. If I didn't know who a player was, I could ask her. Her Poppo would have thought she was a pretty darn good Husker fan. I fought through moments of "What if Curt could see her now?" and tried to stay focused on the good feelings of the day.

Suddenly, our family's favorite player, Shavon Shields, took a horrific fall and landed hard on his head. I gasped, then couldn't keep the tears from coming as I watched him lay motionless on the floor. It seemed like hours before they finally took him away on the stretcher, still motionless. I fell apart emotionally. The last motionless body I saw was Curt's. I felt so much fear for Shavon, this player I've wanted my grandson to emulate. I know Shavon's mom, and she, too, looked so scared as she stood by helplessly. I was so afraid for the outcome and begged God to let Shavon be okay. John kept me updated with news from his Twitter feed and assured me the tweets were saying Shavon was conscious and could move his extremities.

What does this have to do with grief and gratitude? I'm not sure. I just know my heart and soul felt the fear, anxiety, and shock I hadn't felt since May 16th. It was so scary. Later last night, I heard that Shavon is suffering from a concussion, but doing better. I am so glad this talented role model is going to be okay. In fact, I'll bet his life will have even more meaning after escaping such serious injury. That happens, you know. It even happens when one doesn't see a motionless body come back to life.

> *Have you ever had a déjà vu moment that took your breath away?*
> *Is there some deeper meaning to that flash of awareness?*
> *Is déjà vu really just God making connections?*

February 8

Day 261: Our Song

I've always loved Valentine's Day and the days preceding it. I'd probably say it's my favorite holiday outside of Christmas. I remember going to get my mom and other family members Valentine's cards while I was in college. I walked through a bad snowstorm to the local drug store to buy the cards so they would get them in time.

I remember well the Valentine's Day when Curt and I were first a couple. I gave him fudge I had made in a heart-shaped pan. Curt gave me an LP (yes, a REAL record) of the soundtrack from "Camelot." We loved the musical, and had gone to see it on stage. One of our songs was from the musical. "If ever I would leave you, it wouldn't be in summer... spring... autumn... winter." We were eighteen years old, and I didn't know how I'd come to love seasonal changes in the future. Curt signed the card "Not King Arthur, not Sir Lancelot, just me... your knight in shining armor."

Valentine's Day always was a big deal to us. We never missed a gift and special card. Never. Curt often got me cards that fan out. He knew they were my mom's favorite, and mine too. As I recall these Valentine's Day memories, I feel very sad and empty. I could read all my old cards, but I'm not sure I have the emotional stamina for that. I almost didn't put up my few heart decorations, but decided to do it for the kids.

I'm trying to figure out the gratitude today. I will cling to those words of Sir Lancelot, aka, Curt. "If ever I would leave you, how could it be in spring time? Knowing how in spring I'm bewitched by you so. Oh, no, not in springtime, summer, winter, or fall! No, never could I leave you at all."

> *What is your song? How often do you listen to it? Go ahead—listen, dance, sing, and love that song. It's never too late to find your song. It could be an amazing memory someday.*

February 9

Day 262: Grief as Praise

I woke up with sadness in my bones. I try to start each day with some hope and positivity, but the grief was so deep in my soul this morning that I couldn't pull myself out of it. Maybe it was finishing up decisions yesterday on Curt's headstone that did it. Maybe it was the cold, windy February weather. Maybe it was the thought of Valentine's Day this weekend. Maybe it was being with other people and seeing their happy lives. All I know is I had no power to control the sadness of missing Curt and of missing my old life.

During my hour commute to work, I had a continuous loop of pictures reminding me why I'm sad. When I got to work, I read an e-mail sent by a friend who also lost her husband. (Thanks, Michelle.) Some of these grief writings are a bit too much for me, but this one felt different.

> "One of the biggest and most important legacies that our loved ones leave behind is the grief we feel in our hearts. Grief is praise. We must honor these loved ones by allowing our grief to be expressed out loud. Through this process, a person can find tremendous healing. The gaping hole can be filled again."

I've never thought of grief as praise—or that we honor our loved ones by allowing grief to be expressed out loud. That made sense to me on this day when my heart feels empty. I can't say I feel grateful, but after reading those words, I feel a bit like my journey makes sense.

I'm hoping the rest of my day is better. I needed to talk, to be hugged, and to cry. I haven't done that yet, but maybe by the end of the day I will. And I will praise my Curt out loud, because he deserves it, and because I want this gaping hole in my heart to soften and be filled again with joy.

Do you have the courage to express your grief out loud?
How can your grief be praise?

Day 263: Turnaround

As you could tell by my previous post, yesterday was a rough day. I was somewhere between sad and angry about everything. As the day progressed, I found some joy in the stimulation of good ideas, good friends, and good purpose at work.

As I drove home, my headache returned. Then I got a phone message from John saying he'd just left Johnny's school conferences. The teacher said she'd never had a student at that level who had a better understanding of literature. She also said she'd like an invitation to the inaugural ball when Johnny became President. That was enough to give me some newfound joy. Then John told me the teacher also said she could tell Johnny was heavily influenced by his parents and his grandparents. He tries to find the best in everybody. I finally let the flood gates down and cried. Sometimes it takes a great teacher to help a grieving grandma. We've always known that great teachers have an impact on parents, but now I know they can also make the older generation feel like life can still have purpose.

My evening went on to get better. I went to an informational meeting at a non-profit that helped me put things in perspective, and I ended up with a spontaneous dinner invite from my good friends Dave and Patty. They were like my personal coaches and caregivers. They hugged me. They asked me great questions. They laughed. They encouraged. They even paid the bill. A rough day turned around because of a village of people who all took the time to make a difference.

What was your day like today? What little thing can you do to make a difference? Do you have time to do that? I bet you do.

Day 264: Ashes

It is Lent, and I was thinking last night how much I loved being the wife of a pastor. I don't know that all pastor's wives feel that way, but I always felt it was an extension of both my natural self and my own personal mission. Curt couldn't have been more appreciative of my role serving with him in the church, so that made it easy and meaningful.

I was at church alone last night for Ash Wednesday, but Johnny came and sat by me. When I went up to get ashes on my forehead, Johnny walked down the aisle with me, holding my hand. As I watched one of my favorite guys, Brett, put the ashes on Johnny's head, I felt such a pang of gratitude for being with Johnny at that moment.

When it was my turn for the cross of ashes, my emotions gave way. As he put those ashes on my head, Brett simply said, "Ashes to ashes; Dust to Dust. Your body is temporal, but in Christ you are eternal." Wow. Curt had said that phrase many times at funerals and burials, and it pinged my heart like an arrow. Our body does turn into ashes and dust. That's it. But I could also picture eternity through the tears. What grief. What gratitude.

Ash Wednesday was another first. I hadn't anticipated the depth of angst or the depth of love. Ashes to ashes. Dust to dust. But the promise of eternity is real to me, and that's the best Futuristic picture I can imagine.

Do you observe Lent? What can you add to your life during this season to make it a season of meaning? Whose hand can you hold today that needs to feel a loving touch?

Day 265: The Unwritten Book

Curt and I always talked about writing a book on marriage. It was part of our five-year plan we worked on just last year. Well, that won't happen. At least it won't happen as a couple. This week, I had someone encourage me to still do a book. I highly doubt if that will happen, but it's an interesting idea. Marriage, as seen on the other side of the death of a spouse, has new meaning. I don't think anyone can offer marriage advice that fits all couples, but there do appear to be some basics that cross personality types, values, and years.

I hate it that Curt and I can't carry out some of those big dreams we had planned. We had so many plans for post-retirement that had to do with writing, coaching, and teaching. It makes me so sad that it won't be the same, but there might be some of those plans that I can still fulfill.

> *What's your best advice for marriage? What makes your marriage great? Are there things you know you could still do if you didn't have your partner with you on the journey?*

Day 266: Go on with Life

I'll say it again: Saturday mornings are hard, especially when I don't have plans. I often feel so lonely and depleted. This morning, I was excited because I had a date for coffee with Claude, Curt's brother.

Claude knows how to get down to what matters when he's with me. He started by acknowledging my rough week. Sometimes it just takes someone saying, "I can tell you've had a hard week." Then he said he's learned things about his brother that he never knew from my grief and gratitude posts. To know that I've made a small difference for Curt's brother just by sitting down for five minutes to write every day was more than I could hope for.

Then Claude talked freely about his own feelings and times of grief. When I asked him the same question I've asked so many, "What is your advice?" he simply said, "Go on with living. Accept the blessings that come to you."

Those of you who knew Curt and Claude's dad know of Owen's genuine positivity. This morning, I felt that coming from his son too. He didn't say, "It's time to stop grieving." as some people suggest. He just said to proceed with the gift of life. Then he pulled out bag containing a framed picture of two of his roses. A Valentine's gift for me, you know, because this year will be different for me. Inside the bag was a card—a Valentine's card that fanned out like an old-fashioned one. He said, "They're hard to find—but I found one."

On what I thought would be an especially tough Saturday morning, I felt joy. And I felt loved. And I felt understood. And I mostly felt like Curt would be so proud of his brother's love and care for me in his absence.

Happy Saturday, everyone. Enjoy this day.

How can you get on with life today? Is there someone you can listen to or encourage? Is there someone who might need a Valentine's card from you tomorrow?

Day 267: Cards

I decided to sort through all the cards Curt gave me over the years that I could find. I'm sure there are more somewhere, or maybe I just didn't save them in the earlier years. I do seem to have gotten more sentimental as I've gotten older. I'm so glad I kept these cards and little notes that now tell a beautiful love story.

The Valentine from last year was on top, of course. Curt wrote his own words in almost every card, and last year was no exception. "Rosanne, you not only know what love is, you know how to show it. You are an outstanding teacher of many things, but your greatest contribution to my life has been the lessons you have taught me about love. More than anyone else I know, I see God's love in you. Thanks for your love. Curt."

Within a good marriage, we tend to see the other person as even better than they really are. It wasn't that Curt didn't see my weaknesses. He thought I was always pushing to get certain things done, and I was. But his kind words far outweighed any criticism.

Yesterday I organized my cards into categories—anniversary, valentines, birthday, Mother's Day—then I realized the miscellaneous category was just as big as the others. I have so many cards and kind words that Curt wrote just because.

Today I feel like a woman who was loved… and I feel like a woman who has lost. But I will choose the high of being loved over the low of loss. Happy Valentine's Day.

> *Go find a card if you haven't yet. Or just write a note on a piece of paper for someone you love. That works too.*

February 15

Day 268: Travel

Presidents' Day. A year ago, Curt and I were in Birmingham, Alabama. He was teaching there for several days, and I tagged along. Neither of us had been to Alabama, and that state completed his fifty-state visits. (I still have to visit Mississippi to complete mine.) We loved our time together. Birmingham was an awesome city— great homes, great food, and kind of hip.

We then went to Selma. I had always wanted to walk the bridge where so much of the Civil Rights Movement's history took place. Before our trip, we saw the movie *Selma*, so our journey was even more profound. Finally, we ended up in Auburn, though I'm not sure why. We heard it was a pretty town with a loyal university. That's where we had our Valentine's night and a rather romantic ending to our trip.

We loved being with each other on these quick trips. We rarely went on vacations more than a week long, but we did love traveling all over, often tagging on to our work trips. Our travel was mostly about enjoying each other in a new place. When I reviewed the notebook where I keep exciting notes about the weather and what I did around the house, I saw these words: "Had a great time in Alabama."

That was our last trip together. Two months later Curt would be gone. Exotic places were no more romantic than Auburn, Alabama. It's always the people you are with who make a place special.

> *You don't have to be in an exotic location or be gone for days on end to make memories. Plan an ordinary trip with someone you love. It might turn out to be extraordinary.*

Day 269: Nine Months

Nine months today. The amount of time I carried our children. The amount of time in a school year. Three-fourths of a year. Yet it's like yesterday in some ways.

This week I am in a certification training for life coaches. At the beginning of the session, we did a type of ice breaker where we were to find someone and ask each other, "What is your dream?" I said I didn't have a dream, but that isn't true. I have a dream that someday my life will be as full as it was nine months ago. I have a dream that my kids and grandkids will be inspired and loved despite no longer having Curt around. I have a dream that someday I will turn my unwanted life lessons into meaningful teaching. I have a dream that I will someday remember my past with more joy than sadness. I have a dream that I will be the kind of woman Curt thought I was—even though I wasn't that good. I have a dream that I will find meaning in my loss. I have a dream that I will cry less and laugh more. I have a dream that I will help someone, who is still living, know how to die better. I have a dream that I will find new friends who will be brilliant stars in my dark nights. I have a dream that I will find intimacy where I didn't expect it. I have a dream that I will be someone people want to be around rather than avoid because of my lack of life. I have a dream that I will talk more about the future and less about the past.

I do have some dreams after all, and I want to have even more. I do believe dreams are the instigators of change and harbingers of great things.

> *What is your dream? Do you dare say it out loud?*
> *Keep dreaming. It may mean you have new life if you have new dreams.*

Day 270: How Are You?

I think a lot about things that people say that make a difference for me. It's often as simple as asking me how I am. Rarely do I wish someone had not asked me how I am doing. Maybe not everyone would feel that way, but for me, it's a welcome opportunity to just express myself—good, bad, or otherwise.

Asking in person is great, but even a text works wonders. Maybe it's just feeling like someone cares about me. I rarely volunteer how I'm doing, but some days I just need to be asked. It's particularly helpful to be asked by people who are around me regularly because it's those people who could easily assume things about how I'm doing, but don't. Sometimes I can only respond very generally, and even that's okay. Asking tells me that you care. There is amazing power when someone is willing to give up precious time to listen. Your undivided attention is pure gold to me.

What I also need is encouragement. I've been in this coaching class with several people who knew Curt very well and know me well too. Do you know what they do best? They tell me things that buoy me through tender memories and unpredictable feelings. They make me feel more than normal—which, sadly, is what I aspire to. They make me feel strong. They say words that fill up that raw spot in my heart— words that make me feel capable of not just surviving, but thriving. They are encouragers. They are developers. They are not afraid to call out what's best in a person. I'm so grateful for these people in my life. I honestly have no idea what I'd do without them.

Today, ask someone how they are, and be ready to listen. Then tell them what you know about them that will give them a sense of confidence and strength. I doubt if you will ever go wrong doing those two things.

Day 271: Smart Phones

How long will it be before I don't instinctually want to text Curt about something that just happened? Yesterday, at the end a powerful last day of coaching certification, I had the instinct to pick up my phone and call Curt to review this amazing day of learning. As I went with John and his family to one of their favorite musicals in an awesome theatre, I saw two precious faces in awe of the production and wanted to take their picture—to text to Curt.

It doesn't seem fair that we have these very smart phones that let us do so much with communication, and yet I can't send a quick text or picture or even call Curt in heaven. As smart as these phones are, they don't transcend death.

Use those phones for good. Communicate. Call someone. Text a quick check-in message, or take an amazing picture. There are so many ways phones can make us less human, but there are probably a lot more ways they can be used to enhance relationships.

> *Is your phone a stepping stone to relationship growth or a stumbling block? Whom would you text if you could? Whom should you just pick up that phone and call today?*

Day 272: Envy

One of the worst weaknesses in human flesh is envy. I wasn't very old when I realized how envious I was of my playmate's bedroom. It was so perfect—and she had it all to herself. Envy can come easily at any stage of life, and these days, I fight it tooth and nail.

I envy women who still have their husbands. I envy the physical contact between couples. I envy the companionship that others have in a significant relationship. I envy having a mate when I am needing assistance. I envy those wives who are still admired and desired.

Envy is unhealthy, unlovely, and ugly. I also believe envy is closely related to initiative. Many times, what I admired in something or someone gave me impetus to work to find that in my life.

The reality is, we can't always have the things we envy. That's just life. Some people may want children, but can't get pregnant. Some people may want their health issues swept clean, but that doesn't happen. Some people may want one kind of love and devotion, but their partners do not. How does one turn envy into desire, and how does one place new desires in their heart? I'm not sure I know the answer, but I am searching.

For me, two things make some difference. One is gratitude. Finding gratitude seems to take some of the hurt away from not having what I want. Gratitude, in fact, can quickly turn my attitude around. The other is initiative. That one is less clear, but it's about having a new picture and new desires and working toward those. Not the same ones—but new ones. Acting on making some of the new desires a reality is key to life having some meaning and to letting go of envy.

Today, try both gratitude and initiative in turning your envy into desire for the next good thing.

Day 273: Wait

Light was Curt's word last year. My word was *wait*. I have a strong tendency to move things forward—activate—sometimes too fast. In the last nine months, wait has meant something different than I thought it would. It's been more about not getting ahead of myself with grief.

It's been about being patient when I'm lonely and waiting for someone to reach out, or at least waiting for the right opportunity. Last night was a Friday, and I hate being home alone on Friday night. Out of desperation, I wanted to blast out a plea to anyone who would have me, but I didn't. I decided I'd put on my big girl pants and suck it up, even if it meant another frozen meal and Netflix. My niece Rhonda texted later in the afternoon to check in on a mutual friend. Rhonda always told me to ask her and her husband, Terry, if I wanted to go to happy hour or dinner because they often have open evenings. I did, and we ended up having a great night together. It was just what I needed.

Did I wait? I waited until the time and situation seemed right. I waited until I felt like a had a signal from outside my own body. Maybe that's what waiting should be for me in grief. Waiting until I know it's the right time, right place, right people, and right opportunity. Waiting doesn't mean not doing something. It means waiting with patience and awareness. Sounds like good grief counseling to me. Wait.

What do you need to have more patience with? When have you waited too long? How do you find the right time for taking action?

Day 274: Strong Tears

I spent a great deal of this weekend watching Johnny's basketball games. I saw fifth-grade boys who sometimes struggled with their emotions. When things don't go well or they get hurt, the tears still come rather easily, but they seemed awkward when they shed tears in public. I can sure relate to them. Tears come easily, and I wish I could hide my face in my arms just like those boys do.

Curt often said it was a sign of strength when people cried. I think he meant it showed depth of care and a certain authenticity. He would know. His tears came easily most of his life. I cried several times today like a fifth grader. During the songs at church. When I watched my brother-in-law Chris talk so admirably at church. When I saw the defeated faces of members of an opposing basketball team who had been beat by a lot. When I heard that one of Johnny's basketball buddies suddenly lost his grandma today and saw his competitive face scrunch up with tears. And finally, as I watched Johnny's big smile after his team's final win of the season, wishing so much Curt was there to see it.

When will I quit crying? When will I stop being embarrassed to show that emotion I can't control? Maybe never. I kind of hope those fifth-grade boys don't completely grow out of it either. I think men who aren't afraid to cry in public are passionate, caring, and authentic. Don't you?

Are you a man or woman who is embarrassed to cry in front of others? Why? Is it possibly your pride? Shedding tears in public may reveal your strength.

Day 275: Sincere Curiosity

Tough start today, until I received a message from Maika. I've talked about her before. She's an amazing colleague and friend, who is young enough to be my daughter, and like my own coach. She's doing much of the work Curt used to do on the "Theme Thursday" webcast and other Gallup conceptual pieces. That might have made me jealous. Instead, it makes me feel even closer to Curt when I see her do such beautiful work with strengths in such a powerful but humble way.

Here's what she wrote today and why a day that started out with more grief turned into gratitude:

> I'm watching the "Theme Thursday" video Curt did for Command. At about twenty-seven minutes into it, I can see someone open the door in the background, and I know it's you. My immediate prediction was that you'd do what most people would; they'd get scared and jump out of the room, but you didn't. You stood in the doorway a while, and then came into the room and sat down out of the picture. I could tell you were there for the rest of the conversation because the door stayed open.
>
> My point is, I noticed a sincere curiosity you had about Curt. He had the same for you. It was this commitment to discovering what was interesting, beautiful, insightful about each other. And I see that not only in your marriage, but also in the way you love the people you love, beyond that partnership. It's deeper than a belief in talent, but I think that may be part of it. What a sacred habit you both practiced together. Thanks for doing that because it has spilled out and become something bigger than either of you. What a huge gift you've given the world.

February 23

Day 276: Dining Solo

I've never liked eating by myself. When I go on business trips, I've learned to find a restaurant with a bar where I can sit and not be alone at a table. Last night, when I pulled out the leftovers and heated them up, I decided to sit at the table and eat. That was the first time I'd sat by myself at our table since Curt has been gone.

Now I often eat at my desk, both at home and at work. Most lunches and breakfasts sit to the side of my computer. I'll sometimes sit in my chair in the living room, or maybe at the kitchen island, but not alone at a table. I hated sitting at the dining room table by myself last night. I eventually took my plate, left the table, and sat in my chair. After forty-four years of sitting with someone when I ate, it's a hard thing to be alone during meals. Here again, I know many other people have eaten alone much of their lives, so I need to quit whining. I should be grateful I have so many places to sit and eat. I should be happy I have food. I should be glad many people invite me to eat with them.

Research shows the power of eating together as a family. Our family certainly did that, and I remember lots of things we learned about each other over food and drink. No separate meals—we all ate what was on the table and started every single meal with prayer. Maybe that's what I need to do. I can start my meals with a prayer, even when I'm by myself.

> *How about you? Do you take advantage of eating at the table with your family? With your spouse? Maybe you can enjoy the built-in company you might have in your house. Or if you are alone, like me, invite someone else who is alone over for a simple meal at your table. Or maybe just be okay being alone at the table, while reflecting on your day with gratitude. I'm going to work on it.*

February 24

Day 277: Death and Taxes

Taxes. I've never done them before. Our agreement was that I did the day-to-day finances, and Curt did the taxes. I always thought he got the better deal until this year.

I'm so bad at numbers, and I had to follow Curt's system for filing documentation and receipts, which, frankly, seemed like it could use better organization. More difficult was looking at his handwriting on that legal pad where he detailed our taxes, and looking at some of the receipts and notes that were symbolic of our happy life.

His handwriting gets me every time. A person's handwriting is so unique to who they are. When I see his penmanship, I think of all the handwritten notes he gave me, the sermons he wrote, and the powerful thoughts he penned about strengths.

Plodding through taxes is a miserable experience. I hope I'm doing them right. I hope our tax person has a lot of patience. And I hope I don't owe a lot of money! What is there to be grateful for? I once heard somebody say you should send a thank-you note along with your tax payment. For the streets. For the schools. For the financial support of those who need it desperately. For a free country. I'm not getting political, but I do want to be grateful for our country.

So, I will try to finish up these taxes. I will try not to complain, but be grateful Curt could pay taxes to a country that supported him in his dreams and his well-lived life. Now, where are those thank-you notes?

> **What things are you grateful for that your taxes help support?**
> **I challenge you to make a list of those things and remember them when you're paying your taxes.**

February 25

Day 278: Scars

Becky's a good friend and neighbor who has reached out to me to see me in person every few weeks. Last night, the two of us went to dinner and spent almost three hours together. She is an awesome listener and a stimulating conversationalist.

When I got home, I realized our evening had been very different than the others we'd spent together since Curt's death. Last night, the topic wasn't my grief—at least it wasn't the focus of the conversation. We talked about politics, aging, faith, mutual friends, houses, books—and we laughed a lot. It was much different than earlier evenings when she listened to my sad heart and had to watch me cry pretty much nonstop. I had to pause a moment to reflect on how far I've come. Last night, grief danced around some topics, but it didn't dominate the conversation.

I've changed and healed in many areas of my life over the past nine months. I no longer regularly cry with wails, cry until I dry heave, feel like my legs will crumble underneath me, or simply feel like I want to die. The big ugly wound is beginning to heal… but it will leave a scar.

Last night, I found myself being grateful for feeling like myself. For feeling a little normal. For feeling a bit whole. Yet when I went to bed last night, I gently patted the pillow where Curt once laid his head, and I missed him so much. Wounds, healing, and scars. It doesn't happen so neatly, but I'm feeling so grateful for some signs of progress.

> *What scars do you have in your life? Are they physical or emotional? Or both? What stories do they tell? How can you share those stories to help someone else?*

February 26

Day 279: The Boots

Last night, my good friend Linda invited me to go to a Blake Shelton concert. She has amazing seats in a suite, so it was a new perspective on a concert. Linda knows I'm not such a big fan of country music—my radio is preset to NPR and classical music stations any time after 9:00 a.m. Earlier than that, I'm listening to my son's radio show.

I figured it was good for me to have a night out and get a little out of my comfort zone. I planned to tune out much of the music, but there was something about the pounding rhythm and the predictable I, IV, V harmonic progression (with an occasional minor chord thrown in) that got to my emotions. The flow of that country music struck a chord with my current need for predictability, simplicity, and basics in my new world order.

Curt laughed when I told him I'd always wanted to be a cowgirl rather than a farm kid. The cowgirl boots I wore last night were a gift from him on one of my birthdays.

He gave me three pairs of boots over the years. When I pulled them out of the box, I saw his writing: "Some hot boots for my hot cowgirl." Only he could turn my cowgirl envy into something romantic.

So, with those boots on, I listened and clapped and smiled at how the music brought back memories and helped me know what I really hope for at some point: simplicity, predictability, and love rediscovered.

What kind of music do you like? Does it seem to bring order or meaning to your life? Crank up a favorite song, put on your boots, and enjoy!

Rosanne's boots

Day 280: Spring Fever

Spring is in the air. My whole life, I've loved this season best. But this year, I feel a heaviness when I normally would be anticipating green and outdoor living. Going into this spring feels like I'm giving up the last season I had with Curt. I'm already starting to remember "a year ago" more and more intensely.

Stop.

You know what just happened, literally just now? I got a text from Jane saying they put out their outdoor furniture and disassembled winter pots. She said "Doug and I would like to plan a day we can come over and help you do the same. You may not NEED help, but I'm sure it would be more enjoyable doing it together."

The tears just rolled down my face. She's right. I don't like doing all that new season work by myself—more for emotional than physical reasons. Last night, I read another great article by Christina Rasmussen, author of *Second Firsts*. Her writing has helped me so much. One of the things she says that I cling to is, "You can do the impossible because you have been through the unthinkable."

She talks about helping the grieving person with practical things for not just that first month, but for a while. (Some would say it's commanded to do so in the Bible.) When her friends would get groceries or put flowers on her table (Well, maybe that's not so practical, but I like the idea), somehow, she could move forward a little easier. "Empathy with hands and feet," as Curt would say, "is the mature use of Empathy."

I'm not naïve. This season I've loved so much will probably not be easy this year, but I've been so blessed with people who help me physically, emotionally, socially, and spiritually. Come to me, sunshine, daffodils, al fresco eating, geese, crocus, robins, and buds because I will find the will to face new life. New life in spring… for me and for nature.

February 28

Day 281: Music

It must be the week of concerts. For more than ten years, Curt and I went to concerts with our friends Dave and Helen. Early each spring, we'd select which concerts we'd attend. Dave and I always lobbied for orchestral groups. When we'd go, Curt was always so happy and relaxed. He loved having dinner with Dave, and the conversation flowed from grandkids to work to travel.

We usually went on weekends, so when we sat down and got quiet, it was often the first moments of the week where we were side by side and open to whatever the evening would bring. Last night as I sat in the concert hall, I could remember how Curt's pants felt when I would lay my hand on his leg. I remembered how he would cross his hands in front of him and then sometimes slip his arm around me. I remembered how, occasionally, his eyes would shut and I'm pretty sure he took a few winks of sleep. And I remembered how he'd squeeze my hand when the music got passionate. Last night, I was determined to stay focused and enjoy one of the best orchestras in the world—The Russian Symphony Orchestra.

Russian composers are among my favorites. I love Rachmaninoff and Tchaikovsky. The power and ethos that came out of that group of musicians was indescribable. My heart was pounding, and I cried—of course I cried. I cried at concerts even when Curt was with me. The swift bowing of the strings, the unashamed clashing of the cymbals, the perfectly shaped fingers flying over the keys are enough to build my emotions. I guess that's why I loved teaching music and directing choirs. But last night, the tears represented my loss too. Music brings me to my knees.

Today, I'm grateful for my piano teachers, especially Alice Hayman who gave me a love of music. I'm also grateful for the choir members who tolerated my crazy rehearsals and for the students who left my room knowing how a falling third sounds.

> *What about you? What does music mean to you? How are you investing in music with your kids? It might impact their lives for years to come. It did for Curt and it does for me.*

Day 282: 25 Things

Occasionally, I have the emotional fortitude to look at Curt's Facebook page and read things he wrote, look at pictures he posted, or see posts that people still leave in his honor. Today, I happened to find this list of "25 Things to Know About Me." Remember when these were popular on Facebook? Well, here is Curt's list:

25 Things

1. I seem to be best at sports that have either a racquet or paddle (tennis, racquetball, badminton, ping-pong).

2. When I was a pastor and writing sermons, I never finished until early on Sunday morning.

3. I underestimated how much I would enjoy being a grandparent.

4.   February 1st was my ten-year anniversary with Gallup.

5.   My wife turns me on.

6.   I have never met a pizza that I didn't like.

7.   For the past thirty-three years, I have always been a member of a small group with other men.

8.   I wish I could sing and play the guitar like James Taylor.

9.   Writing is hard for me, but it feels so good when I am done.

10. Even though I am good a racquet/paddle sports, I seldom get to play them.

11. I enjoy taking pictures and have over four thousand photographs stored on my computer.

12. I wish I had been as patient a parent as I am a grandparent.

13. I have always enjoyed getting the mail.

14. I can drive and I can talk, but I find it difficult to drive and talk.

15. My first car was a 1961 Corvair, recently recognized by *Time* magazine as one of the fifty worst cars.

16. I love thinking about a person's StrengthsFinder results and helping them capitalize on their God-given talent.

17. I attended a one-room elementary school with one teacher for K-6.

18. My dad was a carpenter, and I worked on his construction crew from seventh grade through college.

19. I was part owner of a roofing company. What that means is that me and another guy (Dennis) shingled a few roofs and got paid for it.

20. While in seminary, I would often skip chapel to play ping-pong with three friends.

21. I often cry when I see other people cry.

22. I have a golf disability, and people laugh at me.

23. Know-it-alls bug me.

24. I am surprised by how much time I spend cutting nasal hair.

25. I am confident about my future, not because of my personal intelligence or integrity, but because of the grace of God.

Don't you love number twenty-five? He often wrote that in his cards to me—how he was confident about the future. These twenty-five things remind me why I miss him every day and why I'm grateful he was my main man.

> *What are twenty-five things people should know about you? Write them down and share them with others, maybe even on Facebook.*

Curt

March 1

Day 283: Slap in the Face

I'm in Phoenix and getting energy from working with a new associate and calling on schools here. I'm still so grateful for my work. Sometimes when I feel so good and so full of energy, it's partly because I've forgotten about my loss.

I rarely go for more than a few minutes without remembering, but on a day like today, I'm swept away for a few hours by the energy of what I'm doing. Then I remember the raw truth about my life. It's hard to describe the feeling that follows those hours of good normalcy. It's like a slap in the face. Maybe it's a good sign I can go even a few hours without remembering Curt's death, but I almost dread those times because, when I wake up to the harsh reality, it's almost harder than if I live in a steady stream of awareness.

If you've not gone through grief, this may make no sense. Maybe in time, the slap in the face won't sting as much. Maybe for now, I need to be grateful for just a few hours when I live with energy—even if it feels naïve.

How do you cope with hard realities? How do you stay charged up when life's challenges slap you in the face? What do you do to extend those feelings of energy?

Day 284: No Regrets

Each day is a bit closer to that one-year mark of Curt's passing. I know it's still about two months away, but something is changing inside my head and heart. I feel a new kind of focus on remembering what these last two months we had together were like. It's quite different than anything I've experienced to date. My guess is that it's not going to be an easy couple of months.

I've been looking back more on Curt's Facebook page. He posted many pictures of our yard. He loved the pond behind our house and snapped hundreds of pictures of it through so many seasons.

I am grateful I still have the pond. I am grateful I still have the pictures. I am grateful Curt loved his life living on Liesveld pond. It makes me want to take the kind of pictures that he could take, but I'm not sure that's my talent.

As we inch into springtime, I will think about his last spring on this earth and how very happy he was. Honestly, just writing that gives me a lump in my throat. I remain hugely grateful that he left this earth in a beautiful state of joy, peace, and contentment. He knew no suffering, and he knew no regret, and that still gives me such great pause and personal gratitude.

If this should be your last spring on this earth, would you be able to say you have no regrets? I hope so.

Early spring on Liesveld Pond

March 3

Day 285: The Necklace

Some years ago, Curt gave me a necklace that had a small cross on it. The gentleman who owns our favorite local jewelry store designed it, and I loved it dearly. I always wore it the whole season of Lent, and this year it had special meaning. It was valuable in more ways than one.

Yesterday when I got dressed to go to my client meeting, I took it off because it just didn't lay quite straight on the top I was wearing. I had no other jewelry with me and, hence, no jewelry bag. I carefully wrapped the necklace in a tissue and put it in my bag of toiletries. Today when I went to put it on, it wasn't there. I have no idea where it went. I was afraid the people who cleaned my room thought the tissue was garbage and threw it out. Tears welled in my eyes as I told the kind housekeeper my story of the cross necklace. The hotel staff bent over backwards looking for it, but it appears to be gone for good.

I cried. I felt cheated. I felt angry. The loss of that necklace was like a metaphor. A tiny lost necklace represents all the hurt I feel. I miss all the tenderness I received the day Curt gave me the necklace and throughout his life. Think of me when you see a cross necklace, or perhaps think what that cross represents. I will work on doing that today when I feel especially vulnerable.

> *Do you have a piece of jewelry that is precious to you?*
> *What makes it special? Be sure to take good care of it!*

March 4

Day 286: A Good Friend

Tonight, I spent time with my friends Dale and Donna. We had an amazing dinner and sweet time together. Curt loved Dale, who was part of the men's group that he met with regularly. I'm grateful for the lives that have touched mine in intimate and joyful ways because Curt was a good friend to so many amazing people. I am now realizing the benefit.

I miss Curt on a beautiful night like tonight, but I feel his presence permeating my every moment. His quiet but profound spirit surrounded us.

March 5

Day 287: A New Cross

I didn't find my cross necklace I wrote about two days ago, but I did get a text from my niece, Elizabeth, that touched me deeply. She sent a picture of a cross necklace I gave her some time ago. I honestly didn't remember giving it to her, but she told me she loved it. What she wrote was even more touching. "The necklace can't be replaced, but maybe you should spoil yourself and buy a beautiful new cross while you are in Arizona. Something turquoise or sterling silver maybe. Because if Curt was with you, I'm pretty sure he would buy his beautiful wife something equally beautiful to adorn herself with. To remember your travels together. To spoil you. And to make you feel wonderful and special, because you are!"

So, today when I was with shopping with Marlene, I found a beautiful cross. It's not like the one Curt gave me, but one like my niece suggested. I sent her a picture of it and said, "I think this necklace is from Curt via you."

I'm so grateful for Elizabeth's inspiration and for my sister who was so patient as I searched for the new necklace. That necklace—just like my new life—cannot replace the one Curt gave me. The new necklace has its own beauty, just as I hope my new life will have someday.

March 6

Day 288: What Can Be

It's been a great day with John and family. We are missing Anne, but I'm planning a trip with her during spring break. Today we went to a Royals spring training game and enjoyed perfect weather. Spring training is a fun, intimate experience for a baseball fan. Johnny got two of his favorite players to sign his hat. Then we enjoyed swimming at the hotel. Who doesn't swim outside in March until it gets dark?

I'm working at not always thinking about their Poppo and what could have been during this trip. Instead, I want to fondly remember what was. Johnny remembers things related to Poppo and food, like how his chocolate ice cream cone once exploded on his shirt. My true goal is to remember the past with joy, to enjoy the present, and not think of the future in terms of what could have been but instead what can be.

Grief and gratitude. I'm so grateful for my kids and grandkids. So, so grateful.

> *Have you been tempted to think about what could have been? Guess what; that's not helpful at all. Instead, learn to think about what can be.*

Johnny and John

Day 289: Arizona Sunset

It's been another great day in Arizona with family. My sister Marlene and her husband winter here, and they were so gracious to teach us about playing pickle ball and let us swim in their pool. Then we found our way to a resort where we had more swimming and hot tub time.

Tonight, I watched the Arizona sun set and looked up in the sky. I know heaven isn't necessarily "up there." In fact, who the heck knows where heaven is? (I don't think I should have used heck and heaven in the same sentence.) I just know it is real. I do look to the heavens sometimes and think of Curt. If I don't look in the sky, I look at the light I placed in my yard in his honor. I can see it from my house and especially from my bedroom window. I often whisper good night to Curt as I look at it.

The sky and the light both draw my eyes to a place where I feel ever-so-sweetly connected with Curt. As I sat in the hot tub under an Arizona sunset tonight, I looked at the sky and felt him smiling down on us. I wish he was here with us. That would be awesome. But he's not, so we will be the best we can be for him. It's all we can do. It's all he would want us to do. That I know.

Look at the sky tonight. What is it telling you?
What power do you feel?

Day 290: Seventh-Inning Stretch

Today was another Royals spring baseball game. It was a beautiful day in Surprise, Arizona, with plenty of celebrities signing autographs, homeruns, and true KC blue fans. During the seventh-inning stretch, as Johnny and I stood by each other singing "Take Me Out to the Ballgame," I had a flash back to Johnny's first baseball game after Curt died.

It was a Monday night—just a few days after Curt's death. John and Meagan wanted to keep Johnny's life as normal as possible, so when he said he would play baseball that night, I felt like I needed to be there for him—and for Curt. What I remembered about that day was in stark contrast to the beautiful time at the baseball game this afternoon.

I remembered the walk up to the ballfield on that painful Monday night with Marlene by my side. When we got close to the benches, my legs gave way, and I literally lost my balance. I remember the surreal sounds and foreign feelings like it was yesterday. I was in a type of purgatory as I sat down on those hard benches and cringed and cried at every ping of the bat. I didn't talk. I stared into space. I had no idea what hell I was facing.

Today, baseball felt more like my healer rather than my horror. Not that I didn't think of Curt a million times—he would have loved this day, but I didn't lose my balance. I only teared up once, and I smiled often and felt a new kind of joy. I'm sure I have some tough days ahead, but for today, I will take singing "Take Me Out to the Ballgame" in harmony with Johnny by my side.

What things in life can you turn from horrifying to healing?
What will it take to make such a transformation?

Day 291: Filling the Void

We spent a big part of today swimming in a beautiful pool and doing a little sun worship. The warmth of the sun rays gave me energy and a feeling of contentment. I loved being with the grandkids again, knowing how very, very blessed I am to have them near to me in both proximity and spirit. Tonight, we went to visit one of my best friends, Linda, and her husband, Phil. They took us to a local artist's home, and Johnny and Norah loved seeing his work and listening to his stories. I was proud of how easily they engaged in conversation with the adults.

We were in the community of Fountain Hills, Arizona, and ate dinner while watching this awesome fountain. I felt Curt's presence with me as the water seemed to catapult into the heavens. It was all so perfect and sweet and full of joy. As I left Linda's house after some Bailey's around the fire pit, she hugged me tightly. Her life is one I hold onto when I need hope. She lost her first husband way too early too, but she is a model of honoring him while continuing to live a full life.

I am so grateful for people like Linda and Phil who reach out to show love and hospitality and generosity. I can't imagine my new life without my family and close friends. I know I've said that so many times, but I can never say it enough. I am so grateful to have people in my life who fill the grief void. As beautiful as the Arizona desert and sky are to me, it pales in comparison to the joy the people on this trip have given me. You know who you are: Marlene, Ron, Ken, Audrey, Donna, Dale, Linda, Phil, Jack, John, Meagan, Norah, and Johnny. You made my trip complete.

Who are your people that fill your voids? Do you invest in people so that someday they fill a hole in your heart? Or you in theirs? People matter.

March 10

Day 292: New Meaning

My great friend Maika asked if I'd write a blog for the Gallup Coaches Playbook, an online publication for strengths coaches. Here is an excerpt. This is my grief. This is my gratitude.

Major Life Changes and Strengths

by Rosanne M. Liesveld

I rarely teach a strengths seminar where someone does not ask, "Do your strengths change if you go through a significant life change?" Our researchers would likely say that we don't have the longitudinal data to make a determination about this question. But based on my understanding of human talent, I know we tend to become more of who we are as things get challenging, so my stock answer had always been, "No, usually one's strengths don't really change that much, no matter what the situation." And then I became one of those people who experienced a major life change.

Now I have a new answer. I truly believe our strengths don't change, but they take on new meaning. Even though I had gone through a lot of the typical life events, nothing was quite as significant as losing my husband suddenly after forty-four years of marriage. For me, those strengths not only remained true, but in some ways, they were even more intense and present.

I noticed that my strengths had more potential to be "raw" after my significant loss. I had little filter, little stamina, little feeling of control, and little energy to be at my best. The behaviors I considered to be my talents took a back seat. It took me a long time to try to reframe my strengths in a mature way.

This was most obvious with my Signature Theme of Futuristic. How could someone who had vivid mental pictures of a beautiful future with her husband proceed when all those dreams are now defunct? Even though my life became more about day-to-day survival, I made sense of those days by conceiving thoughts about what my life would be like in the future.

Another part of my newfound perspective on whether strengths can change came from deep self-awareness that now, more than ever, I needed to lean into certain themes one day and other themes on another day. At times, I knew I needed my Activator to take over and get me going. Other days, my Relator was like a best friend—it brought me best friends when I was lonely or afraid. There were days when my Command was necessary to make quick and hard decisions. And other days, my Significance was leading the charge as I reconsidered my new place in this world.

So, what is the answer? I do believe much of how we experience our themes comes down to our values. New values, new awareness or new paradigms may slightly adjust the trajectory of a strength. But throughout my experience with change, my themes didn't leave me once.

Throughout this journey, I found that I needed stability, reliability and predictability more than ever. And strengths, along with relationships, faith, and work, provided those things for me. What is more predictable than knowing and embracing who you are? I could be myself, for better or for worse. I didn't need to waste precious energy redefining the new me. I knew what my talents were and I knew what they could be. That was a gift. An unchanging gift.

If you've been through a life change, how can you see your strengths still at play? What situations bring out the raw side of your strengths?

March 11

Day 293: Coming Home

I came home from twelve days in Arizona spread over business and family vacation. Driving home from the airport, my heart was so heavy, and the tears would not subside. It feels like I should be coming home with Curt. This beautiful spring weather should feed my soul, but it only makes me stressed about all the work I need to do that I didn't have to do by myself in the past.

Reality has set in after many days of joy. I always thought the best part of vacation was coming back home again, but it feels very different now that I'm alone. It's March here in Nebraska, but the weather feels like May, so I'm reminded of what happened to my life almost ten months ago. I feel like somebody kicked me in the gut, so I need to reach deep within and try to find something to pull me forward. I will fight the thoughts of what could have been, and focus on what I have, what can be, and gratitude for so many amazing years with my Curt.

Thanks for listening when I need to expose my authentic emotions. You have helped just by reading this post, which ultimately has been about my healing.

> *What can be in your life? Are you willing to dream about a bright future even if you've been through a storm?*

Day 294: Curt's Book

I woke up alone again on a Saturday morning and wished I had a coffee partner. I had a lot I needed to get done at home, so I decided to plunge into my chores. Winter decor needed to come down, and it was time to put some spring feel into the house.

I take pictures of how I decorate my house each season so I can just pull them out as a guide. The picture of the coffee table showed a book, but I couldn't quite see what it was. Then it jumped out at me. It was a book Curt gave me for Christmas about three years ago on the tenth anniversary of living in our home. He had spent hours finding pictures of each season on the pond and grouping them appropriately. I found the book, but as I picked it up, I wasn't sure if I wanted to look at it because of the depth of emotions I might feel.

I picked it up anyway and turned the pages—each beautifully laid out with his photographs of the pond. It hurt at first to see the pictures, but I was reminded how Curt loved living on Liesveld Pond for a dozen years. He loved taking photos here. He loved entertaining here. He loved playing with the grandkids here. He loved fishing in the pond. He loved sitting with me on our patio while he watched his favorite ball game. He loved scooping snow off the pond for an ice rink.

I'm so glad Curt loved it here. As with most things, it was my idea first to build here. But in the end, this was his paradise in many ways. I'm so glad he died on this soil that was his piece of heaven, and then went on to the real paradise. I've said it before, but seriously, what a way to go.

We can't choose where or how we will die, but we can choose how we will live. How can you enjoy the place where you live? How can you make it a place where others feel welcomed and comfortable?

Johnny and Curt enjoying winter

March 13

Day 295: Hair Therapy

I should pay my hair stylist, Lisa, for the therapy I get when I am at her salon. She became my hair person more than eleven years ago. I wanted somebody whose salon wasn't far from me, who had flexible hours, worked on Saturdays, and could get me in and out in the shortest amount of time possible. What I got was much more.

This month, I didn't see her much with both of us traveling. In the meantime, she lost her father. Yesterday when we were together, we talked a lot about death and grief and life. She listens and responds in a way only a friend can. She cut Curt's hair too. She knew him as this somewhat quiet, nice man who was always on time. She knew our marriage and our life pretty intimately. I've told her things I only tell my best friends and family.

The morning of Curt's funeral, I sat numbly in her salon along with my daughter and daughter-in-law. I don't remember much. I just remember I was glad it was Lisa doing my hair for this unplanned event. I still had enough sense to want to look good for Curt. Lisa's talent goes beyond how to color hair so the grey doesn't show, or how to cut straight hair at an angle so it lays just right, though she does both really well. Her talent is so much about relationship, about how she treats her customers.

Yesterday, I started the day a bit rough and ended it in Lisa's swivel chair. She didn't just turn me around physically, but also emotionally.

> *Today, I hope you run into someone like Lisa who will turn your day around. Or even better, you do that for someone else.*

March 14

Day 296: Practical Help

Yesterday I felt like I will be okay. It was a beautiful day and I got to work outside. Working in the yard always has been my idea of a good day. I had help yesterday from Anne, Jane, and Doug. They spent a good part of their Sunday afternoon raking, cutting down grasses, hauling outdoor furniture, putting things away in the garage in those areas where I just can't quite reach, and doing many other miscellaneous jobs. I felt less alone and overwhelmed than I had felt for a long time. They spoke my love language when they helped me in the yard.

My friend Ellen tells me the Bible commands that widows be taken care of. I think the culture then warranted a kind of support for widows that isn't necessary today, but helping a recent widow is certainly faith in action. I so appreciated the steady and willing help I had today.

Time with family later in the day was so sweet to me. I felt normal. It made getting up this morning easier because of the people who helped me feel cared for and supported.

I'm so grateful for that kind of help. Maybe helping the widow should be a faith-based responsibility. It certainly grows my faith in people and in a Higher Being.

> **Does your church or place of worship have a ministry for those who have lost their spouses? Does it have a ministry for those in grief? Even if you don't have a formal program, look for practical ways to serve widows or widowers.**

March 15

Day 297: Truth and Hope

Yesterday was a typical day at work. I was booked with coaching calls, many with school leaders. I called a principal who is my age and retiring this spring after thirty-four years in education. Early in the conversation, she told me she'd lost her husband five years ago and was now remarried. I rarely tell my clients anything about my personal life, but I shared that I'd lost my husband ten months ago. She spoke from life experience, which made her a great teacher.

Although I was supposed to be her coach, she began to naturally talk to me about the shock of suddenly losing your life partner. She shared and asked questions. I asked her advice. Like other widows, she emphasized how each person needs to grieve in her own way. She also talked about how work healed her and how she took a big turn in her life when she realized that although her husband had died, she hadn't. She also said she had a spiritual obligation to live out her life fully despite change. The last thing she said was, "I believe something very, very good will come of your life."

This wasn't some goofy person who had only naïve and simplistic platitudes for answers. She is a respected principal and has won many accolades for her work. Her advice was very practical; she was a very realistic person who gave me hope. It felt like a God thing. We eventually got around to me coaching her, but in the end, I received much more than I gave. She changed my day.

> *Don't be afraid to speak some truth to others in a hopeful way. I've seen the difference between realistic talk that is negative, and realistic talk that is positive. The latter helps me heal.*

March 16

Day 298: Not Perfect

Sometimes I think that people get the idea our marriage was perfect. It was far from perfect. There were times we fought, but rarely in front of our kids—at least not the real knockdown, drag-out fights. Neither of us thought fighting in front of the kids was good parenting, but we had our times.

I'd say we fought most about Curt's dedication to work. His mental, emotional, and physical being was so focused on work, and he took his work so seriously. When he left the ministry, I thought that would change. While I would say his stress lessened enormously, he still put work high on his list of priorities. I thought I did too, yet we rarely had fights about my work stuff. His high Responsibility drove him to do what he didn't always feel like doing.

We also fought about me wanting to get things done fast, like projects around the house. I often wanted to move on something more quickly than Curt did. His Analytical slowed him down and he often wanted me to not be in such a big hurry to execute my ideas. We didn't fight much at all about the big three—in-laws, money, or sex. Maybe that helped. And we both believed investing in our marriage was the best way we could be great parents.

So, now you know; we didn't have the perfect marriage, but we had huge value for each other. We were generous with our affection We honored each other's successes and supported each other's work. We didn't let our kids become more important than our relationship. And we involved other people in our marriage and life a lot. Maybe most importantly, we had a shared faith.

So, there it is—not exactly profound, but an effort to be honest, like I've tried so hard to be in all these writings. I wish we could have written that book on marriage together. Maybe these posts are the book we meant to write. Now that thought just blew my mind.

What book should you be writing? Maybe it's not a book with words on paper, but a message that needs to be shared. Can you do it?

Day 299: Control

I've noticed my need to have control of some pretty unimportant things lately. I know exactly why I do it. I feel like I couldn't control the biggest thing in my life, so I grasp desperately to assure myself I can still control some things. Like order in my house. Like putting my recyclables out so that I never miss a week, even though the bin is only partially full. Like turning down my bed at night.

I didn't ever turn down my bed before Curt died, but I started doing it soon after because I was so afraid of my bed at first. I was afraid I would realize he would never be there again. I was afraid I wouldn't sleep. I would get my bed ready so I could get into it without waking myself up when I finally got tired.

Control. Plans. Routines. I always smiled at how old people needed those kinds of things in their lives. Now I feel like I have become one of them—not just because I'm getting older, but because I have a need to control something. Trying to control things can make for a dull life—or at least a very predictable one. It can also cause a bit of paranoia.

But control is such a joke. We don't control anything. Period. Today, I'm going to quit turning down my bed. I'm going to take a risk and change my behavior, and hope it changes my thinking and feeling.

> *How about you? Do you like to have control of things in your life?*
> *Do routines give you satisfaction? What will happen if that*
> *routine is destroyed one day? How will you cope?*

Day 300: Guilt

Sometimes I have an odd feeling that's almost like guilt. Last night, I went to watch some March Madness games at a local sports bar with good friends. I glanced at the table near me, filled with all the guys I know and love. It seemed like I was going to see Curt sitting there too, but I went on and, for the most part, had a good time.

Fast forward to tonight when I will have other good friends over to my house to watch their favorite teams play. Sometimes I feel weird and almost guilty if I enjoy myself, especially when I'm watching sports. I guess it's because I know Curt enjoyed sports so much, and I feel like I shouldn't enjoy it without him. I don't like feeling that awkward quasi-guilt. I know in my mind I'm not doing anything wrong. It's a very weird juxtaposition—doing something fun but thinking I should be feeling guilty. It's all a part of grief. I think Curt would want me to watch sports. I'm probably more compelled to watch them now with him gone. Maybe it's that sports have given me some feeling of being close to him.

The gratitude feels minute today, but I will claim it. Sports and friends who watch sports with me make me feel like Curt is still hanging around.

Who do you watch sports with? How do sports enrich your life?

Day 301: Band-Aids

I can't believe it's been more than three hundred days since I wrote my first post. These last sixty-five days will be filled with anticipation of the anniversary of Curt's death. Last night someone said, "You seem to be doing very well." We both kind of laughed at the idea of what doing well is for a sixty-four-year-old woman who had the earth pulled from underneath her.

What has helped me heal to this point? That's hard to summarize, but I can think of individual things one by one. Today I'm thinking about how people who weren't part of our regular social circle have made a difference. Yesterday, I went to our CPA. She had worked with Curt on our taxes for sixteen years, but I had never met her. I dreaded going to her office, partly out of the fear I would owe yet another chunk of money after so many unplanned expenses this year. Even more, I hated feeling dumb. I'm so bad with numbers and I just didn't know much about how to prepare our taxes.

I went into her office feeling angry, vulnerable, and stupid, but this woman—whom I may have stereotyped because of her vocation—was like an angel to me. I apologized for my lack of excellence in tax preparation. She quickly dismissed that, then talked about how much she liked Curt. How ethical he was. How courteous he was. How he talked about me and our family with pride. She somehow managed to take what I had put together and, in less than an hour, make magic of it. She even said, with a twinkle in her eye, "I think you were even more prepared for this than Curt was."

Twice I choked up enough that I couldn't finish talking. She somehow felt safe and caring and understanding. I truly believe healing comes in little pieces—tiny Band-Aids that eventually cover you like a powerful balm. Even my tax accountant added another small Band-Aid that will help me heal.

Gratitude, you know, for the small things.

March 20

Day 302: My Shiny Black Piano

Another thing that has made a difference for me is my piano. Yesterday I sat down and let my fingers find the song. It's weird how some song comes off my hands even though I don't plan for it. The song that evolved yesterday was one I played many years ago for church. I'm not even sure if I remember the title. I think it was "Feed My Lambs."

As I was playing, I kept picturing Curt singing as he stood in the pulpit. He always sang in public as if no one was watching him, often emphasizing the lyrics with a quick movement of his head as if to say, "I really mean what I'm singing." I spent many Sundays sitting to the right side of the pulpit area, playing the piano, and having a perfect view of the man I loved. Those memories and the words of the song brought me to tears, but I didn't stop playing.

Some people play through pain. I played through tears. Amazingly, it was easy to play passionately with tears streaming down my face. When I finished, I took my hands off the keys and looked straight ahead. I could see my tear-streaked face looking back at me, reflecting off my shiny black piano as if the music rack was a mirror. Even through the blur, I could see the sadness on my face.

So, I did what I try to do when I have pain—I pushed through a bit and put my hands back on the piano. This time a different song came to me. This time I played "Great is Thy Faithfulness." And I played it with my own brand of sorrow-induced bravado.

Part of healing is knowing the right prescription for the pain. For me, some days, that prescription is a piano. A very special piano.

What prescription eases your pain?

Rosanne at the piano

Day 303: Good Work

I think there's a reason God created the seventh day for rest. He suggested we would have six days of work, and then we would need a day to recreate.

Work is a good thing, and it has been a healer for me. When I am in my office at work, I feel like a fully functioning human being. And when I am with clients teaching, like I was today, I feel darn close to my former self. Being productive helps me heal. When I was foggy through those first few months back at work, I had colleagues who were aware of my loss and seemed to always do and say the right thing.

My guess is that we need to work in order to enjoy rest, and we need work to connect us to a bigger outcome. For some, work may be their vocation. For others, it may mean working around our homes or volunteering to make a difference for someone else. I don't think our need to work stops at a certain age. Work has helped me heal, partly because of relationships created from work, the sense of accomplishment, and the good feeling of being tired.

I will be glad for a day of rest, and also for the days that were filled with meaningful work.

What kind of work do you enjoy? How has it contributed to your satisfaction? How can you be a great work partner to someone who may need healing?

Day 304: Home

When I came home from work tonight, I felt a sense of contentment as I entered the house. Over the past ten months, I have found so much solace in my home. I'm so thankful that my house and yard don't feel like a foreign place. Rather, being here feels like… well, home.

It feels like where I can be myself. Where I can find joy. Where I see God's handiwork. Those first few weeks were not easy at home, but even then, I found a sense of connectedness with my Creator and my lifelong love. Although I sometimes feel overwhelmed at the work of being a single woman, I still love the sweetness of this spot I call Liesveld Lottage.

I'm now able to look out to the east in my back yard and see a holy spot where Curt once laid. And that doesn't really make me sad. The new design of the area brings me joy and I love the peaceful nature of that sacred ground.

Part of my healing has come from being in my house and yard. I'm sure that wouldn't be true for everyone. I have read about other widows who moved as soon as they could after losing a spouse. But I will take the precious memories of my home and try to create new ones. Today, as I look at the forsythia, daffodils, crocus, scillia, hyacinth, and plum thicket blooming, I see spring and I see renewal.

I'm grateful I was healed, in part, just by being at home.

> *Where is your place of healing and joy? Is your home that balm you need? If not, what can you do to make it that way?*

March 23

Day 305: Fuel

Words make a difference. As I think about things that have helped me heal, people's words may be in the top five. I've always known there was power in affirmation and encouragement, but never as much as I do now.

Many days, when someone would just reach out and ask, "How are you doing?" it was enough to give me permission to get things off my chest. Other days, hearing the word "Curt" spoken by others made me feel like I wasn't the only person who wanted to talk about the amazing man I lost. If I could ask one thing of people, it's please do not quit mentioning Curt. I hate it when I am the only one to bring up his name in conversations.

Words such as, "I still see and love the person you always were." have also helped immensely. When people say things that show that, though I'm vulnerable, they still think of me as valuable, they give me the ultimate emotional fuel. Today, the person I was teaching with told me about his fourteen-year-old daughter's strengths. She has four of the same ones I do. It's highly unusual to have that many in common with another person. "I'd love to meet your daughter," I said. "Do you think we have some things in common?" He said, "Well, I'm not sure, but I do hope she turns out to be like you."

That small, kind comment filled my bucket, and filled up holes in my heart left by grief. If you've shared words with me in any form, thank you so much. You have made my sad heart happier. You have been a difference maker on this road of grief.

> *Who needs to hear words of encouragement and affirmation from you today?*

March 24

Day 306: Unpredicted

As much as I'd like to control and predict things in my life, I now know I can't really control much of anything. When I think about control, I mostly think of not being able to control the terrible and untimely loss of the person I loved most. But tonight, I realized that I also have not controlled or predicted some of the good things that have come my way.

For instance, I spent tonight with my great friends Nancy and Matt. As few as five years ago, I couldn't have predicted I'd be staying at their home in Omaha tonight, or that they would be included on my list of best friends. My work brought us together in an unplanned way and gave me a new relationship that has fed my soul. As much as I have grieved what I couldn't control, I'm also grateful for a friendship I didn't plan that goes so deep and wide.

Control has less luster for me than it used to, and unanticipated joy is shinier than I ever knew.

> **How's your need for control? Are you sure it's all that it's cracked up to be?**

March 25

Day 307: Grandkids

What else has made a difference for me? Well, of course, my grandchildren.

Today, I picked up Norah and brought her to my house. Within a few minutes, she said, "Your house is a lot more funner than mine. You don't make me wear a coat if I don't want to. You let me eat candy when I want. You don't say 'no' to me as much as my mom and dad do."

I smiled and explained that grandparents can say "yes" more because Mom and Dad's job is to make their kids behave. Then I made some comment about being an old person and she said, "Thirty-one isn't that old." Now you know why she gets to do fun things at my house—she thinks I'm thirty-one!

I will always wonder why I wasn't allowed more time to share my precious grandkids with Curt. It's the part that, in some ways, hurts the most. But Norah and Johnny have done so much to help me heal. They greet me with open arms. Johnny still holds my hand when we walk down the sidewalk. Norah notices my latest necklace and still doesn't seem to notice the wrinkles.

Looking into their faces was the hardest thing I did for many weeks, knowing how much they would miss Curt. Over time, those faces have brought me more joy than sadness. I'm beyond grateful that they are here for me and that they have a similar love affair with me yet—much like their Poppo did.

> *Hug your grandkids today. Embrace your role as spoiler.*
> *Look into their faces and absorb their healing love and affection.*

March 26

Day 308: Paradox

By now you know I am a lover of the seasons. Going through each of the seasons during this year of grief has been so very hard, but I realized today, I have a little more energy as I think about the beginning of spring. I'm starting to realize that the things that gave me the deepest feelings of grief can also give me the greatest healing.

Easter is tomorrow, so I'm thinking about rebirth. I love the hastening of spring to new life, and this year, new life means more than it ever has before. I believe Curt has a new life—a new amazing, bigger-than-words-can-describe life. And I believe I have a new life. Not one I asked for, but, as some writers suggest, a new opportunity to recreate life in the midst of resistance.

Tomorrow, I will face my first Easter without Curt and I will certainly shed tears and feel deep sadness. I will experience the grief of Easter and likely also its joy. A paradox. Curt liked the idea of a paradox, and now, I think I understand why.

Grief and gratitude. Pain and healing—all happening in the same things and sometimes at the same time.

> *What paradoxes do you experience in your life?*
> *Are the things that hurt you sometimes the things that heal you?*
> *Can you experience something that brings you both pain and joy?*

March 27

Day 309: Family

Easter morning came with memories that brought tears, but I was determined to make Easter a day of resurrected hope for the family.

My family came over, and we had a wonderful time together. Commitment to family takes work and priority, but the payoff is huge. I often wonder if the idea of "me time" is just an excuse to retreat and be a bit selfish. Everyone needs some down time, but time alone can be overrated, at least for me. Being with my loving and kind family brought healing and joy. Family—not just my immediate family, but extended family, including Curt's family—has been one of my best healers.

If I could be so bold as to say this to young people in particular, don't forget that your family is what will matter most one day. Keep investing. Keep showing up. Keep contributing. We all need our families, and some of us know it today more than ever.

Meagan took beautiful pictures as we celebrated the Resurrection today. I hope you enjoy her photography. It brings me much joy.

What is your favorite holiday to spend with family?
Who takes the pictures of your family gatherings? Have you
thanked them for capturing the memories?

Easter with the Kats side of the family

March 28

Day 310: Books

What else has helped me heal? I'd say books have helped me more than I would have thought. I'm not a voracious reader, but soon after Curt's death, I found it hard to know what to do when I was alone. TV seemed much too trivial or too depressing. I didn't have the physical energy to work around the house. I also didn't have the inertia to initiate with others. But I could read.

Many people gave me books, and others who had gone through grief recommended books, so I ended up with a stack by my chair. Books like *A Grief Disguised, Lessons on Grief, Jesus Calling, Second Firsts, Widows Wear Stilettos, A Grief Observed*, the Bible, and others I can't remember. I've read only one book that wasn't about grief in the past ten months. Reading seemed to calm me down.

A few books and articles I started and quickly filed under "not helpful," but most were difference-makers for me. *Second Firsts* was one of my favorites. Author Christina Rasmussen writes, "I believe that grief can be used as a catalyst for rapid transformation and personal growth." She talks about letting go of the vision of her first life and surrendering to a new dream. Her grief kept telling her that her new dream would never be good enough to match the first dream. But she, too, searched for the gratitude and realized "we need to listen to life's whispers so that we can absolutely realize that second chapter and second firsts can be happier, dreamier and so passionate."

I'm not there with her yet, but I like the way she pulls me into the future with some positivity. Books seemed to help me process, sometimes helped me emote, and almost always gave me hope and help. In a few months, I plan to put all my grief books away. I want to be done with them. I am a bit tired of reading about grief now. I have a novel recommended by a neighbor next on my list. Maybe that's a good sign.

> **What are you reading now? Is there a book that has changed your life?**

March 29

Day 311: The TV

My TV is broken, so last night, I ran out the door at 6:30 p.m. to buy a new one. I took the measurements for the spot it needed to fit, but other than that, I had no inkling of what I wanted or needed.

I went into my favorite big box store and ran right into my nephew-in-law, who works there and is one smart cookie. He is one of those in-laws that you love having in your family. He's the nicest guy and fits so easily into our crazy tribe. He could tell I didn't want to linger on figuring out the perfect TV, so in about ten minutes, I had paid for the TV, had it in the car, and was heading home.

Curt would have loved looking at all the options and taken the purchase a lot more seriously than I did. And he would have been able to figure out (with a little of my help), how to put it on the wall mount. I had moments of frustration and anger that I had to do this job by myself.

After letting John know I got a new TV, (I knew he'd find that as exciting as his dad would have.) he showed up with the family. He and Meagan got it set up for me. When the wall mount installation required more time than they had, he even arranged for his good friend Jamie to come help him fix it in a few days.

I'm glad I've got my TV back. It's almost embarrassing to admit, but having a TV has made it easier to be alone at night. I need some company, and it provides it in an artificial way.

There are many things I do now that I wouldn't have done before. There are things I need help with, but I try to wait until I am 100 percent sure I can't do it by myself before I ask. I'm so grateful for help. Around number four on my list of what helped me heal is people who helped me in practical ways. So many times, that help was all I needed to feel like I could make it through this overwhelming time. If you've helped me in any way, thank you. Your labor was a sedative for me, or maybe even an upper.

> *Who has helped you with something lately? Did you let them know how much you appreciated that help? How can you pay it forward?*

March 30

Day 312: Kindness

I've learned that many things in life are not worth taking as seriously as I used to, and that some things in life should be taken more seriously. For instance, being right about everything is a joke. I am pretty sure Curt knew that. He didn't have to say things out loud or correct others or be sure the people he was with knew he was uber smart.

The only time I saw him get really angry in the last couple years was when he was with a group of people, and someone made a sweeping statement that was politically charged. Of course, he didn't say anything, but when we got in the car later he said, "I can't believe they think they have to say those things out loud, knowing that there are people in the room who don't agree with them. That's just rude." He didn't have much patience for public criticism, know-it-alls, or people who needed to correct everyone on any minute point. It wore him out.

Today, as I was thinking about what healed me, I realized that as simplistic as it sounds, kindness healed me. Smiles. Greetings. Tender words. Please and thank you. How are you? I did appreciate those things before, but I see now how they add powerful emotional energy to my day rather than deplete it.

People say grief changes you. I don't know that it changed my basic personality or strengths and weaknesses, but it has made me more aware. And I hope that, in the end, that awareness makes a difference for someone else.

> *Can you take more seriously the effort to be kind, or at least try to lift the spirits of others? Can you take less seriously the need to be right? Or be in control? Or be inappropriately influential?*

March 31

Day 313: The Walkers

I spent last night with three of my very precious friends. Like we often do, we hung out over a glass or two of wine and caught up on important things, like the latest yard renovation, the next trip, the cuteness of a grandchild, or the pain of grief.

I don't know how people get through grief without friends. This group of friends is the walkers I've mentioned before and includes two women who have also lost husbands, so they not only care deeply because of our friendship, but also because they have been there.

Here's what I have learned about friends: They don't judge you when you aren't yourself. They show up when you need them—even when you text them at the last minute. They are generous; they find little things that brighten your day. They are encouragers; they say things that help you get up the next morning, even though you hate rising all alone. They are loyal; they show up day after day, year after year, and decade after decade. For me, these four women represent Jesus in the flesh.

We were all initially linked because Curt was their pastor. Today, I am aware of how these four committed, early-rising, honest-talking women helped me heal. And I am grateful.

> *Who is in your tribe of friends? Do they know you love them? Could you just tell them today?*

The walkers: Linda, Deb, Rosanne, Jane, and Rita

April 1

Day 314: Ask Again

I have been working hard to find the future, find the good, find the gratitude, find some joy, but something happened yesterday that blocked my capacity to focus on the good.

I think it was one simple sentence someone said to me. Nothing mean. Nothing stupid. Nothing directly judgmental. Even though I tell myself I am grieving in the way that's right for me, occasionally when people say something like, "I could never do what you're doing." it feels like a commentary on what I've done—whatever the heck that is.

I think most people don't know the extent of my grief, largely because I don't often show it in public, even with close friends and family. Sadly, I don't even share it with my own children, in an effort to protect them, especially with grandchildren's ears and eyes always observing. Because I fight to find the good, it may come off as "doing well." I save my despair for my alone time, in my house, when I have no limitations or expectations on how I express myself. Those times are private and not pretty. Most folks would be sickened to watch me at times.

Yesterday I saw a friend at a restaurant, and she asked, "How are you doing?" I answered generically. Then she asked again, and I told her, "As best as I can be." I realize that after almost eleven months, the way people ask about my grief has changed. In some ways, I need people to ask how I'm doing now more than ever. Earlier on, I had no idea how I was doing.

Now I can occasionally voice it, or emote it. So, please don't judge a book by its cover. Grief often resides in solitary confinement, but sometimes it does need to have another person in the room.

> **Ask. Maybe even ask twice. Take time to ask how someone is doing and really listen to their answer, spoken and unspoken.**

April 2

Day 315: Waiting Room

As the months turn into weeks anticipating the anniversary of Curt's death, I want to be prepared emotionally, physically, and spiritually for that time. I've tried to take some control of my life by anticipating and planning for significant dates—the firsts, the holidays, the birthdays, the anniversary. I've tried to be proactive in making distinct plans so those firsts will be less painful. Even so, many times I was taken by surprise by the traumatic experience of facing significant occasions alone. These next few weeks I will plan how to make the anniversary day/week/month something more than a terrible memory.

When Curt died, I was in such shock and despair that I remember so little about celebrating his life. I have some pretty good memories of the funeral and the night friends and family gathered to share memories, but not much else. I want to enter into this time of anticipation with some ideas about how to honor Curt. I want to dedicate the newly named Light Garden. I want to thank people for what they've done for me. I want to celebrate what I can at this first anniversary. And while I still cannot understand the why (and probably never will), I want to honor life—both his and mine and that of everyone I love.

I know this year has been full of firsts—baby steps on the way to rediscovering a new life. I'm moving out of the waiting room and into the light. The light of life.

> *Do you feel like you're in a waiting room during this season of life? What can move you toward life and light?*

The Light at night

Day 316: Words and Touch

Only our immediate family was at the service at the cemetery. As with so much that happened during those first days, it's a bit vague to me. I do remember feeling bold about letting every family member know Curt would want nothing more than for each of them to have a living and personal relationship with God. I told them I didn't want his funeral to be a time when people were guilted into belief, but that I wasn't above doing that with our families. Guilt or love, one or the other, I implored them to consider their personal faith.

Then I asked each family to do something for me. I said that the Liesvelds are great huggers and the Kats are good communicators. I urged the Liesvelds to consider communicating more often. Pick up the phone. Talk. Express themselves. And you know what? They have all done that beautifully and with ease this year. And the Kats side—I asked them to consider hugging more, and we do that better now. Even though communicating affection can sometimes be flippant, like a quick "Love you" at the end of every phone call, I will take hearing precious words any day of the week. And hugs may feel like an obligation, but I'll still take that touch any day. I needed touch today and my son touched me lovingly during church as I was crying, and hugged me in front of his friends tonight at the end of the evening.

I know both words and touch matter. They have healed me. The kind words. The encouraging words. The love yous. The touch on my hand. The side hug. The front hug. The lingering hug. They are all good. Touch and words work like medicine to a hurting heart. They have healed me, and I still covet the great communication and loving touch.

> *How do you show affection? Do you hug? Do you say,*
> *"I love you"? Do you write beautiful notes? Words or touch—you may*
> *be better at one, but practice doing both.*

Day 317: Risks

Curt and I took many risks during our adult life. They weren't all big risks, but they were, at some level, a less-than-typical approach to life.

For starters, we decided to get married at a relatively young age. We tied the knot after our sophomore year in college. The risks were financial, the ability to maintain focus on our education, and immaturity. Those are probably not risks we would want our kids to take, but, clearly, that one worked out. Then we moved to Michigan for Curt to start seminary. This may not have been a huge risk, but I cried lots of tears as we drove our U-Haul down I-80, believing I'd never really be back home again.

Going into the ministry was a big risk for a young couple. It certainly wouldn't be financially rewarding. We wouldn't live private lives, or have an eight-to-five work day. We most likely wouldn't live in the same spot all our lives. Above all, it meant we often felt the weight of the world on our shoulders, but that risk worked out well for twenty-three years.

Then Curt decided to go back to school for yet another degree. We decided it was okay to risk leaving the profession he'd gone on to graduate school for. And a pension. And the reputation he'd built. We pulled up stakes and took our five- and eight-year-old to a new city where we needed to buy a house with no cash and would depend primarily on me for our income again.

Then there was the risk of me taking a job with a company I'd never heard of instead of holding out for a teaching job that seemed a bit more secure. Thirteen years later, Curt took the risk of leaving his first love, pastoral ministry, without knowing what he would be doing after he resigned. But we did it. And in a short time, he had a new role at this company we now know as Gallup. Those risks made quite a difference for us for sure.

Then we took the risk of leaving our comfortable home on 74th Street and buying a lot where we'd build a home—and take on a new mortgage.

Lots of risks. Big ones and some small ones—but it always seemed to make sense. At times, Curt was the instigator. At times, I was, but the outcomes were the same. We trusted that things would be okay. We trusted that God would lead us. And we trusted that our love would see us through. And it did.

I still ask myself as I get older, "What risk is next for me?"

What risks have you taken? What might you need to risk to make life even fuller? How risk-aversive are you? How much trust do you have that things will work out for the best because someone else is ultimately in control?

Rosanne and Curt, 1971

Day 318: Faces

Grief has so many faces. Early on, it had a face of fear. I wasn't even sure what I was afraid of. I just knew I was afraid of what I'd see or hear or find. Then there was the face of shock and the face of dread. The face of utter defeat and the face of exhaustion. Many of the feelings were more about me than about my lost relationship with Curt. Grief can make one selfish.

As time has gone on, some of the feelings that were more about me have settled down. On a day like today, I simply miss Curt. I miss our long talks. I miss him sitting in a chair beside me. I miss being held and touched. I miss him in our bed. I miss him taking pictures. I miss his interest in anything sports. I miss his inclusive, grace-laden faith. I miss a dinner partner. I miss a coffee partner. I miss his smile. I miss his kind words about me. I miss going on trips together. I miss staying home together.

I miss him.

Though the waves of grief have lessened in intensity, they still come, and tonight, the face of grief is Curt's face. I will face his strong, distinct, loving face and acknowledge the loss. Then I will work at honoring my own face, my being, and my life that still has meaning.

Whose face is on your mind today? Perhaps there's a reason a certain face is front and center in your thoughts. What do you see? Why is that face so special?

April 6

Day 319: Milestone

Last month marked thirty years since I came to Lincoln looking for a house and a job. Curt wanted to go back to school and was considering a career change. So, we made the decision, after ten years of ministry in Mitchell, to return to our home area so he could go to school, and I could go back to full-time work.

I remember so well sitting at my sister's house in Lincoln reading the want ads to find a job—any job—because we needed my income to survive. I answered an ad for a company that became my work home for the next three decades.

I remember how awesome it was to have my sister and her husband help us find a house, find friends, and do some life reentry. The first week of June, it will be thirty years since we moved to Lincoln, I started at Gallup, Curt started his second graduate degree, and we bought a home for the first time. Those memories are so sweet, and I wish I could celebrate them with Curt.

I miss celebrating with him. We loved to talk about those days and we would likely have figured out how to celebrate thirty years of work at Gallup. I don't have my partner to enjoy this milestone with, so it's a bit anticlimactic.

Everyone thinks I was the person who loved to celebrate, but Curt loved marking important occasions too. I am still so grateful we made that move—crazy as it seemed at the time. The work I've done has been a highlight of my life, and being close to family, well, nothing trumps that. Plus, I love being a Husker.

What milestones should you celebrate? How does celebrating make you and others better people? What's keeping you from throwing a party?

Day 320: The Shower

I often have flashbacks to the first couple weeks following Curt's death. They seem to come to me at odd times. I usually have no idea what instigates them.

Today, I took a shower and had a very difficult memory. I had been working in the yard the morning of Curt's death; I was dirty when I was at the heart hospital. I had mud on my clothes. My pruners were in my back pocket and kept jabbing me as I sat in the waiting room, but I didn't have the presence of mind to take them out of my pocket. But what I remembered today was about the shower. A few hours after returning home, I knew I had to clean myself up, but I was afraid to be alone. I was afraid to go into the bathroom. I asked Meagan if she would come in there with me. As I took a shower, trying to wash the horrid reality away, Meagan and Norah sat on the floor right by the shower door and sang. I don't remember the songs. I just remember there was some sound, and they were physically right next to me. I wonder how many women would ask their daughters-in-law to do that? I could do that because I loved and trusted her. And I needed her.

Tonight, I think back to those individual images from the first few days and almost feel like I need to remember them—hard as it might be. I need to know the depth of the grief, and I need to know the things that I'm grateful for that I could not realize at that time.

> *Who would sit by you on the floor next to the shower and stay with you when you are in the darkest moments of your life? I hope you have someone. And I hope you would ask them so that they know they are special and a part of the healing—even on the worst day of your life.*

Day 321: Room Cleaning

Today I went to the funeral of an amazing woman who made ninety-four look pretty darn good. Shirley Clifton was remembered as having a life well-lived and well-loved. The funeral was at the same church where we held Curt's funeral, and many of the same people were at both.

I was doing well until I walked into the fellowship hall. I remembered exactly where I stood as the long, long line of people gave me their condolences and kind words. As I looked over the crowd this afternoon at some of the same amazing people I saw that day, it brought back memories of one of the hardest days of my life.

I drove home with a heavy heart. In part, my sadness was for the Clifton family as they had to say good bye to the family matriarch. But I was also sad for my own loss. I felt like I could reach out and be right there again.

I sought out my grandkids for some solace. I asked if Norah and Johnny wanted to go for ice cream, but they were on "clean your room" duty. I helped them clean their rooms. The rooms were covered with clothes, papers, toys, and books. Among their things were many mementoes of their Poppo. Pictures of him. The *Paired Up* book Curt wrote. The cowboy hat he got for Johnny. The snow globes from trips we took to Chicago, the Badlands, and Colorado. The Husker trivia game Curt bought them so he could ensure another Husker-crazed generation. The dress he brought from Singapore. And the Bible we gave Johnny for his baptism.

I'm glad those grandkids still live in rooms that speak so loudly of their Poppo. Grief over my memories of Curt's funeral. Gratitude over treasures in grandkids' rooms.

What do the items in your bedroom tell about your life story?
What items do you have from a favorite grandpa or grandma?

Day 322: Mulch

God blessed me in an unexpected way today.

When we built this house, I read several books on design and placement of a house on a lot. One of the books said, "No matter what your view, if it isn't your property, don't consider that it will ever be your view in the future." So, when I drew our first rough draft of this house, I drew a neighboring house to the west. It took thirteen years for someone to actually buy that lot and build on it. The buyers were two architects who knew how to position the house to get maximum use of the lot.

When I saw the first stakes go up, I started praying that I would be a good neighbor. I told Curt that if I prayed for our new neighbors, maybe someday they would take care of me when I was an old lady.

Fast forward. Today I had one hundred bags of mulch delivered. I started early with the job of carrying bags, opening those tight seals, and spreading the mulch. By noon, my back and shoulder were complaining, so I took a lunch break. I was working on the west side of the house when my new neighbor Michael came out and asked if I could use their three sons to help me move the mulch. He said they were bored over at the new house and he had run out of things to have them do. "It would be a win-win for both of us," he said. Tears welled up in the corners of my eyes.

Just like that, they carried and placed the bags throughout my yard, so I could open and spread the mulch without dragging another fifty bags around. I wish I could tell Curt how my prayers were answered—I am that old lady who needed help and got it today. When I prayed for those neighbors a year ago, I didn't know I would be handling yard work as a widow. Forty-six bags of mulch to go—but I know now I can do it.

Which neighbors should you be praying for? Which neighbors should you be helping? How can you be a good neighbor today?

April 10

Day 323: Influence

My life was changed when I became Curt's wife. More and more I realize how my attitudes have been shaped by Curt's life philosophy, and even more strongly by his behavior as he lived out his beliefs.

One thing I learned from him is that it is better to be for something than against something. He felt that one influences more by being positively in favor of something, rather than negatively attacking the things, person, or idea that may be contrary, or the enemy. For example, someone might stand for something very worthwhile, perhaps even extremely other-focused, yet they can't get their point across because they prefer to attack the people or ideas on the other side. The negative attack is always louder than the worthiness of their cause.

As I watch all of the political, spiritual, and personal discourse, I often think about how Curt would come home and say things like, "It's hard to support their good cause because they are more in love with finding an enemy to be angry with." Today I think about people like Kathy Campbell, our retiring state legislator, who figured out how to do what was right for a state, and seemed to win respect and admiration while still being respectful of others. People like Kathy are the authentic influencers. These are the people who promote the good and turn their back on the bad. They are the people Curt admired and wanted to be more like.

I'm so grateful Curt's influence rubbed off on me. In some ways, I think I am more impacted by Curt's life thinking and behavior now than when he was alive. That's sad in some ways, but it is a small bit of gratitude in my life today.

> *How about you? What are you for? How can you maximize that and minimize being against things? I know it's possible. I've seen it done, and it is brilliant.*

Day 324: Giving Back

Anne has been a great example of someone who gives back to the community. She works at the local community college during the week, but on Saturdays, she very often volunteers at a community center for low-income people. Saturday night, she, among others, was recognized for giving of her time and her talent. She also often uses her breaks to help with Vacation Bible School or to do other volunteer work.

Curt would be so proud of her. She has an awareness of others' needs that most of us don't have. I found myself missing Curt as I was thinking of her yesterday. Parents never tire of hearing of their children's successes. Even more, they never tire of hearing how their children make a difference.

Life is not always easy for many people, and I realize that now more than ever. But even when life is hard, I've found that the times I've given back during this grief, I have come away healed a bit. My days as a mentor to a high school student didn't end with my loss. Even though it was so hard to get myself to go and do my volunteer work, I always felt like my life still had meaning afterwards.

Healing comes in the form of giving back. I need to do more, and I'm starting to have more desire and energy and will to give back.

How do you give back? Can life be as much about giving back as pleasure? Or maybe giving back and pleasure are the same thing.

Rosanne and Anne

April 12

Day 325: The Arbor

The tulips at my house are in their full glory. These are many of the tulips my family helped plant last fall. They look particularly beautiful in the new Light Garden.

I've been so attracted to that area of the yard, and especially the birch arbor that was designed and built by some very talented people. It is almost magnetic for me, and I find myself looking longingly at it. Yesterday I think I realized why; it feels so symbolic of an entry. It reminds me of a doorway to somewhere. And then I knew—it seems like Curt's doorway to heaven. The physical structure feels like a picture of entering into something special. That doorway may be symbolic for me too. It's a doorway into an uninvited, unwelcomed but new life—a life I would rather not have had but will work at making significant.

As I continue to look at the birch arbor, I will continue to think of Curt's doorway to paradise, and maybe even the doorway to my second chapter. Symbols can be powerful reminders of truth.

What's your gateway? Where does it lead you?

The arbor in the Light Garden

April 13

Day 326: Golf Lessons

Today when I was driving, listening to my son on his radio show, he read a Facebook post written by a college friend. The friend happens to be Michael Greller, the caddy for professional golfer Jordan Spieth. Now I'm less interested in golf than about any other sport, (probably because Curt loathed it) but I do follow Jordan and his caddy. Maybe because John knew Michael in college, or maybe I have a soft spot for Michael because he was a fifth-grade teacher before becoming Jordan's caddy.

The post John read contained Michael's thoughts after Jordan's loss in the Masters, after going into the final round with a big lead. He talked about hating to lose; then he talked about putting loss in perspective. He said loss is a part of life and will happen again. "A wise coach reminded me recently, winning shows your character and losing shows ALL of your character," Michael wrote. "Jordan continues to model grace and humility through wins and especially losses. The student continues to teach the teacher, and now millions of others as he did at Erin Hills. Jordan Spieth is the same genuine, grounded, and humble person he was five years ago, in victory or defeat."

Loss is loss. I lost this year too, and I'm choosing grace, humility, and positivity. And yes, loss does show ALL your character. I'm not the model that Jordan and Michael are, but I will believe that life will go on and should be lived with anticipation, instead of anger and fear. Who would have thought golf would help heal me today? Wow.

What losses have you experienced? How have you handled them? What's your strategy for better handling loss?

Day 327: Tokens

I've seen lists of dos and don'ts for helping a grieving person, and most of the time, I find them pretty accurate. But the truth is, each person in grief needs different things.

One of the things that helped me heal was tokens of affection from family and friends. It feels weird to say, but gifts often made me feel loved and special. I remember the floral arrangement on our anniversary. I remember the bracelets that were so personal and meaningful. I remember a heart-shaped stone that was given to me very soon after Curt died and is outside in my yard. I remember a magnetic board to hold notes and sweet thoughts during this difficult time.

I remember many gifts at Christmastime, including a pillow with a cardinal on it (From work, but I still don't know who gave it to me.) and a bottle of perfume left on my counter right after Curt died. It was from someone who wore that perfume, and I had commented on it because I liked it so much.

So as odd as it is to say, things helped in my healing. They are symbolic and felt a little like what Curt would have given to me. So, thank you for the tokens—the gifts, the physical symbols of your love. Everyone has a love language and needs different things. Curt knew my love languages were words and tokens. I knew his well—touch and words.

What's your love language? How can you help someone by individualizing your gifts for them?

Day 328: Realistically Determined

Reality thought I was not spending enough time with it, so yesterday it came for an unwelcome visit.

I had that feeling of deep sadness over not getting to have what couples nearing retirement have. I don't have a big trip planned with Curt. I don't have Saturdays when I get to work outside with Curt. I don't have someone to talk with about the kids and grandkids and how to handle things with them. I don't have his extra income to help pay for the stupid expenses I now have… or for some fun things either, for that matter.

I don't have someone to haul the dang river rock bags out of the car. I don't have someone to sit on the patio with tonight, when the weather is beautiful and I have nothing to do. I don't have Curt here to go on the inaugural boat ride of the spring with me. Heck, I can't even get the boat in the water without him. I don't have my best friend to share a meal with me. I don't have anyone to make plans with for a summer vacation. I don't have someone who will care about my latest success at work. I don't have someone to give me his opinion about the length of my hair. (He did do that the day he died—"No shorter than that.")

I don't have him to program the sprinkler system—which may be the most complicated thing known to womankind. I don't have anyone whom I can watch fish, and who will yell, "Hey, Rosanne, get the camera."

So, it was a long day yesterday. Reality stole more time than I usually let it. I went to bed feeling like I couldn't face the future. Then morning came, and I had a great job to go to. I had an idea-laden friend who wants me to meet her friends for dinner. I have two grandkids joining me in the morning for coffee. I have so many things that cannot be replaced. I'm realistically sad and realistically determined. So today, if you haven't gone through the loss of a spouse, please know how hard it is, and that even after eleven months, this widow is still so raw and hurt and envious of those who have a future I wish I could have. Thanks for listening. Grief still outweighs gratitude on some days despite me giving it a good fight.

> *How do you give the edge to gratitude? Do you fight for gratitude, even when you feel sad? What are you grateful for? Make a list.*

April 16

Day 329: *Thirty Days*

Today is April 16th—one month until the anniversary date of Curt's death. I don't know what the next thirty days will be like. I keep trying to prepare myself and finding time to celebrate his life.

Although I don't celebrate that he died, I can celebrate how he died... and how he lived. The last eleven months sometimes seem to have gone fast, as odd as that might seem. In many ways, it seemed like he was here with me, loving life, just yesterday.

In other ways, this year has been an eternity—except this eternity felt like hell. All those firsts. People think that firsts are big observable days. No, they are ordinary firsts, like the first time I drove a car as a widow. The first time I walked into a grocery store. The first time I went to Johnny's game by myself. The first time I had to use a tool from his workbench. The first time I played the piano. The first time I walked to the east side of our yard. And on and on and on.

Soon there will be many less firsts, though in some ways, I'll have them the rest of my life. Today, I had a first. I deadheaded some of the early blooming flowers in the Light Garden, and I sat on the boulder under the arbor and looked at the beauty around me. I felt somber, but not utterly sad.

So, walk with me for another thirty days, and I will be done posting my grief and gratitude. And please pray for me as I go through the next thirty days and prepare for a season of reasonable grief and profound gratitude for what was.

> *What do you have coming up in the next thirty days? How will you make the next month one of impact, joy, and gratitude?*

Day 330: Learn

These are the things I have learned to do since Curt died. Change the ink in the printer. Jumpstart the car. Do the taxes. Get the boats out. Take out the garbage each Sunday. Find and carry bags of river rocks for the grandkids to throw in the pond. Take the car to get oil changed. Entertain groups by myself. Work the TV remotes. (Yes, this one is true.) Fix a table with wobbly legs. Turn on the underground sprinklers. Feed the birds. Clean off the patio.

Here are things I want to learn to do: Use Curt's camera. Use the grill. Paint easy things like the garden benches. (I hate painting, but I probably need to learn.) Enlarge and print Curt's photos off the computer. Launch the kayak in the pond by myself. And many more.

Some of what I've learned to do may seem minor, but I'm working to find some gratitude in growth over these past eleven months. What I am most grateful for is that I have the stamina and determination to still learn and grow, even though it wasn't my idea. Mostly, I've learned about life and how to live it with a nod toward gratitude, and that trumps everything else. Learning to do things is good. Learning to live is best.

What are you learning to do? What can you do now that you didn't know how to do last year? What things aren't worth your time? What do you need to learn to do? How can you learn more about how to live?

Day 331: Deep Conversations

Sometimes I miss the depth of conversation I had with Curt. He always had time to talk about big things with me. We spent a lot of time talking about the concept of strengths. He sometimes liked to share theological concepts with me that I had not thought of before. Sometimes he just liked talking about us. He'd analyze why I did something, or felt something, and then think about how that made sense of us as a couple.

He sometimes talked to me about things people said or did that bothered him. He got tired of negativity, and hated when people made assumptions, or made another person feel guilty because they didn't do or see things the same way. He particularly didn't like veiled opinionated statements—the ones where someone would say what they never do or always do in a way that makes other people feel slightly guilty. He was sensitive to how people made others feel when they spoke.

I miss those big conversations, but I'm grateful for how his words still ring in my ears advising me when it's sometimes best to just not say anything. Or to say something positive, accepting, or not judgmental. Sometimes I think, "What would Curt say... or not say?" He sits on my shoulder and whispers in my ear. I can't be him, but I can follow his example. I don't think that will ever go away.

Because of Curt, I'm more aware of the impact of important topics and important words. I hope that out of grief comes growth. Even in my raw, immature state, I hope that every day.

Do you take time for deep conversations? Who do you go to for important talks? What topics are so important that they demand your attention?

Curt and Rosanne

April 19

Day 332: Spokes

I never anticipated how hard it would be to grieve Curt myself while watching my children with their own grief. I feel so badly about how little help I've been to them.

Today on a plane, the mom of a six-month-old had her hands full. The baby was unhappy during most of the two-hour flight. Finally, the flight attendant picked up the baby and walked up and down the aisle with him. Instantly, that little six-month-old was happy and smiling. That mom had to rely on an unknown flight attendant to give her a break and soothe the crying. It made me think about how I've had to rely on other people to help my own kids through this. Part of me hates that.

As Mom, you always want to take care of your kids' aches and pain. Even if I could help my adult children with their grief, there's rarely a time when one of the grandkids isn't around, when we can talk and cry freely without impacting those young hearts too much. So, I feel utterly useless. I wish I could talk to them more about our feelings, but it's hard to find the time or the energy.

Last night, some of my friends gave me a bracelet made from the spokes of a bike. The spoke is symbolic. The artist views the spoke as representing people working together. On a bike, the spokes all work together, yet the spoke nearest the ground bears almost no load because the load pressure is distributed among the top and side spokes. Friends and family take the pressure off when we are on the bottom. We are supported by the spokes around us. I've had to rely on human spokes to support my kids.

I'm quite sure I don't know all the support they've been given in prayers, conversations, and kindnesses, but thank you—thank you for being there for my kids and grandkids. They are my world, and you have made my world better by caring for them.

> *Who needs you to be their grandparent? Or aunt? Or uncle? Can you fill the gap for someone? Who are the spokes who have taken some of the load when you've been at the bottom?*

April 20

Day 333: Last Words

I had no real preparation for this journey of grief. Today is the anniversary of my dad's death. I'm horrible with dates, but I think it was about twenty years ago. His death was not expected either. After being in the hospital for about ten days, he died from complications of fibrosis of the lungs and pneumonia. Although we never expected he would die, we had watched him struggle to breathe for many days, and in the end, his death was almost welcomed, albeit so sad.

I was alone with my dad right before they put him on a respirator, and he told me two things. First, through gasps of air he said, "I'm not afraid to die, but I would rather not suffer." Then, tenderly and unselfishly he said, "I don't know what your mom will do if I die." I assured him we would take care of her, and we did. Almost every day for the next few years, mom saw one of her kids, and she did amazingly well.

All this to say, I wonder how my last year would have been different if I had heard Curt's last words of instruction. Or wishes. Or devotion. I'm glad he didn't have to face saying those things to me. His last words to me were not significant. "Yeah. I will pick up the clippings when I finish," he said before starting up John's lawnmower again. He looked happy.

When I saw his lifeless body just a few minutes later, you could tell he had only one more round of picking up the clippings to go. The bag laid beside him. No dramatic life and death comments preceded his death, just our normal routine. Him doing a good thing that needed to be done: me expressing my appreciation. I'm okay with that. I'm glad the last thing I said to him were words of appreciation. I'm glad he didn't have to see my face knowing he was dying and feel the guilt of leaving me alone. I'm glad he was happy. I'm glad he didn't have to say a hard goodbye. It didn't make it easy on the people left behind in shock, but it's the way it was.

We don't get to choose if death comes suddenly or slowly. In the end, it isn't about those last few days or minutes with your loved ones that matter anyway. We had multitudes of days full of life and love that are making it possible for me to continue with my new life. For that, I'm grateful.

> *What would you say to the people you love if you knew you had only minutes to live? Can you say those things now instead?*

April 21

Day 334: Just Talk

Last night I couldn't sleep. I'm not sure why. I was tired from working in San Antonio and flying home, but it wasn't like I'd had an overly stimulating evening, which often is the reason for my insomnia.

I think I needed some conversation. I realized I had presented and taught for almost three hours that morning, yet I'd had very little real conversation with anyone the rest of the day. I don't think of myself as negative about texting, but sometimes I just want to hear a voice and respond in real time to another human being, or at least have a real reciprocal conversation. I know many people don't like talking on the phone, so I hesitate to call anyone like I used to.

So, at the risk of sounding like an old person, I just need to say that sometimes it's nice to talk to people instead of reading a text. The efficient part of me finds texting helpful for transactional purposes, but my emotional part prefers a human voice for transformational purposes. I'm grateful for both efficiency and for depth in communication. Mostly I'm grateful for people who communicate in any form. They fill a lonely void with their words.

Today, try a phone call instead of a text. Hear a voice.
Use your voice. Just talk.

April 22

Day 335: And

It's hard to even imagine a day more beautiful than today. I put on my playlist of easy listening music and spent some time outside.

And sadness slapped me in the face.

This is the kind of day I normally would feel like I had the world by the tail. Now, I inch toward that feeling without having full consciousness of my new life. Then— bam! I descend quickly into reality. I believe the only way to avoid that awful smack of reality is to create new reality that has a new kind of unique joy.

Curt loved the concept of the genius of the *and*. I'm trying to embrace that concept by believing and trusting that I can celebrate the joy I had for the past forty-four years with the love of my life, and still anticipate some unplanned and God-ordained joy into the future.

That's it for today. The genius of the *and*. Can you have joy both before *and* after grief? I will do my best to live my life with gratitude so that I am drawn toward what can be.

> **Where do you need to embrace the and *in your life?***
> **Think about it. It might be just what you need to embrace true joy.**

April 23

Day 336: Beauty

Last night was a great night. (Did I just say "great"?) I had some friends over in this perfect weather to see some copper artwork from a new friend I met at a lawn and leisure show. He had his own art show right on my patio, which was a first. This artwork was quite beautiful, and the conversation, wine, and beauty of the evening made me feel happy. At times, one of my friends would wander over to the Light Garden and spend some time there.

Curt knew me well. He knew I loved beauty of many kinds. He would say aesthetics were one of my core values. And you know what? He liked that. He never made me feel bothersome when I wanted to go see a renowned botanical garden. He was never surprised when I found some artwork that I loved for the house. He wasn't cranky (well, not most of the time) when I wanted something adjusted here or there, or tweaked for maximum artistic and aesthetic presentation.

He told me once that my love of visual beauty may be the best representation of my Significance theme and my Belief theme blended. Curt knew I felt closer to God amid beauty. He also knew that I loved beauty most when I could share it with my friends and family, so he encouraged it in me. Better yet, he celebrated beauty in his own way too. He took pictures of beautiful tablescapes or my flowers or just the natural beauty surrounding him.

I was very blessed to have a husband who enjoyed what I enjoyed in terms of beauty. I think it filled both our souls. I know that without beauty, my world would be even more empty than it often feels now. I will take beauty for what it offers me yet and be grateful.

> *What is beautiful to you? What causes that reaction of "wow"? What do you see with your eyes and heart that brings you close to your Creator?*

April 24

Day 337: Perfect Rhythm

Seldom a week goes by that I don't hear from someone whom Curt touched with his teaching or coaching at Gallup. Today, I was on the GallupStrengthsCenter.com site and, for the first time, looked at some of the responses to the blog I wrote recently.

One of the people who responded was Mary Sue, a certified strengths coach. I've never met her, but wish I knew her after reading her very thoughtful comment. The last paragraph said this: "I was among those lucky to have been taught by Curt, and it was clear that his love and respect for you knew no bounds. Through the wisdom you have shared in your post, I and others can see the wisdom and genius that is within you. May doors open for you to share this richness even more broadly with a world that needs it."

I've found healing in the words of people I know—but also from those I know only through Curt. I needed that today. It's raining lightly—the kind of weather that brings out the strongest feelings associated with my love for Curt. You'd think it would be a bright shining day like the day he died, but no. We both loved watching it rain and just a few days before he died, we had a very romantic evening watching the rain come down with such a perfect rhythm.

I'm a little achy today for my former life. Mary Sue's words gave me a bit of a lift. She honored the past and moved me into the future. So, thanks to those of you who don't know me personally, but have made the effort to comfort me with your words. Your long-distance care has up-close impact. Thank you.

> *Have you read something online that encouraged or inspired you? When you read a blog that impacts you for good, take time to leave a positive comment.*

April 25

Day 338: Journals

For years, I've kept two journals. One is a more formal gardening journal where I record such things as the weather, activities in the garden, maintenance, wildlife sightings, and notes. I have gardening journals going back thirteen years. On the blank back page, I often summarize the week and depart from the theme of horticulture.

The other notebook is less impressive. I've mentioned before that I scribble in it every few days, depending on if I'm around or have anything to notate. It's very practical, listing things like where I found a good buy on something, what I accomplished that day, and sometimes general reflections on how I'm feeling about life. I often go to these notebooks and look back at the year before. I read them month by month. Curt always said it was my Futuristic strength that made me want to look backwards so I could create or anticipate the future.

It's been hard to read the entries I made last April and May. I found myself physically shuddering as I peeked at the last entry before Curt's death, but I did it. There are no entries for a long time after May 16th. Then the entries are heartbreaking, even for me to read. On May 26th, I wrote simply, "Unreal. I loved him so much." It also hurts to read the naïve writing I did all those days leading up to May 16th. On May 4th, I wrote, "I'm feeling content." On April 24th, "Praying for God's grace and for me to put things in perspective." Wow.

The good part is, everything I wrote during those last days was quite positive. As I realized how much I've documented in these notebooks over the years, it's not all that surprising that I've documented my grief and gratitude on Facebook. I have a need to write and document and reflect.

Soon I will be done with this documenting, but I know I will continue keeping notes in other ways. I've filled out my gardening journal each week since March 18th this spring. That's progress.

What do you document? What is important for you to put into writing? What does your diary say about you?

April 26

Day 339: Unplanned

Many people offer advice on life after they've had a close call or lost someone near to them. Much of this advice is about living life to the fullest, taking everything in. Seeing things. Doing things. Experiencing things. Although I wouldn't argue with much of that philosophy, I think my advice would be different. I would say just live ordinarily, knowing that the ordinary things in life are the extraordinary.

My most profoundly satisfying memories are of our ordinary life experiences. Not that I didn't love the big things, but it's the everyday things I miss the most. I'm a planner, an Activator, an initiator, so I tend to move quickly on efforts to turn ordinary things into the extraordinary. I've mentioned before that the word I chose for the previous year was wait—and that's hard for me. After this past year, I would NOT advise people to try to squeeze in every experience, every trip, every game, every social occasion. Do some of that, but don't live for those things. Live for the day and let it unfold, knowing that some rather mundane things give the most satisfaction.

My sweetest memories are things like a spontaneous ride in the convertible on a beautiful night; catching a glimpse of Curt fishing on the pond; Curt running out to get us our favorite ice cream at 10:00 p.m., cuddles in bed on a Saturday morning; picking up Chinese food on the way home from work for al fresco dining; watching the joy on Curt's face when Johnny had a good play on the field; watching him run inside and get his camera to capture that perfect shot; touches and kisses and looks and smiles that were—unplanned.

> *Yes, grab life from each day, but maybe don't always plan what that will look like. Sometimes just wait and trust that great memories can come out of the ordinary. Be ready to embrace unplanned moments of joy.*

Day 340: Distracted

I look forward to the day when I don't get distracted by grief. I am quite sure that grief has made my memory worse. I forget where I put things. I leave things lay when I am supposed to take them with me, and I lose focus when on a task that requires detailed attention. It's like I always have two tracks running in my head (and heart). One track is what I am currently thinking or doing, and one is about… well, anything about Curt and me and my new life. I imagine it's probably somewhat how a person who has an attention disorder feels. Two conversations often go on in my head. Two pictures are often in my mind. I'm often not fully present.

I know I may have experienced some of that anyway, given my age and my tendency to multi-task, but grief has made it worse. Eleven months ago, ninety-nine percent of my thinking and doing was about my grief. I had virtually no other thoughts or actions that weren't directly related to my loss. As days turned into weeks, then months, and soon a year, that percentage has evened out a bit. I have no idea what the percentage is now, but I know I'm still distracted. For brief periods now, I can turn off the grief track and be in the moment, but a quick thought or picture or feeling from the past jumps in to confuse my focus.

I said at the beginning that my grief outweighed gratitude about 99-1, but that over time I hoped at least to even them out to 50-50. One day, maybe gratitude will trump the grief and win. It will knock the heck out of the grief. Grief will be disabled, ineffective, and the loser. I'm not quite there yet, but I've made progress. And today I will try to focus on things without being distracted.

How's your focus? In what areas do you need to be single-minded? What will help you kick the heck out of that negative part in your life?

Day 341: Endorsement

So many people have told me how much Curt talked about me and our family. Curt used to tell me he had people in his classes who wanted to meet me. I'd look at him like, "Why?" And he'd say, "Well, I've talked about you a lot, and they just are interested in meeting you."

In truth, I think they loved Curt and wanted to meet me to see if this guy got lucky enough to marry someone equal to him. I always found his out-loud endorsement of me and our family a pretty sweet thing. Both of us considered each other to be a gift. His most-often written words in cards were, "Of all things I am most proud of, my marriage is at the top of the list."

Ours was not a perfect marriage, but it was a great one. I try to hold that as comfort. I wish we could have written that book on marriage. I know Curt would have had a much better way of saying things than I do. Perhaps, as often happens, there's a message we were meant to share that wasn't planned.

Today, my wish for each of you is a meaningful relationship. Lessen the harsh words and tone of voice. Increase the words of praise. Think twice before expecting your partner to be something he or she is not. And go the extra mile. Show up at things you don't feel like going to. Remember special days, even with a five-dollar grocery store bouquet. Talk together about things that matter. Ask his or her opinion. Work on romance. Make games out of showing affection. And above all, put your relationship before your kids. In the end, your kids will benefit from your model of a great marriage.

Day 342: Examples

I've mentioned before that having role models has always helped me. Even as a little girl there were people in my life whom I admired and looked to as examples: my Sunday School teacher Blanche, my friend Linda, my 4-H leader Jeannette, and my fifth-grade teacher Mrs. Whitmeier. As I got older, the models were often peers, but I still looked up to several older people: my friend Susan, my music teacher Mrs. Oestmann, my piano teacher Alice, and my pastor Reverend Dykhuison. My models were teachers, friends, family members, older acquaintances, and many others

As a teacher, I had very specific role models: Alice, Rick, and Jean. And at Gallup, I've had too many models to mention, including some young people, young enough to be my kids. I've had models even during this tough time of life as well. Last night I had dinner with one of the women I admire, want to study and learn from, and hang out with when possible. I have other friends who have survived huge life challenges. They have experienced horrible losses, but they've modeled how to recreate a life that is confident, contributing, and caring of others. They have joy. I will continue to look for examples to help give me focus and keep me on the road of hope.

What about you? Who is your example? Who has inspired you?
Who helps you make it through—not just in a survival mode, but in a
thriving mode? Have you told them that they are a model?
Take time to do that. It might encourage them and inspire you.

April 30

Day 343: Flowers

It's flower season. I went to get some of the annuals I put in my pots. I have a hard time retaining the control to buy a reasonable amount. I lose common sense when I enter a nursery. I used to wonder what Curt thought when I came home with all those flowers. Some men might question the sanity of someone who spends so much money, time, and thought on pots of flowers that last about six months.

But honestly, Curt loved that I loved flowers. When I'd apologize for spending money on them, he'd say, "Hey, when the money runs out for me, it runs out for you too." We were always in things together. He knew one of the best days of my year was when I'd turn on the classical music, dig into that soil, and let my creative juices flow while potting. He would look at each pot when I finished and make comments like, "This one is my favorite." Or "I've never seen you do one like this one before."

I'm afraid potting day will be lonely this year and another hard first. I will miss my admiring husband. I will miss his strength to move some of the big pots. I will miss the way he encouraged me to do things that made me happy. I will probably cry often while doing what in other years would have brought me pure joy. I'm grateful I still have flowers, and that I still feel his blessing when I pick up the umpteenth petunia. And that I know he's in a place that probably makes my garden look rather ordinary.

> *What's your favorite flower? What feelings do you have when you walk into a nursery full of flowers? Can you imagine it's a little like heaven? I can. At least my corner of heaven.*

The view out of my office is one I adore. The red Adirondack chairs announce that summer is on its way, and the flowers and water confirm that even more profoundly.

May 1

Day 344: May

I've always loved turning the calendar over to the new month. It always brought me anticipation of good things, but today was different. It's May.

A year ago this month my life changed forever.

I've always loved May. How could you not love May? It's the beginning of summer, the month of school ending, the month of outdoor dining, and the month of beautiful weather. Tonight, I sit here in denial that this is the month when Curt died.

I have a feeling each day leading up to the sixteenth will find me searching to relive those last significant days before his death to make them a bit sacred. I don't want to dread May. I don't think Curt would want me to dread May. I'm going to enter these last days of this tediously difficult year with my eyes and heart wide open. I know I can't avoid the obvious memories and the emotions, but I can work at making new memories and new emotions to mark May. I can ask friends and family to be near me and help me find peace and purpose, and to walk with me throughout this anniversary month so that May can be a month that's not dreaded but met with meaning and hope for the future.

What is your favorite month of the year? What do you love about it? What month do you dread? How can you turn dread into gratitude?

May 2

Day 345: A Habit

Last night was a hard night. I had repeated dreams about me being left behind (literally) while others were leaving. It felt like I was supposed to go somewhere on a trip, but everyone forgot about me and drove away. I had that dream over and over and over, or so it seemed.

Looking ahead to the summer is not easy. Normally we would be planning what we would do and where we would go. Last year I was in such awful shock that I didn't realize how my life would be different. I read a pretty depressing blog recently where a widow said year two was worse than year one. Wow—talk about something that took the wind out of my sails. This blog described how people forget about you, how in year two you are no longer in shock, and the realism about your future sets in.

Maybe that was what I was feeling last night. I know there is nothing magical about being done with year one, yet part of me feels a sense of relief. I've survived the hardest firsts. I've found out how difficult things are as a new, yet old, single woman. I've also navigated through many things I didn't think I could do.

The sun is out this morning, and I am still trying to start my day with gratitude. I'm grateful I'm almost done with year one, even if year two may be more difficult. I'm feeling a bit feisty this morning and would like to prove that blogger wrong. Maybe she just didn't live in gratitude in year two. That makes me know that this gratitude thing must go on. I'm hoping 345 days of looking for gratitude has created a disciplined habit that will last the rest of my days and make my life full and even a bit amazing.

What habit should you be intentional about developing? What do you need to do to create that habit? How can discipline make you a better person?

Day 346: The Bruise

Of all the things to give me reason to be normal and happy and energetic, it is my grandkids. They now occasionally refer to Poppo in a way that makes them smile.

The other night, Norah had food on her face, and Johnny mentioned that if Poppo was here, he'd pull out his handkerchief and wipe her face—whether the handkerchief was clean or not. I don't think they loved Curt's multi-use piece of white cotton. It was an item that had a plethora of purposes, and we laughed at the memory.

The sitting boulders in the Light Garden will be a good place for me to sit with them and talk about what we learned from Poppo. I guess that's what I want most for them—that they will have learned something from Curt that will make their lives more meaningful. I know one thing they learned—that he loved them so much. I miss the look on his face when he smiled, tucked his chin in his neck, and crinkled his eyes in response to something one of them did or said.

I try sometimes to be both Poppo and Grammy for them. The bruise on my leg is a testament to that. I was playing basketball with Johnny and tripped and fell right on my behind. I'm not always successful playing both roles. In fact, I know I can't take his place, but I love to at least be all I can for them. They are the best continuation of Curt I can imagine, and I'm grateful beyond measure for the healing they have brought me this year. I don't know how I would have navigated this last year without them.

> *Do you have a good spot in your yard or house where you can sit and think or talk about important things or important people? Can you create a spot like that?*

May 4

Day 347: Swing Batter

Tonight, I'll go to Johnny's first baseball game of the season. I vividly remember going to the first game last year. I rode with John and Meagan because Curt was driving home from Omaha after teaching his strengths coach class. I remember him standing at the ballpark with his dress clothes on, jawing with John or the other players' dads or grandpas. And of course, I remember him trying to lead the batter and the ump with his well-timed suggestions that they should "swing batter" or call "stee-rike." I also remember walking up to the first game after Curt died, knees buckling underneath me, tears coming down my face, numb and in shock.

I'm no longer numb and in shock, but I'll still miss watching my main man enjoy watching his grandson's baseball games. I will never understand why he wasn't given more games to watch. That, along with hundreds of other things, often makes me feel cheated and hurt.

What brings me gratitude tonight? I'm grateful Marlene and Ron picked me up and took me to Johnny's games last year. That was a huge thing for my emotional state. And tonight, well, no one had to pick me up. I drove to the ball park and felt grateful to see Johnny play—grateful to have something to do on summer nights this year. Grateful I can sit by my daughter-in-law and granddaughter and feel included, cared for, and a bit needed as a cheerleader too. I may have to throw out a "swing batter" or two just for Curt's sake. I'm pretty sure he'd want me to do that.

> *Could you show up at someone's games this summer and cheer them on? That's a high calling.*

Johnny at the ballfield

May 5

Day 348: The Dance

I heard a song on the radio today that reminded me of dancing with Curt. We didn't dance very often—at a party or a wedding reception, or occasionally at home where no one was looking. The music and the memories that quickly invaded my mind and heart reminded me again that what I miss most is Curt's physical presence, his touch—dancing or not.

I had a moment today when I thought that if I were granted just a few more minutes with him, I'd want to touch his face. I miss the feel of his face. I miss rubbing against his whiskers. I miss his cheek against mine. There's absolutely nothing that can take the place of that physical closeness. I felt a sense of deep sadness that forever is a long time when it comes to wanting to touch someone again.

Years ago, for some class we were taking, we each needed to write down three things we liked that our partner did to or for us. One of his was, "run your fingers through my hair." I remember being so surprised that he wrote that. But I guess I did that a lot, and he liked it more than I ever knew.

This is kind of personal stuff, but after almost a year of candidly exposing my grief, I don't find it inappropriate. What I do find inappropriate is not being grateful for the closeness we had for all those years. It was like heaven. When I wonder what heaven is like, I know it must have the same high as a touch from someone you love.

> *What kind of touch means something to you? Are you willing to let your loved ones know what kind of touch you enjoy? Do you know what kind of touch your partner enjoys? Don't waste time being selfish with your touch.*

May 6

Day 349: Education

Tomorrow I will go to my niece Elizabeth's graduation from vet school. She worked hard for this degree, and it will be so neat seeing her get some celebration and applause for her tenacity and commitment.

I can't help but remember the education adventures Curt and I had. We got married in between our sophomore and junior year in college, so even getting through college had its challenges. In Curt's junior year, he managed to take classes only on Tuesdays and Thursdays so he could work with his dad doing construction the other three days of the week.

Then came three years of seminary, complete with summer classes in Hebrew and Greek. As if that wasn't enough, Curt went back for another master's degree when our kids were six and nine. We all moved back to Nebraska for his studies and lived on a rather meager salary. After that, I went back for another degree when the kids were nine and twelve. We did school a lot. It probably didn't pay off for us financially. In fact, it probably set us back a bit, but Curt liked the learning, and I liked the environment of learning.

So tonight, I reflect on how our educational endeavors made us strong. Wisdom always trumped knowledge for Curt. I learned a lot from him, but the most powerful lessons were always more about character than anything a degree could bring. His walk spoke louder than his talk every day of his life.

I wish he could be there to celebrate with Elizabeth. He would say something meaningful to her. He would be supportive. He would enjoy being with family. Congrats, Liz. I'm proud of you, and Curt would be too.

> **What part of your education has meant the most to you?**
> **What would you still like to learn? What's holding you back?**

May 7

Day 350: Mother's Day

Tomorrow I face the last first holiday—Mother's Day. As you know by now, Curt's generosity in words and gifts were unmatched. I still have the card he gave me just a little over a year ago lovingly displayed.

Tonight, as I made a rather lonely three-hour drive back home from a great graduation celebration, all I could think about was how last Mother's Day Curt was so diligent in going to see his mom at the care facility where his dad was in hospice. As I was driving down I-80, Curt's sister called saying Mom had cut her ankle and needed some stitches. Although my day tomorrow will be filled with good things, like watching the grandkids play soccer and football and doing the annual potting of flowers with my daughter-in-law, I knew nothing is more important than making time for Curt's mom on Mother's Day.

When I called her, she sounded so glad we were coming. She insisted we plan to stay long enough to eat some of the chocolate cake that she had made. When I hung up, I finally cried and let out all the emotions that had been dammed up for some time. I realized that the best Mother's Day gift I could have was to do what Curt would want me to do for his mom.

Tomorrow will be a tough first for his mom too. There will be three generations of Liesveld moms spending time together tomorrow. We all love each other. We all need each other. And we will all do what it takes to honor each other, even when two of the key men in our lives are no longer here.

My guess is Curt and his dad will be with us in spirit tomorrow and would be grateful we are spending some time together—all those women they loved all in one place.

Who do you honor on Mother's Day? Is there a mother you can borrow for the day? Or maybe you can be a mother figure to someone.

*Great Grandma
Liesveld with Norah*

May 8

Day 351: Sacred Spot

This Mother's Day may go down as the best day I've had since Mother's Day a year ago. I squeezed in several moments of joy today.

The day started out potting flowers with Meagan—with Johnny and Norah's help. It's been our tradition for more than ten years, and it's always pure joy. Then we went to the soccer game where Norah scored the only point for her team. Next we cheered at Johnny's football game where he scored touchdowns and looked so confident and comfortable out there throwing the pigskin. Finally, we headed down to Holland to see Curt's Mom. Although we both shed many tears, we also shared hearts full of memories and gratitude for each other.

After our usual Mother's Day dinner at John and Meagan's house, God had something special in mind. We moved most unpredictably but naturally into an evening of honest, poignant, tearful, and loving conversation about Curt. All of us said things we've needed to say for almost twelve months. We loved on each other in a way that could never have been orchestrated.

I asked the family to consider approaching the next couple weeks with more than just sadness. To embrace the *and* of grief. We can be sad *and* thoughtful. We can be sad *and* wiser. We can even be sad *and* grateful. I asked them to think more about what we all learned from Curt. Johnny said he learned "eighty-five percent of everything from Poppo, either when they were fishing or when they were riding in the convertible." That made a lot of sense to me. Most of us are impacted by others through our everyday, ordinary experiences and interactions.

As much as I wish I could still stand at the back door with Curt, arm in arm, watching the rain on the pond as we did last year, I am grateful for what I have today. And that's all we should and can do—be grateful for what we have in this very day. Give us this day our daily bread... For Thine is the Kingdom, and the Power, and the Glory Forever. Amen.

> *What sacred space do you have where you can help someone learn? Maybe it's not a fishing hole or a convertible, but it might be a back porch or a kitchen table. How can you make the most of the opportunities you have there?*

Johnny and Curt on the Pond

Day 352: Ruin

I sit here in the house watching the rain and hail and wind destroy so much. Our normally serene pond is raging and making its way higher and higher in the yard. Even worse, for me, is that after spending a lot of time, money, and effort on my flower pots, they are totally decimated. I'm not exaggerating. Every plant is totally stripped of the leaves. There are only bare stems in several large planters I just finished on Friday. And the rain and storms are not even over. The night supposedly has more in store.

I feel like someone is trying to punish me on this anniversary week. I know pots of flowers aren't a life and death matter, but I am angry because I know if Curt would have been here, he would have carried them all in and made sure they didn't get ruined. But I wasn't even home to try to be strong and brave.

I feel a huge sadness after such determination to be grateful and positive these next few days. I probably love my pots too much. Maybe I'm being taught a lesson. I don't know. I just know I am deeply disappointed, a bit overwhelmed, and tremendously discouraged.

But so far, I'm safe. I know what real life and death issues are. Believe me, I know. I will try hard to put things in perspective, and try to fight the evil force that wants to bring me down to nothing.

I hope you are safe tonight. I am safe, and my family is safe. So, I need to realize that what my mom always said is true—"It could have been worse."

> It what situation would Opal's words, "It could have been worse," actually make things better? Context, folks. Put it all in context.

May 10

Day 353: Prune and Fluff

In the last twenty-four hours, I've felt more defeated than I have for weeks, if not months. It all had to do with the wreckage the storm did to the yard last night. On top of feeling bad, I felt guilty for feeling bad.

Working with flowers and doing yard work has been so healing for me, then BAM! The wound opened again. This morning at my bi-weekly coffee time with my best friends, I let out my anger, resentment, and despair. I used bad words. And they listened and didn't make me feel guilty for feeling angry. On the way home from work today, I stopped and got a few filler flowers to try to salvage the wreckage of pots I have now. Then I prayed the rest of the way home. I'm not sure what I said. I think I asked for forgiveness for being so self-focused. And I asked for peace. I may have asked for my pots to recover.

I got home and did what I advise people to do with their pots—fluff them and prune them back a bit. I stuck some new plants in a few bare holes, all the while realizing the analogy to my grief. Flowers and life are not the same after they are hit by a storm, but they can still be good. That pruning—or shaping—of flowers and of life can make things look better and clearly improve the prospects of a better future. That fluffing—or giving some tender touch—helps the flowers and one's life to feel more beautiful. And when necessary, add a new plant for immediate improvement. I'm not sure how that correlates to life, but maybe it means to occasionally splurge and make yourself feel better.

Lots of Grief. Little Gratitude. Less Grief. Slightly more Gratitude. "To everything there is a season…"

What in your life needs to be pruned? What needs a little fluffing? Is there something new you can add just to brighten your day?

May 11

Day 354: Notes

I needed a new spiral notebook to lay beside my desk—the one where I jot down simple notes and reflections. When I went to put my old one away, I took a minute to look at the upcoming month from a year ago. I wondered if I had even written in it; then I saw phrases like this:

5/15   *John's Walk of Shame. Pouring Rain. Good day.*

5/26   *Tuesday after Curt's funeral. Unreal. Loved him so much.*

6/1   *I hate all this financial crap and bills. Why did I cancel his life insurance?*

6/4   *Rainy and dreary.*

6/5   *I'm exhausted and feel so futureless.*

6/8   *So many thank-yous and so hard to face the future.*

6/9   *Norah talked about Curt being able to see Switzerland.*

6/11   I noticed I made my first list of to-dos for the day—something I usually do.

And finally, a month after Curt died,

6/16   *I'm writing here as if I'm normal. I'm not. It's a beautiful day, but not the same without Curt here.*

As you can see, my personal notes were so full of shock and pain. Today, I'm thankful that I won't be going through that again this year. That is such a weird thing to say, but I find myself thinking, "Wow, I'm glad I don't ever have to do that again." As if it's done. As if everything is okay now.

I don't write this to invite pity. I write it to remember what reality was like less than a year ago, and to be grateful it's behind me. It is very odd to have gratitude about not having to face Curt's death again. Once is enough. I'm so grateful I can begin to see some future—just a little peek of the future.

> *Do you keep a simple journal or jot down your notes every few days? Maybe you should. All it takes is a cheap notebook and some will.*

Day 355: My List

Many of the things I've read this year were written by people who went through the death of a loved one then advised people on how to help others after a loss. I think everyone is unique in what they need and how they want to be treated. This list isn't to suggest everyone would be like me, but here goes my advice on what helped me, and what didn't.

In the early days of shock and grief:

1. Don't ask what needs to be done. Just do it. I had no capability to think ahead. This was especially true of the things that needed to be done immediately after Curt's death. I needed someone to make the decisions, then ask if that was what I wanted.

2. Help keep things neat and in order. I had a compulsion to have things cleaned up around me, even those first few days I was in shock. I'm always kind of that way, but the junk around the house almost made me crazy. I felt like I'd lost control of everything and I was desperate for order of some kind.

3. Stay overnight for a few nights, but let me get through being alone before too long. I think it was important for me to face reality and force myself to be strong.

4. Saying, "I don't know what to say." seemed to mean the most to me for some reason.

5. Pick up some work slack. I knew immediately my colleagues would take care of my work load (including rearranging a whole trip to Switzerland that was to happen in a month). It was huge to have my work taken care of immediately.

6. Help with work at my home and my personal responsibilities. This one never gets old, but I remember how much it meant when my sister and brother-in-law helped clean my daughter's apartment.

7. Touch me.

8. Love on my kids and grandkids. Taking care of them when I couldn't was perhaps the greatest gift of all.

9. Help with thank-you notes. I felt such a need to write them, but also felt overwhelmed. If you can address the envelopes, that frees the grieving person to just write the note.

10. Realize that when death comes as such a shock, the person in grief will likely say and do things that don't make sense, or are inappropriate. I dread to think of all the things I did or said. Use A LOT of grace when advising or judging a person in shock.

Later, after shock has worn off:

1. Ask me to do things; then offer to drive. Something about being driven to things helped. Sitting home alone at night was the worst thing, so I did appreciate getting out even for an hour or so once I was past the first few months.

2. Remember special days. It was meaningful when people were extra sensitive on anniversaries, birthdays, etc.

3. Help with physical work around the yard and house. The exhaustion of grief is unfathomable, and physical work was so hard for me. On the Fourth of July, I had help cleaning up, and that was such a gift. I had help again this week. Huge emotional stamina comes from that help.

4. Ask "How are you doing?" I needed an open-ended question that invited me to share. I often needed to talk, and sometimes I needed people to ask.

5. Talk about Curt. I need to talk about him, so it helps when someone besides me says something about him.

6. "I'm sorry." just fell flat on me. For others, those words may be perfect. I do best with some encouragement (not a lecture), but hopeful, kind words of encouragement.

7. Ask me to do something with you. Just being included helps.

8. Pray. Many of you have told me you prayed for me. I know you did, and I still lean into that.

9. Share good books and articles. Some are terrible, but I found some good ones that helped me.

10. Be generous. People's generosity with time, money, help, and words never got to be too much. It has changed the way I think and feel and—I hope—behave for the rest of my life.

If you know someone who has experienced a loss, lean in and dare to do something. Action is always better than inaction.

May 13

Day 356: A Beautiful Day

It's been almost a year since Curt had his last full day on earth. It was a Friday like today. I know I've shared parts of this story before, but these memories are so vivid again.

Curt arrived home from teaching two very long weeks of strengths classes; he was so glad to be home. We hurried to find John doing his walk across Lincoln to raise money for a young man who had recently lost his leg in an accident. We found John and the three of us posed for a picture in front of Memorial Stadium before John went on to finish his walk.

We met him at the end of his walk, along with some of his radio fans, and some of my sweet family. We admired our son as he took to the air and talked about his walk and interviewed this brave young man who had just undergone such a tragedy.

Then it was time to hustle home and get ready for Johnny's Boys' Choir concert. We held hands during the concert, as we were prone to do, and both of us had tears in our eyes as we listened to this choir of boys sound quite angelic singing, "River in Judea," almost as if someone had planned that song for the last evening of Curt's life. We finished the night together at the kids' house and finally went home, happy and tired.

So, the memories were whispering in my ear all day. I don't know what the next three days will be like, but I do know today I simply wished I could go back to a year ago and experience it all again. Not because of any regrets—there are none—but because it was a beautiful day.

Today I had a heavy heart and several moments when the tears came uncontrollably. Tonight, I went to Johnny's concert, and the music brought me emotionally to my knees. The tears ran down my face onto my chest. Anne sat beside me, and put her arm around me, patting my shoulders—much like I did for her when she was a little girl and hurting.

Music, especially when sung by my grandson, pierces my heart like an arrow. I'm working with all my might to be grateful. Grateful we spent our last night together watching our family use their strengths in such a powerful way. Grateful we were together and had fun with each other. Grateful we were in love and loving toward each other. Grateful for the powerful words of "River in Judea."

There is a river in Judea
That I heard long ago.
And it's a singing, ringing river
That my soul cries out to know...
May the time not be too distant
When we meet by the river, by the shore
'Til then dream of that wonderful day
As we sing once more, once more
There is a river in Judea

What memories do you have of a sweet day you'd like to relive?
How can you have more days like that?

May 14

Day 357: The Rose

It's Saturday. Saturdays have been hard this year since that was the day Curt died, but today was different. It was so much harder. I tried being proactive about the day by inviting some family to join me for breakfast. John and the grandkids met me for a tour around the Farmer's Market, which was sweet, but a reminder that the morning Curt died, we went to the market with such happy hearts.

I saw all of Curt's family at a graduation celebration for our niece. Seeing the faces of his siblings and mom reminded me of that Saturday a year ago. Their grief was real too. On the long drive home from the graduation, I had plenty of time to get pictures in my head, hear voices, and remember details I hadn't thought of for months. I remembered my pleading prayers and wondered where this year of grief has gone. I went down a road of fear, of wails, of daily tears, of loneliness, of doubt, of hurt, and of brokenness. Now, I sit in the evening hours of a beautiful night, alone—trying to face the next few hours with some gratitude.

Today, Norah was with me for a few hours in the middle part of the day. I took her to a nursery with me to buy a rose. I'd found a spot in the Light Garden that seemed a little empty. Curt would probably be laughing at that since I'm always finding spaces that needed more flowers. We picked out a rose and went to my house to plant it. She told me she was good at digging through roots to make the hole. Well, we kind of did it together.

While we were digging, I asked her what she likes to remember about Poppo. She paused then said "Fishing." I liked that memory too. Then I looked at my watch.

It was about 1:15 p.m.

Although I'm not exactly certain what time Curt died, I am pretty sure it was very, very close to the time. I stood with my Norah in the Light Garden, where Curt died on another beautiful Saturday almost a year ago, alive and grateful.

I can promise you tonight I am trying desperately to hold onto the gratitude, but it is very, very hard. I've thought a lot about the verse in the Bible, "In all things, give thanks." I realized only recently, the verse doesn't say, "Give thanks for everything." I think I know the difference after 357 days of seeking gratitude.

Tonight, I will find something to be grateful for... something.

> **What does it mean to give thanks in all things? How is that different than giving thanks for all things? Where can you find gratitude today?**

May 15

Day 358: Life-Givers

It's the eve of the anniversary of Curt's death. I strategically asked my small group from church to spend the evening with me. You see, Curt loved these people.

Some of you may wonder what a "small group" is. The term is neither creative nor appropriately descriptive, considering it's such a significant group of people. It's simply a group of faith-minded people who gather to eat, drink, and talk about our spiritual selves. The men in this group meet every Friday morning at 6:30 a.m. and were the men Curt leaned on in tough times and in good times. I knew I wanted them to be with me on the eve of the one-year anniversary of my husband's death.

It's the same group of I people I knew needed to be called immediately on that Saturday afternoon, to tell them the worst news I've ever had.

They showed up.

They showed up in disbelief and in belief, these friends who have a common love of each other and of God, the Father, Son, and Holy Spirit. I've talked a lot about my faith in the past 358 days. Tonight, let me say that without my faith, I would never have made it through this year. It is a faith of power, a faith of ambiguity at times, but a faith that has endured through life and death.

Tonight, we gathered around the light in the Light Garden. I told them that if they ever wondered if they were significant, all they had to do is know they were the best friends of Curt, a supremely significant man. And for me, they were life-changers, and life-givers, and life-sustainers.

We gathered in a circle around the light and the marker that says,

Curt Liesveld

Dominus Illuminatio Mea

"In His Light, We Saw Light" - Psalm 36:9.

As the dark encircled us, we circled around each other and sang the song we sang at Curt's funeral, "Great Is Thy Faithfulness," voices strong despite the tears. It was more beautiful than I can explain—much like heaven is not to be explained.

> *So tonight, I ask you to consider if you have friends who bring the kind of faith you may need someday when you make that horrible call. If you don't have faith-filled friends, it's not too late to find them. Just create a small group. And maybe call it something more appropriate—like "The Group of Life and Light"—a name that fits, especially in this death-filled year.*

The small group

May 16

Day 359: A Sacred Day

This is the day I've wondered about for many, many months. It's almost a bit ordinary. I'm working, and don't have any special plans. I woke up feeling oddly strong after a weekend of tremendous moments, and gut-wrenching memories. Today, I want to share not my own words—as I have for 358 days and will for another eight days—but the words someone sent me soon after Curt died. I read this most days. It became the strength I needed and the credo by which I tried to live my life this past year. It presented gratitude as a goal and necessity for me to be able to live with some joy.

You can shed tears that he is gone,
or you can smile because he has lived.
You can close your eyes and pray that he'll come back,
or you can open your eyes and see all he left.
Your heart can be empty because you can't see him,
or you can be full of the love you shared.
You can turn your back on tomorrow and live yesterday,
or you can be happy for tomorrow because of yesterday.
You can remember him only that he is gone,
or you can cherish his memory, and let it live on.
You can cry and close your mind, be empty and turn your back,
or you can do what he would want:
Smile, open your eyes, love, and go on.

I believe this day is like a holy day—a day that is sacred. Go live your life in a sacred, joy-filled way. Curt would want you to.

Day 360: The Journey

Six more days to write this rather long experiment of being public about my grief and gratitude. Throughout this journey, I've had numerous people say, "You have so many friends who have been there for you." Yes, I do. One of my core values is relationships, and all I could think about yesterday was the power of friendships.

Although I don't have high Woo (people strong in the Woo theme love the challenge of meeting new people), I do love the development of human interaction known as friendship. So many places brought me great friends: school, my childhood church (Holland), high school (Norris), schools where I taught, seminary and Michigan, the Mitchell church and community, Gallup friends, Gallup clients, Hope Church, neighbors in Fox Hollow, small group friends, flower and nursery people like my dear friend Angie, New Covenant Church, friends of my children, Preserve neighbors, graduate school, mentees, the hair salon and the nail salon, strengths coaches, and my family—who are perhaps the best friends of all.

I cannot even begin to tell you how much my life has been touched by friends— hundreds of people who I consider friends. My dear sister-in-law, Sandy, observed that the investment Curt and I made in people (friends) over the years, has come back to help me through this difficult time.

Today I want to just encourage, urge, entice you all to invest in friends. It's so easy to let work, your immediate family, or your to-do list consume your time, but people (friends) are important. Find a place for them in your life. A few times in the last few weeks when I was tired, busy, or overwhelmed with work, I wanted to say no to some invitations. But I said yes because in ten years, or maybe in one day, life can change. And in that second, I will never regret choosing to invest in friends.

> *I don't care how busy you are, how old you are, how tough you are— you will need friends. Invest, value, take care of, and prioritize the most important thing in the world—people. You will never, ever regret it.*

Day 361: True Essence

At the beginning of last year, Dave from our small group challenged each of us to come up with one word that we would focus on during the coming months. As you know, Curt's word was *light*. Looking back, it seems predestined—a divine, and even holy choice.

Benjamin, Curt's go-to at work, spent some time thinking about Curt's pursuit of light and the impact that it had. Thank you, Benjamin, for your thoughtful reflection on Curt's essence.

> "The *presence* of light illuminates our darkness. We all experience the darkness that prevents us from seeing who we really are. Curt's light shone brightly on who we are so that we could see the true talents we brought to the world.

> "The *absence* of heaviness enables us to experience lightness. We all experience the heaviness of the burden to be who we are not. Curt lightened our burden by helping us let go of who we are not so that we were free to bring our talents to bear in the world.

> "The *essence* of who we are capable of being is illuminated by the presence of light and empowered by the absence of burden, which leads to lightness.

> "Presence. Absence. Essence. Three SENCES that Curt has enlightened.

> "He awakened us to the presence of our true essence that we could not see. Curt's wisdom was enlightening.

> "He freed us from the burden of expectation of a false essence that we could not realize. Curt's understanding was enlightening."

May 19

Day 362: *Real* and *Strong*

As we wind down these 366 days (yes, I got an extra day of grief and gratitude thanks to leap year), I realize I've learned a lot about myself. I've learned that I wanted to be both authentic in my grief *and* strong. Those two desires sometimes fought with each other.

My determination to be strong is just a part of who I am, grief or not. Most of this year I landed hard on weak—unable to perform simple tasks, tired, and discouraged beyond words. I often just couldn't muster up strong, but I wanted to be strong for the people around me. I wanted to be strong for my kids and grandkids. I felt like they had enough grief and pain with the loss of Curt without having to take care of me when I fell apart. I also found myself hating to ask people for help with things, or even more, to burden them with my emotional pain. I wanted to be strong for Curt's mom and his family. I wanted to be strong for co-workers. I wanted to be strong for people who told me they couldn't stand to think of Curt's death. Heck, I even wanted to be strong for people I hardly knew.

There still are times when I don't quite know how to take care of something Curt would have done, and I feel so inept. Yet I've tried to do most of the things that he did with a few exceptions. So, my head says, "be strong," and my heart says, "I'm weak."

I've truly tried to be honest and real and authentic in my talk and my walk. I've wanted to be myself, even when I didn't feel like myself. Even when I wanted to be real in my grief, I still wanted to be strong—the genius of the *and*. More than ever, I wanted to be true to myself.

I'd been through hell and knew I didn't need to invite more hell by trying to be someone other than who I am. I needed to be true to the strength inside me that I can arouse when I need to. Hard *and* soft. Rough *and* smooth. Loud *and* quiet. Dark *and* light. Pain *and* joy. Strength *and* weakness. Grief *and* gratitude.

> **What things do you balance in your life? How much do you get to be yourself, even in difficult times? How can you be authentically more of who you are while continuing to become a better version of yourself each day? It may be okay to be both strong and authentic in your feelings. In fact, it may be the only way to live.**

May 20

Day 363: Words

Communication is powerful. During the past year, I've longed for someone to talk with me so many times. Days like today still seem to be thunderously quiet. I have missed sharing my thoughts, ideas, plans, excitement, and fears with Curt.

Sometimes the words we exchanged didn't have much significance. Other times, words were hugely impactful. It's been an adjustment to be alone with my thoughts. Curt was a great listener, so I had a perfect sounding board for almost forty-four years. I often talked to him for long periods of time, and he let me because he knew how important it was to be vulnerable and open with one's thoughts.

I don't think I talk as much as I used to. Maybe it's because I just don't feel like talking about what now seem like trivial things or because I know the ridiculousness of trying to be right about things that really don't matter. Maybe I just don't have the energy to talk. There have been times I've wanted to talk, and it just didn't seem like the space was there. Maybe I've learned to listen better. I continue to try to figure out what to do with my thoughts that want to come out in verbal language.

I'm grateful for the texts, phone calls, cards, Facebook posts, and one-on-one conversations that keep me connected and feeling like I matter yet to someone. I'm so grateful for people who ask great questions and wait for an answer. I'm grateful for people who reach out and let me know what's happening so I feel included. I'm so grateful for grandkids who still run up to me and say, "Grammy!!!" as if I'm the treasure they have been looking for.

> *Today, whatever you do, have a meaningful conversation with someone. Ask good questions. Wait for the answer. Look into their heart as much as their mind. Words matter. Use them wisely.*

May 21

Day 364: The Funeral

A year ago today, we had Curt's funeral. The funeral is one of the few things I recall vividly from those first muddled weeks. I remember asking Johnny which dress I should wear. I remember putting on some makeup for the first time in six days. I remember the way the church looked—like a beautifully-lit garden. I'd certainly never had the time, reason, or anything that enticed me to envision what the stage would look like for Curt's funeral, but it was simply beautiful. I wish I had a good picture of that stage now.

I remember how the keys felt on the piano when I played "Great Is Thy Faithfulness." I remember the authentic and loving way our pastor communicated to aching hearts. I remember each word that was spoken—perfect words that went beyond eulogy to healing. I remember listening to John talk and thinking about how proud Curt would be of him—and kind of believing Curt heard John's words. I remember the verse, "In Him, there is no darkness at all." I remember the music, "Legacy" and "No More Night."

I remember the long, long line of people who patiently waited to greet me. I remember the shock of how many people had given up part of their Memorial Day weekend to travel miles and miles to attend Curt's funeral. People came from DC, from Minneapolis, from Denver, from LA, from Oregon, and even from international destinations. I remember seeing each face and feeling each hug. I remember feeling the power to physically and emotionally stand for a long time and love with and on people.

I have thought many, many times about the difference when a relatively young person has a funeral versus an older person. Unfortunately, I think there is more awareness of a person's contribution when they go out in their prime. I think Curt got to go out in his prime and have a funeral that spoke to his impact. I remember how that funeral reflected, so beautifully, Curt's life. He was known for something. He made a difference. His life was not just about his own comfort and enjoyment. He was admired. He was loved. He was adored. And so, he was celebrated.

> *What will your funeral say about you? What will be your legacy? How can you live today so that on the day we attend your funeral, we can also rejoice in the unique greatness you have brought to life? Maybe you should start imagining your funeral and then live out that legacy today.*

May 22

Day 365: Ashes to Ashes

We made the decision that Curt would be cremated. Both of us were clear that was our wish. We buried some of his ashes in the plot in the Holland cemetery the night before his funeral. Later, the mortuary called my sister and said the remaining ashes were there if we wanted them. She picked them up and stored them at her house until just a few days ago.

Doug brought them to me so I could spread them in the Light Garden. He lovingly handed me the black plastic box. I took it and held it tightly to my chest and put my cheek down on it as if I could give Curt one more sign of love and affection. I took the box in the house and let it sit there on my desk. The white label affixed to the box read:

Curt Liesveld, May 16, 2015, 64 years old, #24830798

When I saw those numbers, I wanted to scream. Didn't they know Curt could be described in so many amazing words rather than a set of random numbers? But, you know, they didn't really know him. I did.

Yesterday, I planned to have some of our closest friends over for dinner. I wanted to be with them when I spread his ashes, so I took the box and opened it. The tears came down my face as I felt so alone pouring the ashes into a generic, small, black container. My hands were shaky, and I spilled some of those ashes on my kitchen counter. I looked at them and didn't know what to do. I didn't want to wipe them up with a rag, or suck them up in a vacuum. So, I took my sweaty hands and rubbed them all over the spilled ashes. Then I rubbed the ashes into my face and chest and hands until they were all gone. They felt like one more time to be close to Curt. I told him I loved him and cried some more.

Last night, standing in the Light Garden, I read some verses and finally took the small black bottle and spread Curt's ashes over the area where he'd died. I cried, but the tears were not of desperate pain, but something between gratitude and grief.

"For then the dust will return to the earth, and the spirit will return to God who gave it." Yes, God got back a saint when Curt died.

Where would you want your ashes spread? What does that say about you? Do you know that in the end, we are all just ashes? Ashes with eternal souls.

Day 366: The Last Post

A year ago, I somehow found myself on Facebook, several days after losing the love of my life. So many people had sent me messages on my Facebook page, and I decided I should try to read those personal efforts to reach out to me. But the reason I put my fingers on the keys that first day was because I was overwhelmed by the support I'd received during the worst days of my life. Not only did I have emotions of the deepest grief, but also of inadequacy in not being able to communicate my sincere appreciation for others. I remember finishing that first post and feeling an amazing sense of healing. Clearly, I was given a message from somewhere that perhaps I should continue to look for tiny lights of gratitude in my days of horrific grief.

So, I wrote the second day, and the third, not naming them as Day 2 or Day 3 because I had no plan to continue doing this for a year. I just did it because I knew I was a little better after I wrote about my grief and gratitude each day.

Well, a year later, I am finished writing these posts. There are more than 123,400 words about grief and gratitude. Grief trumped gratitude most days, but that balance shifted as the days went by. When I first started, I had no idea what my life would be like a year later. I had no idea how people would remain in sync with my life just because they read a short blurb I wrote each day. I had no idea that some days it took a lot of discipline to find gratitude for anything I was experiencing. I had no idea that these words would help me be the most authentic person I could be, despite a drastic change in my life. I had no idea others would be willing to read my words. I had no idea I could encourage, bless, and recognize people who made a difference in my life almost daily. I had no idea that people would tell me these posts made a difference in their marriages or in their lives. I had no idea how my posts would deepen relationships in a way that could have never happened otherwise.

This was almost a spiritual discipline for me. Most days, my fingers hit the keys easily and words jumped on the page. Some days, I had to think so hard to find something to be grateful for. But I wrote quickly; I wrote without worrying about what people thought of me, and without guarding my heart. Many people told me it's not something they would or could do. I get that. For me, it wasn't something I planned. I honestly think God led me to this experiment of faith, honesty, discipline, and gratitude.

Here's what I know: It's easier to be authentic with people than to try to pretend or hide things in your life.

I also know that after writing about my grief for a year, that grief has taken on a new face. I have worked hard to be strong and to carry on in the way I believe I was intended to carry on. I've tried to intentionally and naturally reframe my new life. I want to continue to have a full life and I believe with all my heart that this writing and your support has allowed me to start this new journey of life reconstruction.

Finally, let me just say this: Being grateful makes a difference. I'm sure I've overlooked many people, many things, and many days as I tried to express the gratitude I had in my heart. But I've tried so, so hard to find and express how thankful I am for what I was given. And in doing so, I have released a lot of my pain and found some joy. The munificence of gratitude is not overrated. It changed my mind, my body, my spirit, and it healed so much of my heart.

Thank you for your support along the way. Please continue to never be afraid of encouraging too much. Of showing care too much. Of loving too much. Neither Curt nor I would want you to hold too tightly to what is good, true, and right. Release it and let it make a difference for someone.

Now it's your turn. Take your own journey toward seeking gratitude each day. Trust me, it's there, even on our darkest days.

Postlude

During this year of grief and gratitude, Curt's sister Sandy sent me poetry. She lovingly selected poems from her vast collection that she felt might pour light into my soul. So often, the right words arrived on just the right day.

We read this poem that Sandy shared with me as we scattered Curt's ashes in the Light Garden. It seems a fitting end to this journey of grief and gratitude.

You can choose, you know?
You can see the dark clouds,
You can stare at the shadow on the mountain
You can wish for the winds to calm and rain to dry.
Or.
Or.
You can let your jaw forget to close
and let it fall free towards the floor
in awe and appreciation
for the tiny slice of light that pools up in the foothills.
You can realize that without the dark,
it wouldn't be light at all.

—Tyler Knott Gregson

Acknowledgments

I've always wondered if anyone reads the acknowledgments in a book, except those who are acknowledged. I hope so, because the following people have been my rocks as I ventured through the unknown territory of putting this book together.

First and foremost, I must thank Cindy Conger. Years ago, I met Cindy shortly after we attended New Covenant Church for the first time. I was a bit bruised from twenty-three years of ministry and, frankly, wanted to remain anonymous as I searched for a new church. But Cindy was different. I felt like we had connected long before we ever met in person. She had a way of thinking about things that appealed to me. Her husband, Kirk, and Curt and I became great friends and always knew that when we were together, the day would be perfect. Cindy is the primary reason I decided it was okay to write this book. She never pressured me, but she helped me realize this book could be a good and God thing to share my grief and gratitude.

I didn't know then how much she would be involved in the production of this book. She is a genius at writing, editing, concepting, and mostly, encouraging. She helped me know the book was my best way of honoring Curt.

Early on, I created a type of support group to help me make decisions and generally advise me on the book. That group included Kim Berg, Tosca Lee, Meagan Liesveld, Elizabeth Cavazos, Sandy Westra, Deb Brown, Nancy Oberst, Maika Leibbrandt, Cicely Tuttle, and Becky Breed—it was Becky's early nudging to journal that became this book.

Cicely is a friend who was also a client at one time. She lives in Dallas and after being in one of my classes, she asked to friend me on Facebook. She then read all my grief and gratitude posts in a relatively short time. It was her compelling writing to me that gave me the real push to move forward with the book at a time when I was questioning myself.

"Should there be a book?" she wrote in an email. "I believe there already is. I believe God birthed it in your heart long before May, 2015. See, one doesn't get to reap a harvest like what came out of your heart during your first year of grief if they haven't sown seeds in fertile soil that allow the harvest to come to fruition. Your and Curt's life was lived to the fullest, lived with intention, and built upon a foundation of love. What qualified you to write those posts (or shall I say this book) was not you becoming a widow; it was the fact that you sowed years of seeds together which grew deep roots of life, love, abundance, and wisdom. Your posts are an outpouring of those things. I believe this is your and Curt's book, and you did write it together in a life lived well. You are simply adding lyrics, after the fact, to the beautiful piano score that has already been written."

The photos in the book are a labor of love. Most of them were taken by Curt with some of them taken by Meagan, who now uses Curt's camera as her own. Meagan Liesveld and Cori Waters spent hours and hours working on them, categorizing, assessing, and pouring raw love and passion into that effort. Having lost their brother and father-in-law, that work was one of emotional sweat and tears. I love them both.

As I entered this publishing venture I met Lisa Pelto and her team at Concierge Marketing. Their expertise in the publishing and distribution processes buoyed this project. They've gone beyond the role of advisors and become friends.

I need to thank the many, many people who helped me survive those first days, weeks, and months after Curt died. My children, John and Meagan Liesveld and Anne Liesveld, who struggled through their own grief while taking care of me in untold ways. My sisters, Jane Vander Broek and Marlene Auman, along with their spouses, who did the hard and heavy work during those first days of weighty decisions. They gave me the strength I needed to put one foot in front of another those first few weeks. Curt's sisters and brother, Claude Liesveld, Sandy Waters, and Cori Waters, who in spite of losing their brother, still managed to care for me as if I were their blood sibling. The many, many friends, too numerous to mention, who held me up and showed me they wouldn't ever go away.

And finally, the biggest appreciation goes to the all my Facebook friends who read my posts and supported me as I hammered out my daily ritual around grief and gratitude. I cannot tell you how much it meant to me that you encouraged me through your words, your "likes," and in so many other ways that most people will never be aware of. I know it wasn't easy, but you did a sacrificial and Godly act by walking beside me as you supported me in profound ways. Helping people can be hard and messy and sad sometimes. In many ways, you are the true authors of this book.

About Curt and Rosanne

Curt and Rosanne were both born in Lincoln, Nebraska, just eight months apart. They grew up going to the same church in the small town of Holland, Nebraska. Both graduated from Norris High School where they were high school sweethearts. They attended Northwestern College in Orange City, Iowa, before getting married on August 6, 1971. After they were married, they finished their undergraduate education at the University of Nebraska where Curt majored in sociology and Rosanne in vocal music.

After college, Curt and Rosanne moved to Holland, Michigan, where Curt attended Western Theological Seminary, and Rosanne taught school in Hudsonville. After three years, Curt received his Masters of Divinity degree and accepted a position as Senior Pastor at First Reformed Church in Mitchell, South Dakota. Shortly after moving to Mitchell, their son, John, was born. Three years later, their daughter, Anne, joined the family.

While the children were small, Rosanne taught piano lessons and exercise classes and was active in the church where Curt was the pastor. Rosanne later taught music in the area as Curt built a reputation as a strong leader in the community and the church. Under Curt's leadership, the church doubled in size and was known for attracting young families.

After ten years in Mitchell, the Liesvelds returned to Lincoln in 1986 so Curt could pursue a master's degree in counseling psychology. While in school, Curt worked part time at Hope Church, and Rosanne worked at Selection Research Institute (later to become Gallup) as a client development leader, teacher, and analyst. Her work was primarily with K-12 schools, but she also worked with leadership development as a coach and consultant.

After Curt received his degree, his original desire to do counseling had less appeal when he realized he did not see himself working primarily with dysfunction.

Instead, he accepted a call to become the full-time pastor at Hope Church. He was a pastor there for thirteen years, again growing the congregation many times over. That growth demanded another major addition to the church, and Curt felt it was time for the neighborhood church to move to a new location and become a "church on main street." He also realized it was time to have someone else lead the church to the next stage.

Curt attended a Leadership Week at Gallup, where he won the vision award and was extended a job at Gallup within days of his resignation from Hope Church. In his role at Gallup, he quickly found alignment with the strengths philosophy and could use both his writing and teaching talent to promote the beliefs he naturally held so dear. In nineteen years at Gallup, Curt became known around the word as a strengths guru and favorite strengths coach of leaders, corporations, and organizations.

Curt and Rosanne both traveled extensively for their work and found great joy in being partners both in work and at home. They loved supporting their children and grandchildren in all they do.

Curt's unexpected death on May 16, 2015, changed life forever for Rosanne.

At this writing, she continues to work at Gallup as a coach and teacher for strengths theory and practice, while contemplating the next chapters of her life.

About Gallup

"Rosanne Liesveld has a rich history with Gallup—as a teacher, a business leader, and an author. She won an award for *Teach with your Strengths*—a philosophy she has carried in all her endeavors. She looks at children through the eyes of an adult with extreme individualization. She lived in a marriage admired by her friends. Her visible and emotional drive was matched with the wise counsel of a pastor, presenter, and coach. Curt and Rosanne spent a combined forty-five years with Gallup during the time the science of strengths was developed, tested, and used by an audience of over fifteen million people. Both have been critical players in helping individuals and organizations grow by better understanding of talents, leadership, and successes."

—Connie Clifton Rath
President-Clifton Foundation
Gallup Board of Directors

Throughout this book, you read about Curt's and Rosanne's work with the Clifton StrengthsFinder™, an assessment of normal personality from the perspective of Positive Psychology developed by the Gallup organization. Curt Liesveld was known as a strengths guru and was a highly sought-after strengths coach and consultant who worked with thousands of individuals, businesses, and non-profit organizations around the world. He is the author of three books about strengths: *Living Your Strengths* with Albert L. Winseman and Donald O. Clifton, *Engage Your Strengths: EYS 4.0* with John Edgar Caterson, and *Expanding Your Strengths*.

Rosanne used strengths theory to help school districts identify and engage the most effective educators. She is the author of *Teach with Your Strengths* with JoAnn Miller and Jennifer Robinson. She currently serves as a mentor and coach.

Strengths theory shaped Curt's and Rosanne's life. They sought to help people identify, develop, and use their strengths, and considered their work at Gallup as their life mission. The definitions of the thirty-four strengths identified on the Clifton StrengthsFinder are listed on the following pages. You can learn more about strengths and take the StrengthsFinder assessment online at the GallupStrengthsCenter.com.

Signature Strength Themes

Curt Liesveld's Signature Strength Themes

- Responsibility
- Relator
- Maximizer
- Learner
- Analytical

Rosanne Liesveld's Signature Strength Themes

- Futuristic
- Activator
- Relator
- Significance
- Command

Clifton StrengthsFinder™ Strengths Guide

Achiever: People strong in the Achiever theme have a great deal of stamina and work hard. They take great satisfaction from being busy and productive.

Activator: People strong in the Activator theme can make things happen by turning thoughts into action. They are often impatient.

Adaptability: People strong in the Adaptability theme prefer to "go with the flow." They tend to be "now" people who take things as they come and discover the future one day at a time.

Analytical: People strong in the Analytical theme search for reasons and causes. They have the ability to think about all the factors that might affect a situation.

Arranger: People strong in the Arranger theme can organize, but they also have flexibility that complements this ability. They like to figure out how all of the pieces and resources can be arranged for maximum productivity.

Belief: People strong in the Belief theme have certain core values that are unchanging. Out of these values emerges a defined purpose for their lives.

Command: People strong in the Command theme have presence. They can take control of a situation and make decisions.

Communication: People strong in the Communication theme generally find it easy to put their thoughts into words. They are good conversationalists and presenters.

Competition: People strong in the Competition theme measure their progress against the performance of others. They strive to win first place and revel in contests.

Connectedness: People strong in the Connectedness theme have faith in the links between all things. They believe there are few coincidences, and that almost every event has a reason.

Consistency: People strong in the Consistency theme are keenly aware of the need to treat people the same. They try to treat everyone in the world with consistency by setting up clear rules and adhering to them.

Context: People strong in the Context theme enjoy thinking about the past. They understand the present by researching its history.

Deliberative: People strong in the Deliberative theme are best described by the serious care they take in making decisions or choices. They anticipate the obstacles.

Developer: People strong in the Developer theme recognize and cultivate the potential in others. They spot the signs of each small improvement and drive satisfaction from those improvements.

Discipline: People strong in the Discipline theme enjoy routine and structure. Their world is best described by the order they create.

Empathy: People strong in the Empathy theme can sense the feelings of other people by imagining themselves in others' lives or situations.

Focus: People strong in the Focus theme can take a direction, follow through, and make corrections necessary to stay on track. They prioritize then act.

Futuristic: People strong in the Futuristic theme are inspired by the future and what could be. They inspire others with their visions of the future.

Harmony: People strong in the Harmony theme look for consensus. They don't enjoy conflict; rather, they seek areas of agreement.

Ideation: People strong in the Ideation theme are fascinated by ideas. They are able to find connections between seemingly disparate phenomena.

Includer: People strong in the Includer theme are accepting of others. They show awareness of those who feel left out, and make effort to include them.

Individualization: People strong in the Individualization theme are intrigued with the unique qualities of each person. They have a gift for figuring out how people who are different can work together productively.

Input: People strong in the Input theme have a craving to know more. Often, they like to collect and archive all kinds of information.

Intellection: People strong in the Intellection theme are characterized by their intellectual activity. They are introspective and appreciate intellectual discussions.

Learner: People strong in the Learner theme have a great desire to learn and want to continuously improve. In particular, the process of learning, rather than the outcome, excites them.

Maximizer: People strong in the Maximizer theme focus on strengths as a way to stimulate personal and group excellence. They seek to transform something strong into something superb.

Positivity: People strong in the Positivity theme have an enthusiasm that is contagious. They are upbeat and can get others excited about what they are going to do.

Relator: People strong in the Relator theme enjoy close relationships with others. They find deep satisfaction in working hard with friends to achieve a goal.

Responsibility: People strong in the Responsibility theme take psychological ownership of what they say they will do. They are committed to stable values such as honesty and loyalty.

Restorative: People strong in the Restorative theme are adept at dealing with problems. They are good at figuring out what is wrong and resolving it.

Self-Assurance: People strong in the Self-Assurance theme feel confident in their ability to manage their own lives. They possess an inner compass that gives them confidence that their decisions are right.

Significance: People strong in the Significance theme want to be very important in the eyes of others. They are independent and want to be recognized.

Strategic: People strong in the Strategic theme create alternative ways to proceed. Faced with any given scenario, they can quickly spot the relevant patterns and issues.

Woo: People strong in the Woo theme love the challenge of meeting new people and winning them over. They derive satisfaction from breaking the ice and making a connection with another person.

Endnotes

Day 36:   Riddle, Jeremy. "Sweetly Broken." (Music Services, Inc.)

Day 37:   Chisholm, Thomas O. "Great is Thy Faithfulness." (Carol Stream, Ill.: Hope Publishing Group. 1923. Renewed 1951.)

Day 80:   Ecclesiastes 3:1. (King James Version).

Day 119:   Jim Clifton, email to Gallup Associates, May 17, 2015.

Day 184:   Rasmussen, Christine. *Second Firsts: Live, Love and Laugh Again*. Carlsbad, Calif. Hay House Publishing, 2013.

Day 187:   Chapman, Steven Curtis. "Glorious Unfolding." (New York: Universal Music Publishing Group, BMG Rights Management US, LLC.)

Day 191:   Chisholm, Thomas O. "Great is Thy Faithfulness." (Carol Stream, Ill.: Hope Publishing Group. 1923. Renewed 1951.)

Day 200:   *Today Show*. "Facebook's Year in Review." Interview with Savannah Guthrie. NBC, December 9, 2015.

Day 213:   Jo Ann Miller. Personal email to author, December 21, 2015.

Day 230:   Rasmussen, Christine. *Second Firsts: Live, Love and Laugh Again*. Carlsbad, Calif. Hay House Publishing, 2013.

Day 231:   Nike Slogan.

Day 241:   Young, Sarah. *Jesus Calling: Finding Peace in His Presence*. Special and Revised Edition. Nashville. Thomas Nelson, October 2004.

Day 258:   Young, Sarah. *Jesus Calling: Finding Peace in His Presence*. Special and Revised Edition. Nashville. Thomas Nelson, October 2004.

Day 258:   Numbers 6:24-26 (English Standard Version Anglicised).

Day 261:   Lerne, Alan Jay and Loewe, Frederick. "If Ever I Would Leave You." (Nashville. Warner/Chappell Music, Inc.)

Day 280:   Rasmussen, Christine. *Second Firsts: Live, Love and Laugh Again.* Carlsbad, Calif. Hay House Publishing, 2013. Also quoted on blog at www.secondfirsts.com/content/blog.

Day 292:   Liesveld, Rosanne. "Major Life Changes and Strengths." Gallup Coaches Playbook online publication, March 9, 2016.

Day 310:   Rasmussen, Christine. *Second Firsts: Live, Love and Laugh Again.* Carlsbad, Calif. Hay House Publishing, 2013.

Day 356:   Feldman, Jack and Marcus, Linda. "River in Judea." (Shawnee Press.)

Day 357:   1 Thessalonians 5:19. (Douay-Rheims Bible.)

Day 359:   Based on "Remember Me." A poem by Harkins, David. David Harkins Poems. Poemhunter.com, 2011.

Day 365:   Ecclesiastes 12:7. (New Living Translation).

Postlude: Gregson, Tyler Knott. "You Can Choose"

Clifton StrengthsFinder™ Guide and References. Used with permission of the Gallup Organization.

Seasons of Life
Photo Gallery